The Kabbalah
and
Jewish Mysticism

The Kabbalah and Jewish Mysticism

by
Israel Gutwirth

Philosophical Library
New York

BM
526
.G87
1986

Library of Congress Cataloging-in-Publication Data

Gutwirth, Israel.
  Kabbalah and Jewish mysticism.

  1. Kabbalah   2. Mysticism—Judaism.   I. Title.
BM526.G87   1987   296.8′33   86-18693
ISBN 0-8022-2516-0

Copyright 1987 by Philosophical Library, Inc.
200 West 57 Street, New York, N.Y. 10019
All rights reserved
Manufactured in the United States of America

Contents

Preface by Chief Rabbi Ovadia Yosef of Israel	9
Introduction by Dr. Yosef Burg, Interior Minister of the State of Israel	11
Foreword	13

Significance of the Kabbalah, the Zohar, and the Great Jewish Mystics

The Kabbalah	17
The Zohar	21
The Sanctity of the Zohar	23
The Prophet Elijah	27
The Messiah as Redeemer	33
Daniel's Prophetic Vision	38
The Holy City of Safed, Cradle of the Kabbalah	42
Rabbi Yehuda, the Hasid of Regensburg: A Revered Figure of Jewish History	46

6 THE KABBALAH AND JEWISH MYSTICISM

Eliezer Ben Yehuda Rokeach: Kabbalist Known for His Work *Rokeach*, a Guide to Righteousness	51
Ari the Saint: A Star That Shone with a Light of Its Own	56
Rabbi Chaim Vital: The Faithful Disciple of the Ari Hakadosh	60
Rabbi Yeshayahu Halevi Horvitz: Shela the Saint	64
Rabbi Solomon Alkabetz: Kabbalist and Religious Poet	69
Rabbi Chaim Ben Atar (Or Hachayim): Sage and Kabbalist	73
Rabbi Yehuda Liwa Ben Bezalel, The Grand Kabbalist: The Maharal of Prague	77
Teachings of the Kabbalists on Sin, Repentance, and Penitence	82
Rabbi Jacob Emden (Ya'abetz): Influential Scholar	90
The Paths of Heaven and Their Mysteries	94
The Jewish View of Astrology	97
The Sages' Attitudes toward Magic, Spiritualism, and Sleight-of-Hand	100
Dreams as Explained in the Talmud and the Kabbalah	104
The Evil Eye: Belief and Exorcism	107
Belief in Demons and Evil Spirits	110
The Golem and Its Creator, the Maharal of Prague	113
Dybbuk and Gilgul in the Light of the Kabbalah	115
The Jewish People and Their Eternal Longing for Redemption	118
The Significance of Jewish Prayers	122
Attitude of the Polish Gonim toward the Kabbalah	126
Rabbi Malbim: Interpreter of Holy Writ and Kabbalah	132

Hasidic Leaders Who Were Also Outstanding Exponents of the Kabbalah

The Kabbalah and Hasidism	139
Rabbi Leib Sores: One of the Thirty-six Just Men	143

The Baal Shem Tov, Creator of Hasidism: His Relation to the Kabbalah	147
Rabbi Nahum of Tchernobyl: Kabbalist and Defender of the Meek	155
Rabbi Jacob Isaac Horowitz, The Hozeh of Lublin: Grand Kabbalist and Visionary	160
Elimelech of Lizensk: Author of *Noam Elimelech*	165
Simha Bunem of Przysucha: Philosopher and Founder of Polish Hasidism	169
Rabbi Nahman of Bratzlav: Hasid, Scholar, and Kabbalist	174
Rabbi Shneer Zalmen and His Famous Book *Taniah*	178
Rabbi Moshe Leib Sosover: "Lover of Israel"	183
Rabbi Israel, The Maggid of Kozienice: Kabbalist and Mainstay of Hasidism	188

Noted Figures of the Jewish Golden Age in Spain

Rabbi Saadya Gaon: Philosopher and Talmudist	195
Menachem Ben Saruk: Author of the First Dictionary of the Bible	202
Rabbi Moses Ben Hanoch: Initiator of Jewish Religious and Cultural Life in Spain	207
Rabbenu Gershon	210
Rabbi Samuel Ha-Nagid and his Protégé, the Philosopher and Poet Solomon Ibn Gabriol	213
Rabbi Shlomo Yitzhaki (Rashi): Commentator of Holy Writ	217
Rabbi Yehuda Halevy: Physician, Philosopher, and Poet	220
Rabbi Samuel Ben Meyer (Rashbam) and His Brother Rabbenu Tam	224
Rabbi Abraham Ibn Ezra: Jewish Poet of Spain	229
The Great Maimonides (The Rambam)	233
The Rambam's Monumental Work *Yad Hazakah*	238
The Rambam's Letter to His Son Abraham	241
Rabbi Joseph Kimche: Defender of the Jewish Faith	245

8 THE KABBALAH AND JEWISH MYSTICISM

Rabbi Moses Ben Nahman (Ramban): Kabbalist, Philosopher, and Renovator of the Jewish Community in the Land of Israel	250
Rabbi Bahye Ben Joseph Ibn Paquda: Religious Philosopher and Author of *Hovot Halevavot*	254
Rabbi Abraham Ben Samuel Abulafia: Philosopher, Kabbalist, and Jewish Community Leader	258
Rabbi Jacob Ben Asher: The Baal Ha-Turim	261
Don Isaac Abravanel: Sage, Statesman, Poet, and Interpreter of the Bible	265
Rabbi Joseph Caro: Compiler of the *Shulhan Arukh*	270
Rabbi Moses Isserles (The Rema): Commentator of the *Shulhan Arukh*	274
Index	279

Preface

Israel Gutwirth, the Argentinian activist, writer, and journalist, has completed his second Spanish-language book under the title *The Kabbalah and Jewish Mysticism*. The book comprises three sections: the significance of the Kabbalah and the Zohar and the great Jewish mystics; Hasidic leaders who were distinguished Kabbalah scholars; and outstanding figures of the Jewish Golden Age in Spain.

The author, an outstanding Torah scholar and a student of the world-famous Yeshiva of the Sages of Lublin, has drawn from the purest sources all the facts concerning the themes of his new book; the reader will appreciate the warmth and authenticity of his descriptions.

The book has been strongly recommended by the scholarly Chief Rabbi of Argentina's Jewish Community, Don Shelomo Benhamu, who has written to me in glowing terms of the author's personality. Israel Gutwirth's contribution to literature and journalism have done much to further the cause of Jewish traditional education.

10 THE KABBALAH AND JEWISH MYSTICISM

During my visits to Argentina I had the pleasure of meeting with Israel Gutwirth, whose literary articles have served to bring young people nearer to the spiritual sources of Judaism.

Therefore my best wishes and gratitude go out to Israel Gutwirth for offering us this very important and instructive book, which I recommend.

May the Almighty bless his efforts to explain the Torah, and may his purpose be successfully achieved.

Chief Rabbi Ovadia Yosef of Israel
Spiritual Guide of World Sephardic Jewry

Introduction

It is with great pleasure that I contribute an introduction to this new book by Israel Gutwirth, a valued friend.

For more than thirty years this talented writer and journalist has expressed in the columns of the Jewish press his message of the Torah, of tradition, and of love of the people and State of Israel.

Throughout those years of brave and honest journalism, Gutwirth has had a commonsense, dignified approach to the daily events of Jewish life, illuminating it with original and independent thinking rooted in the Jewish tradition of the Torah.

Particular food for thought is contained in his essays and articles on Jewish education; he has made an outstanding contribution to its depth and growth, bringing wide circles of youth nearer to the original source and thus fulfilling the glory of the Torah.

For several decades, Gutwirth held the position of president of the two eldest and most respected Rabbinical schools and seminaries in Argentina, which have saved thousands of Jewish children from assimilation.

We live in times when Jewish youth seek access to Jewish knowledge, initiation in our spiritual treasures and into their own past. They are keen to know why they are Jews and why they belong to a generation that has been much neglected by its elders, that knows little or nothing of religion, Torah, or the great spiritual values of Jewry, its history and traditions.

Many peoples have disappeared and been forgotten because their youth were not interested in knowing their history.

That is why I hold that, whoever can do so, is in sacred duty bound, particularly after the Holocaust, to give new generations a written account of our cultural treasury, explaining and illustrating it. And Israel Gutwirth, an erudite graduate of the famous Sages of Lublin rabbinical seminary; one whose noble and sensitive personality combines Jewish and world knowledge, is certainly the right man for the task.

I firmly believe that his new book on adepts of the Kabbalah, Jewish mystics, and illustrious figures of the Golden Age of Spain will arouse at least as much interest as his first book, *Anthology of Hasidism*, of which a second edition has appeared.

Dr. Yosef Burg
Interior Minister of the State of Israel

Foreword

The subject of the Kabbalah—Jewish mystical doctrine—is not an easy one to approach. To popularize it is difficult enough; to provide the reader with insights into its mysteries is too formidable a task within the framework of this book.

During recent years the Kabbalah aroused widespread interest in the Jewish and Gentile cultural worlds and has been disseminated among ever-widening circles. Unhappily some alleged experts have drawn on material other than the original Jewish sources. This fount of knowledge, instead of being sanctified, is being desecrated—its contents distorted and downgraded. That is why I set out to demonstrate the beauties and sanctity of Jewish mystical doctrine, hoping to achieve my aim through this modest contribution.

Our generation, which has moved away from Judaic learning, seems in need of a guiding light—something to show the way, to animate and reanimate it. That is why I thought it very important, even essential, to take a retrospective glance at the great personalities of the past and reassess the meritorious part they played in

Jewish religious and cultural life, bequeathing an everlasting heritage to posterity.

I have divided the book into three parts: (1) the significance of the Kabbalah, the Zohar, and the great Jewish mystics; (2) Hasidic leaders who were distinguished exponents of the Kabbalah; and (3) notable figures of the Jewish Golden Age in Spain. I hope this work will help to stimulate interest in this captivating subject.

Israel Gutwirth

Significance of the Kabbalah, the Zohar, and the Great Jewish Mystics

The Kabbalah

The name Kabbalah is derived from a three-letter Hebrew root—kbl—which means "to receive." It occurs in the Mishna and the Gemara when referring to reception of religious traditions; thus *Avot* I reads: "Moses received the Torah of Sinai."

The term *Kabbalah* is used to designate Jewish mystical teaching, which, being considered secret, was not written down but communicated by word of mouth, so that each generation of the chosen might receive it from the foregoing generation.

It is thus extremely difficult to determine the period in which this mystical Jewish doctrine originated. Even in the Bible there are whole words and verses that transcend their apparent meaning and seem to contain occult references to mysterious relationships between man and the Divinity. Note, for example, the passages in the Pentateuch that refer to angels or to the names of God: "I am that I am" (Exodus 3:14); the prophecies in Isaiah 6 with his visions of God's throne and the seraphim; those in Ezekiel 1, on the divine chariot; or those in Daniel, which have a definite mystical character. At all events there is a consensus on the existence of Jewish mystical doctrines during the period of the Second Temple.

18   THE KABBALAH AND JEWISH MYSTICISM

That which is known today as Kabbalah was undoubtedly revealed much later—in the 13th century, as the Kabbalists themselves admit—although it had already been "gestating" for many centuries. According to Jewish tradition the principal work of Jewish mysticism, the Zohar, was written by the Tanna Rabbi Simon Bar Yohai in the 2nd century, and all the Tannaim and Amoraim were Kabbalists.

The earliest Jewish mystics, starting from the 13th century, were Rabbi Abraham Abulafia, Rabbi Isaac Sageh Nahor, and Rabbi Moses Ben Nahman (Ramban or Nahmanides), and their disciples. Jointly with this upsurge of mysticism in Spain was its counterpart in Germany: that of the Hasidic Ashkenazim, whose leaders were notable personalities such as Yehuda Ha-Hasid and Rabbi Eliezer Rokeach.

Even in those times, the Kabbalah had both a theoretical and a practical side. The former is concerned with problems of the essence of the Divinity and with the influence of the Torah and its precepts on the world; the latter, conversely, aims at giving a practical application to secret divine powers, using them for determinate purposes, enacting miracles, or producing the supernatural through the use of Holy Writ.

Theoretical Kabbalah developed in Spain; the practical side was rooted in Germany. During that period minor works on theoretical Kabbalah began to appear, culminating with the appearance of the Zohar by Rabbi Moses de León in Spain, in the 13th century. After the publication of the Zohar, the Kabbalah gained increasing importance in Jewish religious life.

According to mystical doctrine, ten Sefirot (spheres) emanate from the Divinity: (1) *Keter* (crown), (2) *Hochma* (wisdom), (3) *Bina* (reason), (4) *Hesed* (grace), (5) *Gevura* (strength), (6) *Tiferet* (beauty), (7) *Netzah* (constancy), (8) *Hod* (majesty), (9) *Yesod* (foundations), and (10) *Malchut* (empire).

Much has been written about the significance of the word Sefira, but little is known about it. There is even less clarity regarding the essence of the ten spheres, but some authorities believe that these are attributes of God according to His influence on Creation; others think they are separate elements.

The highest and most important sphere is the first, *Keter*, whence derives the second, *Hochma*, which comes next in importance, and so on to the tenth and last, *Malchut*. The ten spheres form the World of Emanations (*Olam Haatzilut*). From the tenth sphere emanates the world of Creation (*Olam Habria*) or of finished matter, formless and in the chaotic state, whence emerges the shaped world (*Olam Hayetzira*), which in turn is transformed into the present, ordered world (*Olam Haasiya*).

This teaching clearly aims at establishing that the world forms part of Divinity, even if part of it is divine material of a lower level. All this leads to the conclusion that man, who is a part of Creation, may and must aspire to unite with the Divinity, to which purpose it is sufficient to pursue a path of contemplation, profound meditation on the Torah and its precepts, and a life of sanctity.

For the different levels, forms, and expressions of Divinity and its influence on the material world, the Kabbalah created many terms in Aramaic, such as *Dohrah Venokvah* (male and female; active and passive influences), *Nitzotzot* (sparks or remnants of Divinity), and many others.

The Kabbalah stayed with the theoretical and philosophical content as described until the 16th century, when Rabbi Isaac Luria, the Ari, set up in the holy city of Safed a yeshiva for Kabbalists, in which he taught to his disciples, and especially to his favorite pupil Rabbi Chaim Vital, a new approach to the Kabbalah, amplifying the concept of Divinity.

The Ari emphasized the need of spiritual change in order to be worthy to undergo transmigration. Such souls descended into the material world for purification, so that they might return to their original state of sanctity; it was therefore the duty of man to help them return to the path of righteousness.

Ari's influence was a decisive factor in the emergence of practical Kabbalah, which led to the messianic movement of Rabbi Solomon Molho, Sabbatai Zevi, and Jacob Frank on the one hand, and to the Hasidic movement on the other.

Many Jewish religious authorities, on becoming aware of the abuses of the followers of so-called false messiahs, opted to prohibit young people from studying the Kabbalah.

20 THE KABBALAH AND JEWISH MYSTICISM

In Jerusalem and Safed until recently there were yeshivot that offered courses in Kabbalah.

Many books have been written on the subject of this mystical science, indicating the enormous interest that it awakened among Jewish scholars, from Moses Chaim Luzzatto in the 18th century to Gershom Scholem and his numerous disciples in the 20th century.

The Zohar

The Zohar (Brightness) is the holiest book of the Kabbalah. Its name derives from the verse "And they that be wise shall shine as the brightness (Zohar) of the firmament" (Daniel 12:3).

It was written in difficult Aramaic and consists of mystical interpretations and commentaries from the *sidrot* (weekly readings) from the Torah, the Song of Songs, Ruth, and Lamentations of Jeremiah, and others.

The Zohar is the fundamental work of the Jewish Kabbalah for its mystical teachings, its references to religious terminology, the problems of the infinite, the divine emanations, and others.

According to Jewish tradition the Zohar was written in Israel by the Tanna Rabbi Simon Bar Yohai in the 2nd century of the Common Era. The Talmud, in its tractate Shabbat XXXIII, recounts that in order to escape Roman persecution, the Rabbi hid with his son Elazar in a cave and lived there for thirteen years, at the conclusion of which the prophet Elijah appeared before them to announce that the danger had passed.

According to tradition, the Zohar remained hidden for a thousand years, until at the end of the 13th century Rabbi Moses Ben Shem Tov de León discovered the manuscript and made it known.

Although the authorship of the Zohar is a subject of controversy, there are writings on the Kabbalah from very remote times, long before Rabbi Moses de León. His contemporary Rabbenu Bahye Ben Joseph Ibn Paquda mentions a Midrash of Rabbi Simon Bar Yohai as a primarily Kabbalistic work; other authors of that period and subsequent researchers make the same assertion.

The Zohar was made public in 1290. Two printed editions appeared in 1559, one in Cremona and the other in Mantua, and it has since been published many times, with the addition of many commentaries such as *Or Hachamah* (Light of Wisdom) and others.

The contents of the Zohar were translated into Yiddish in the 17th century by Rabbi Hirsch Hatash under the name of Nahalat Zevi. A Hebrew translation has been published in Israel by Reuben Margulis, on whose writings this book is based.

In Hasidic texts, the Zohar is considered so sacred that readings from it are recommended even if one does not know the meaning of the words. To this day Sephardic Jews are in the habit of reciting daily passages of the Book of Brightness, even without knowing its contents.

As a historical curiosity, it is of interest in the 18th century a "Zoharist" movement considered the Zohar superior to the Mishna and the Gemara. This trend, of course, made no headway, inasmuch as the mystics themselves rejected it strongly.

The Sanctity of the Zohar

The Zohar became deeply rooted among the Jews, much as the belief that the Talmud, like the Torah, was delivered on Mount Sinai. There were also those who claimed that the writ of the Zohar was as holy as the Torah of Moses, and the Kabbalists came to sanctify it even above the Bible and the Talmud, considering it the "fundamental book of Judaism." Some even asserted that study of the Zohar could accelerate the coming of the Messiah.

A Jewish mystic wrote: "Study of the Zohar will produce the redemption of the Jews of the Diaspora, who will return to the Land of Israel.... Then freedom will reign over all men, who will live in a calm never before known on the face of the earth."

The Kabbalists interpreted the words of the prophet Daniel, "...and they that be wise shall shine as the brightness of the firmament" (12:3), as referring to those who had become initiated in the secrets of the Zohar.

This holy text is very difficult to interpret, since besides the difficulty that it is written in hard-to-understand Aramaic, it also contains very profound thoughts, so that very few people are able to comprehend it from the Kabbalist point of view.

24 THE KABBALAH AND JEWISH MYSTICISM

The Zohar states in its third book that "in one city, only two persons can interpret it, and two in one family." The Kabbalists therefore claim that no one should grieve at failing to understand that work, since this is a privilege reserved to a few wise men. It should nevertheless be studied, since it is Holy Writ, and whoever does so, even without proper comprehension, will be privileged to receive the Holy Spirit and with it Divine Grace.

There is no definite knowledge concerning the author of the Zohar, or where it was created. These aspects have been subject to controversy among scholars to this day. Be that as it may, the Kabbalists have always asserted that the authorship of that work belongs to the great Tanna Rabbi Simon Bar Yohai, who lived in (what is now) Israel in the 2nd century of the Common Era.

According to the Zohar, Rabbi Simon gathered together a select group of sages and revealed to them the secrets of the Torah and of the celestial world, which he had heard from the "Faithful Shepherd" (Moses), from the prophet Elijah, and from the Almighty Himself.

Rabbi Simon Bar Yohai has always been venerated by the Jewish people as a true saint who had marvelous knowledge of terrestrial and celestial mysteries. The Talmud abounds in legends about him and his son, Rabbi Elazar. In times of Roman rule, when study of Jewish Holy Writ was strictly forbidden, both went into hiding in a cave for 13 years, risking their lives. At the entrance to the cave there grew miraculously a carob tree and water sprang from the ground, providing them with food and drink throughout their concealment. At the same spot, according to the Talmud (*Shabbat* XXXIII) the prophet Elijah appeared before them and revealed to them all the secrets contained in the Torah.

The Talmud also says that Rabbi Simon Bar Yohai was considered a true saint in his time and that by virtue of his merits no rainbow ever appeared in the sky, which meant that God did not intend to unleash the fury of the Universal Deluge over the Earth.

For these reasons, only he alone could have written a book so holy and full of secrets as the Zohar.

Some scholars of centuries past expressed serious doubts in that respect; most sages rejected it outright. Among the rejections

Significance of the Kabbalah, the Zohar and the Great Jewish Mystics 25

were such notable mystics as Rabbi Moses of Córdoba, Rabbi Isaac Luria (the Ari), and Rabbi Chaim Vital, all of whom lived in the holy city of Safed in the 16th century.

Rabbi Moses of Córdoba wrote a commentary on the Zohar, maintaining that its text had been created by Rabbi Simon Bar Yohai. In that respect the weight of the opinions of the Ari and of his favorite disciple, Rabbi Chaim Vital, also made itself felt, since the Ari was greatly revered, his word being held sacred and incontrovertible. The Ari similarly affirmed that only after the coming of the Messiah might the content of the Zohar be understood in all its splendor.

It was thus with good reason that the book's first printers entitled it *The Sacred Book of Zohar on the Torah, by the Holy Tanna Rabbi Simon Bar Yohai*.

Contemporary researchers nevertheless hold that in reality the Zohar is a compendium of fragments from various authors who lived in different epochs, some of them very remote. They must have included Rabbi Abraham Abulafia and Rabbi Moses de León.

The Zohar, an incomparable book in Jewish literature, is of a mystical-religious character. In its words there burns continuously the sacred fire of praise of God. Each one of its phrases contains a deeply felt spiritual sentiment, brimming with love of our Lord. It proclaims the almighty power of God and asserts that everything lives and moves by virtue of His works and thanks to His secret power of creation. On the other hand it declares that all the concepts of the Torah, even those that seem superficial, constitute a sacred and inexhaustible mystical source.

The Zohar emphasizes the sanctity of the Book of Books. Like the Zohar, every expression, word, syllable, and letter of the Bible contains some secret or veiled symbolic allusion. That which we have read, studied, and understood, though it is important, is nothing more than the outer crust, the cloak that covers the body of the Torah and its enigmas still to be solved. The Zohar says:

> Only fools see the external garb of aspects of everyday life in the Torah, without noticing what lies beneath. All the words of the Torah are divine and each one of them contains a secret. A flesh-

and-bones king does not use common speech, nor write it himself. Why should not God (who is the King of Kings) use loftier and indeed celestial words, rather than those used by Esau, Hagar, Lavan, Balaam and his mule, Balak and Zimri?... The Torah is holy and complete. Everything written in it is divine...so one should interpret its text correctly and seek to unravel the mysteries and sacred thoughts that it contains.

The Prophet Elijah

Elyahu Ha-Navi (Elijah) is, after Moses, the prophet most venerated by the Jews. They have always believed, in times of exile, that at the hour of redemption Elijah would reappear.

In the Talmudic tractate *Baba Metzia* CXIX, some Tannaim tell that they had the privilege of meeting with Elyahu Ha-Navi. Similar accounts were disseminated at later periods between the Kabbalists and the Hasidim, these being generally known under the name of Revelation of Elijah. The Gemara, for its part, steadily reiterates the firm belief that the prophet Elijah will return to announce the times of the Messiah.

Every Sabbath, *zemirot* (Sabbath canticles) are sung in honor of Elijah, that he might return as soon as possible and with him, Redemption. Those songs include *Ish Hasid Hayah* (There Was Once a Hasid), which tells how Elijah rescued a Jew from his impoverished state. The Gemara, like the Zohar and later creations of Hasidic literature, contains many stories of Elyahu Ha-Navi, who always appears at the most critical moments for Jews, to bring them succor and save them from grave danger. Usually he appears in the guise of a simple, ordinary person such as a peasant, a shoemaker, a tailor, or the like, and only the most believing Jews can recognize him.

The Bible tells wonderful stories about him, more than about the other prophets: he brings rain, or stops it; resuscitates the dead, and brings down fire from the sky. That is why the People of Israel say that "he was a Divine and the word of God is in his mouth."

His life and death were shrouded in mystery, and many wonderful legends sprang up after his disappearance. According to Holy Writ, Elijah did not disappear like other mortals, but at the end of his life "a chariot of fire and horses of fire parted them both asunder and Elijah went up by a whirlwind into Heaven" (2 Kings 2:11).

The Jewish mystics wove innumerable legends around events that occurred during his life, his disappearance from this world, and thereafter. Thus it was recounted that the cave in which God appeared before him was made by God during the six days of the Creation and that it had been intended for Elijah ever since then; that his belt was made of the sheepskin which the patriarch Abraham offered in sacrifice to God in place of his son Isaac; that Elijah and Phineas, son of the high priest Elazar, were one and the same person, who lived in the times of the prophet Ahiah of Shiloh. According to popular belief Elijah stayed hidden in Paradise and took note of the conduct of each generation. Similarly, that he descended onto Earth and flew over it like a bird, revealing himself to a few elect—mainly Tannaim and Amoraim—to teach them the secrets and mysteries of Heaven.

In the Zohar he is repeatedly mentioned, mainly in connection with his frequent appearances before Rabbi Simon Bar Yohai and his adepts, in whose meetings he took part in order to reveal to them the secrets of the Torah. Elijah figures prominently in mystical and Hasidic literature. Together with the Ari, the Baal Shem Tov, and many other pious men, he acts as a mediator between God and the righteous.

The mystical authors compare Elijah to Moses. On equality with Moses, who redeemed the Jews as an emissary of God, Elijah

Significance of the Kabbalah, the Zohar and the Great Jewish Mystics 29

will be sent on Earth to redeem them and, like Moses, he too will know the decisions of the Almighty. Moreover, he was gifted with divine powers: "God stops the rain, Elijah does the same; God brings down fire from the sky, Elijah does the same." Even more: from time to time Elijah upsets the harmony of nature, as God does; God ordained that winter be the rainy season and summer rainless; then came the prophet Elijah and changed winter into summer. He said to King Ahab: "By the will of God, Lord of Israel, from whom I have come, there shall be no more rain or dew this year, except at my word" (1 Kings 18:1).

Elijah is immortal. Both in Heaven and on Earth, he has been entrusted with innumerable missions to fulfill. In Heaven, for instance, he had to act as protector and defender of the People of Israel. The Aggadah tells that in the times of King Ahasuerus, edicts prejudicial to the Jews were decreed in Heaven and that Elijah complained to the Patriarchs, exclaiming: "How long will you remain asleep, patriarchs of the people, to avoid seeing the disaster that threatens the Jews?"

Every time, he showed himself before men in a different guise. During the siege of Jerusalem in the year 70 of the Common Era he sought out the hungry to feed them; on other occasions he appeared as a community leader, a Bedouin, a horseman, and even as a bear, always adapting himself to the circumstances, in order to help the Jews. These accounts show what high hopes the people put in him and how closely he was bound up with the idea of redemption. If Moses freed the Jews from slavery in Egypt, Elijah will bring them liberation in the future. Moses succeeded in freeing his people from its first Dispersion—a situation which would recur and from which the prophet Elijah would liberate them finally.

While all the prophets predicted the coming of messianic times, it was given only to Elijah to prepare the way for the fulfillment of that prophecy. He will announce the good news of salvation, revealing himself as the "final day of days" approaches. And Malachi said: "Behold, I will send you Elijah before the coming of the great and dreadful day of the Lord" (3:23). Thus it was entrusted to Elijah to prepare the people of Israel, awaken it to the need for its purification and sanctification, and thus make it deserving of salvation. "And he shall turn the heart of the fathers to the children, and the heart of the children to their fathers" (Malachi 3:24). Elijah would come to a city and make known the good news; he would go from one man to another, announcing redemption. Nobody would see him speaking with the people; he would arrive and say to the People of Israel: "I am Elijah." Three days before the coming of the Messiah he would grieve disconsolately high in the mountains.

The Bible has little to say about the earthly life of Hanoch (Enoch); in exchange it abounds in details of the life of Elijah. Likewise as regards the amazing disappearance of both, accounts differ widely. As regards Hanoch, the matter is mentioned in a few words: "And Enoch (Hanoch) walked with God, and he was not; for God took him" (Genesis 5:24). From those words one might well conclude that Hanoch died like any other mortal; in contrast, the approach to the disappearance of Elijah, as seen in 2 Kings 2:11, is entirely different.

The post-Biblical accounts that are affectionately concerned with both figures generally differ widely, even after their ascent to Heaven and their transformation into angels. "Hanoch immediately changed into a cloud of fire. He left Earth forever and had nothing more to do with men." As regards the prophet Elijah, however, it was said that when he entered Heaven he was given a new body of heavenly light, and that he took his place among the angels. Nevertheless, when he appeared on Earth before men, he did so in his terrestrial body. His figure is intimately bound up with the People of Israel throughout its history.

After his ascent to Heaven, Hanoch received the name of Metatron and became the "prince of the angels." There he served before the Heavenly Throne and with the prayers of the Jews he wove crowns for the Creator; from then on, he lost all contact with this world. Elijah remained in contact with the Earth despite having likewise been changed into an angel of Heaven. That is why he is so beloved of the Jewish people, for he accompanies them from place to place, from dispersion to dispersion, sharing all their sorrows and joys. With time, he has been changing into a

Significance of the Kabbalah, the Zohar and the Great Jewish Mystics

symbol of love and peace, a bringer of glad tidings and a comforter of hearts. He who in the Bible had been a "zealous avenger" was converted by the Jewish people into an "angel of peace."

The Biblical Elijah is an energetic upholder and champion of truth and justice and a zealous fighter against idolatry. He fought unsparingly against the high priests of Baal and their four hundred and fifty false prophets on Mount Carmel. By performing a miracle, he showed that the Lord of Israel was the true and only God. It was enough for him to pray to the Highest to show His power before the assembled Jewish people in that place, and fire from Heaven fell upon the altar. Thus he caused the Jewish masses to turn away in disgust from idolatry and to return to the path of the Jewish faith. And this occurred at such a critical period, when the country was practically overrun by the cult of Baal and lapsing into chaos. King Ahab's Phoenician wife Jezebel had brought from Sidon hundreds of idols and priests. She built pagan temples throughout the territory of Israel with the intention of eradicating the Jewish faith and attracting the people to idolatry. She also gave orders for the masters of the Torah to be killed and for the true prophets to be expelled from the country.

The confrontation on Mount Carmel saved the faith of Israel. When the Jews saw the divine miracle they could only exclaim: "The Lord is our God!"

The following story further illustrates Elijah's courage. On one occasion he went to the royal palace and denounced the king in strong terms, predicting that he would come to a tragic end. Sentenced to death by Ahab and his wife Jezebel, he took refuge in the desert and hid in a cave. Jezebel sent armed soldiers to capture and kill him, but they failed to track him down.

In the meantime, King Ahab and his Phoenician wife had committed a dastardly crime against a neighboring relation. The king wanted to take possession of Naboth's vineyard. He wanted to buy it, but Naboth refused to sell, since he had inherited it from his ancestors. The wicked Jezebel then rigged a trial with false witnesses and had Naboth sentenced to death for slandering and ridiculing the king. Naboth was executed and his property was confiscated in favor of the crown.

As Ahab and Jezebel were about to take possession of the vineyard, the prophet Elijah suddenly appeared before them, exclaiming in a wrathful voice: "So you have killed and also inherited? Hear the judgment of God: In the very place where Naboth's innocent blood was spilled, your own blood shall be spilled. The dogs shall drink your blood in this vineyard and shall feed on Jezebel's body in the palace garden. Every male of Ahab's dynasty shall be mown down and not one heir shall be left alive."

And Elijah's prophecy was inexorably fulfilled.

If that account and similar ones found in the Bible picture Elijah as a strong and resolute prophet, a tireless seeker after truth and justice, the Talmudists and Exegetes give a different description of him: as an affectionate figure who deeply loved his people, whom he tirelessly helped and counseled. According to commentators, Elijah was changed into an angel and was given God's permission to appear under various guises, extend a brotherly hand and comfort the righteous in moments of distress.

The Gemara recounts that the prophet Elijah could fly faster than the angels Michael and Gabriel. He was thus able to bring immediate help to those in need and protection to those in danger. In that respect, Jewish folklore abounds in fascinating stories. One of them tells that Elijah allowed himself to be sold as a slave in order to work on the construction of a great building. The product of the sale was intended for a very poor but righteous and believing man. The building was completed in a single night with the help of angels from Heaven and Elijah was set free. This story is told in the Sabbath canticle *Ish Hasid Hayah*.

The Messiah as Redeemer

The idea of the Messiah (the Anointed) is one of the fundamental principles of Judaism. According to it, the "Divine Redeemer" will come to liberate the Jews from the oppressive chains of the Dispersion.

The term "anointed" appears in Isaiah 45: "Thus saith the Lord to his anointed, to Cyrus" the King of Persia, who allowed the Jews exiled in Babylon to return and to resume building their Holy Temple.

But the belief in a Jewish Messiah, who would come to bring final redemption and establish on Earth a new order of things, of justice and divine power not only among the Jews but over all peoples, appears in subsequent books like the Talmud and the Midrash. These books tell that the Messiah was announced by a number of prophets as in Isaiah 2: "And it shall come to pass in the last days," "For out of Zion shall go forth the law for the peoples," "And he shall judge among the nations," "Nation shall not lift up sword against nation," and other prophecies of Isaiah about the ideal ordering of the world. Similar ideas may be found in Jeremiah, Ezekiel, Zechariah, Malachi ("Behold, I will send you Elijah the prophet"), Daniel, and others.

This belief is expressed more fully in the later books of the period of the Second Temple and also in the historical works of Josephus Flavius, who tells of certain persons who turned that idea to their own advantage, proclaiming themselves as the Messiah.

This belief is mentioned in the Mishna in the tractate *Berahot*, at the end of Chapter I: "For the days of the Messiah" or simply "the other world." The Gemara, in its Sanhedrin tractate, mentions the verse "I the Lord will hasten it in his time" (Isaiah 60), opining that if the people proves deserving of it, the Lord will hasten the coming of the Messiah. Otherwise, he will come at the appointed time.

The Gemara further asserts that if the Jews succeed in accumulating sufficient merits, the Messiah will come on the clouds of the sky, and if not, he will come "in poverty and riding on an ass." In the same book, the Redeemer is referred to under a variety of names (Khanun, Menachem, Shiloh, Haninah). On the other hand, the Gemara's *Pessachim* LIV asserts that the name of the Messiah was created before the world and that his coming will be preceded by a terrible famine in which many people will die. Similarly, the Jews will suffer many sorrows, referred to in the expression *Khevleh Mashiah*, the "sorrows that would precede (the coming of) the Messiah."

It was also declared that there will be two Messiahs: one Messiah will be the son of Joseph, who will unleash the war of Gog and Magog and perish in it; after him will come the Messiah descending from King David, who will bring redemption. The explanation of this belief in two successive Messiahs is that redemption will come for the ten tribes that in earlier times formed the Kingdom of Israel (the Kingdom of Ephraim and Joseph) as well as for the remainder, who constituted the Kingdom of Judah.

It was further affirmed that before the coming of the Messiah, the prophet Elijah will ascend the mountains of Israel to announce

Significance of the Kabbalah, the Zohar and the Great Jewish Mystics 35

the redemption. Elsewhere in the Gemara it is written that Elijah will blow the "shofar of the Messiah" which is a greeting among Jews.

The Talmud often mentions that the Messiah will be King David ("David, King of Israel, lives and is"), or one of his descendants. This belief is based on a verse of the Psalms, "If you serve David, you will not reject the Messiah," and on others that include expressions such as "the Messiah, son of David" or "David, the Messiah King" or the blessing before the reading of the *Haftarah* (which is complementary to that from the Torah): "We rejoice—and in the kingdom of David, thou anointed—the shield of David."

Relevant Jewish personalities of the post-Talmudic period were likewise concerned with the subject of the Messiah, especially the Rambam (Maimonides) in his well-known *Epistle to Yemen*, listing the signs of the coming of the Messiah and denouncing false redeemers.

The subject of false redeemers originated in the period of the Second Temple, in which was begun the subjugation of the Jewish people by other peoples, especially by the Romans in the 1st century before the Common Era. Out of despair on realization that their own forces were inadequate to free themselves from the oppressor sprang the belief in the Messiah, who will enact the miracle of redemption. Ever since those days there have appeared from time to time false messiahs claiming to be the divine envoys who will bring liberation to the people.

Josephus Flavius considered the problem in his historical works. The most prominent aspiring messiah of that period was the heroic soldier Bar Kochba. After his disastrous defeat, other false messiahs appeared who made insistent appeals in Israel for rebellion against the Roman power.

In the course of time these messiahs appeared in various guises: as military heroes, mystics, visionaries, or reformers of the Jewish religion. The best-known were David Alroy, David Haruveni, Sabbatai Zevi, and some of their disciples.

According to the Rambam, the idea of the Messiah is one of the fundamental principles of the Jewish faith. He further asserted that the Jew who does not believe in his coming cannot be considered a believer and loses his place in the other world.

He likewise held the idea that the Messiah had power to bring total redemption. The Zohar emphasized that the Jewish people felt a tremendous longing for the Messiah. His temple or abode was called *ken tzipor* (bird's nest); there the Messiah awaited the time of his coming, of his generation full of longing, and when he became aware of the terrible sufferings of his tortured people, he would sob disconsolately.

If the Messiah had not taken upon himself the weight of the Jews' sins, they would not—as the Zohar points out—be able to bear it. The Redeemer is full of infinite mercy and helps his people in disgrace, despite their sins. On his coming, he would treat his flock as a father his well-beloved son.

The Rambam included belief in the Messiah in his thirteen creeds, which the Jews recite daily. The twelfth of them reads as follows: "I fully believe in the coming of the Messiah as sent by God to redeem the Jewish people and the whole world, and even if it is delayed we shall not lose hope in his coming and in the liberation that will follow."

Without this belief it would have been impossible for the People of Israel to endure the innumerable privations and sufferings of its millenary exile.

At the end of the tractate *Suta*, the Mishna gives a lurid description of the moral decay that will befall the generation preceding the coming of the Messiah. Nobody will believe in God, people will reject truth and pursue their moral misconduct, turning a deaf ear to the calls of conscience. The judges and the sages will become corrupt and there will not be adequate censors, for they themselves will be immersed in the mire of sin. Youth will have no respect for age, the aged will stand before them in fear; the son will bring shame to his father, the daughter will rise against the mother. All will lose a sense of shame, members of the same household will become enemies, and the faces of that whole generation will resemble those of dogs.

Just as a dog looks into its master's face to see if he is satisfied with it, so the governors will scan (the faces of) the governed in order to satisfy all their whims. And the tractate ends with the cry: "We have nobody on whom to rely but our Father in Heaven, whom we implore to hasten the coming of the Messiah."

Daniel's Prophetic Vision

Daniel was a sage, a man of God and a prophet. His visions, both in dreams and in the waking state, were fulfilled. The Book of Ezekiel 14 also tells of a pious man named Daniel. The Book of Daniel is part of the Bible as Holy Writ and belongs to Scripture. Why was it written partly in Aramaic? Perhaps because it was written in Babylon and in those times the language of the people was Babylonian Aramaic. In the matter of language the Jews were already half assimilated, and Daniel wanted his words to reach the whole people.

As a youth, Daniel was taken to Babylon together with other young aristocrats of Israelite lineage. He was much liked by King Nebuchadnezzar, who received him at the palace, where he became famous for his wisdom and his interpretation of dreams, so much that the king regarded him more highly than all his own sages and counselors.

The Book of Daniel also tells that the last of the kings of Babylon, Belshazzar, held a great banquet for his princes and courtiers. He ordered that the gold and silver vessels that had

Significance of the Kabbalah, the Zohar and the Great Jewish Mystics

belonged to the Great Temple of Jerusalem be brought so that he might drink from them. He also ordered that the Levites of Jerusalem whom he held prisoner should appear before him and that they should sing and play the melodies of the Great Temple, while the king and his courtiers mocked Jerusalem and the invisible God of the Jews. Suddenly there appeared in the air a hand that wrote incomprehensible words on a wall of the palace; nobody could decipher them. Daniel alone explained their meaning as an announcement from the God of the Jews, who had decided to destroy Babylon. The words were MENE, MENE, TEKAL, UPHARSIN. And that same night, the Persians broke into the palace and killed the king and his courtiers.

The same book tells how three pious Jews—Ananias, Michael, and Azariah—were thrown into a furnace as punishment for not prostrating themselves before an idol, but miraculously the fire did not touch them (Meshach, Shadrach, and Abednego). Daniel too was sentenced for praying to the God of the Jews and thrown into the lions' den, but he emerged from it unscathed.

Chapter 7 tells of his visions and his prediction that a mighty state would arise in Greece and conquer all countries, including Persia. It would later be divided into four states; bad times for the Jews would supervene; the Great Temple would be defiled; the sacrifices would be held for naught; and unbelieving Jews would unite with enemies.

The historians hold that Daniel's prophecy foretold the rise of Alexander the Great, who conquered many countries, including Media and Persia. Thereafter Greece was divided among four generals and bad times came of the Jews. Daniel's prophecy was fulfilled during the period of the reign of Antiochus Epiphanus, who, helped by Jewish Hellenists, set up the statue of Zeus in the Great Temple, defiling the altar and the whole edifice.

In the same book are mysterious allusions to the coming of the Messiah, and many historians have tried to interpret Daniel's predictions for the future.

The Talmud speaks of a Great Temple that bore the name of Daniel, and the traveler Benjamin of Tudela asserts that he saw Daniel's tomb in Shushan, Persia.

The Midrash tells that when Daniel grew old, he sought out Zerubabel from among exiled Jews, brought him before King Darius of Babylon and said to the king: "O King, my strength is failing and I am unable to serve you properly. For that reason I have brought with me a fine youth who should occupy my position in the palace. He is honest, intelligent, and of royal ancestry. His name is Zerubabel, son of Jehaniah, king of Judea. What thing I have done, he will do much better. He knows many languages, is intelligent, and can give you good counsel." And Darius answered: "You have done well. It hurts me much to part from you. I well know that nobody can replace you since you were a Divine, gifted with a heavenly intelligence. Go, my good friend, and live out in peace your last days among your brethren."

Daniel died soon afterward and was buried on a hill near the capital Shushan, beside a river. And there was an abundant harvest in those parts and fortune smiled on the doings of men.

Then the people on the other side of the river said: "Because the tomb of Daniel is not among us, our land is not blessed." That led to arguments and quarrels between the two sides; each side stole the remains of Daniel from the other. And they came to an agreement: the coffin with the body would rest on one side of the river one year, and on the other the next. The king of Persia finally came to that place and inquired about the strange custom of carrying Daniel's coffin from one side of the river to the other. The matter was explained to him, to which the king replied that it was not right and proper to proceed thus—that it was disgraceful that the coffin of such a noble person should not rest in peace. He advised them that on the bridge that crossed the river, at its exact center, they should set iron columns. The coffin of Daniel should be set within another of shining copper and suspended with iron chains from the columns raised in the middle of the bridge. They agreed to that proposal, and the bronze coffin hung above the bridge. And as evening fell, the rays of the setting sun illuminated the coffin and gave it the appearance of a celestial object.

There was a legend among the Jews that if a boat sailed under the bridge with an honest and pious man aboard, that man would have good fortune; but if sinners or thieves were in the boat, it would sink and the villains would be drowned.

For his part, the king ordered that a temple be built near the bridge where one could pray, and ordered that fishermen should not approach with their nets closer than one mile from the coffin of Daniel.

The Holy City of Safed, Cradle of the Kabbalah

One of the main reasons that impelled me to go to Israel was that I felt obliged to visit the holy and historic city of Safed (Tzfat) toward which I have felt attracted since childhood, when I was taught that every corner of it held memories dear to the Jews and redolent of spiritual glory.

The interesting trip along the fine road, with a thriving Jewish population, *moshavim* and *kibbutzim* on both sides, the handsome houses and villas brilliantly reflected in the translucent waters of the Mediterranean; the mountains, with the tall, bright-green olives and grapevines that clothed their slopes—all this was genuine delight.

At times I had a feeling of having been in those places before. There rushed into my memory names and figures of Jewish history, mystics with whom I would be meeting shortly; also side-streets, *yeshivot* (Rabbinical seminaries) and synagogues about which I had read and heard and which had deeply impressed me.

Safed, the ancient city of the Upper Galilee, is the undisputed center of the Kabbalah. Together with Jerusalem, Hebron, and

Significance of the Kabbalah, the Zohar and the Great Jewish Mystics

Tiberias, it was one of the four sacred cities of ancient Israel. It was the home of the most prominent mystics such as Ari the Saint and his disciples Rabbi Chaim Vital, Rabbi Moses Alsheikh, Rabbi Solomon Alkabetz (author of *Lecha Dodi*), and many others.

In its ancient cemetery lie the mortal remains of many saints, including those of the Ari, Rabbi Moses of Córdoba, Rabbi Jacob Moses Beirav and others. The Jews of Safed traditionally assert that the tomb of the prophet Hosea is in a neighboring cave.

In the time of Ari the Saint and Rabbi Joseph Caro there were eighteen Rabbinical seminaries and over twenty synagogues and schools in Safed; also the Halacha center that served as a guide for the Dispersion. There Rabbi Joseph Caro wrote his *Shulhan Arukh*[1] and other works.

Safed was destroyed by an earthquake, but within a short time it flourished again thanks to the influx of students from all parts of the Jewish world who came for purposes of study. Noted Hasidic leaders such as Rabbi Menahem Mendel of Vitebsk and Rabbi Abraham of Kalisk, disciples of the Maggid (preacher) of Mezricz, settled in Safed, which eventually became an important Hasidic center.

Alongside the historic city of Safed has risen another settlement known as "New Israel," where luxurious houses and villas have been built along with comfortable hotels on the mountainsides. Thousands of tourists from within the country and from abroad visit there, attracted by the picturesque scenery; Safed's ideal climate during the hot summer months is a delight.

Thanks to its marvelous scenery Safed has become a permanent home of noted artists and painters. They can be seen seated before their easels, beside broad roads or in narrow by-paths, painting pictures and displaying them for sale.

Saturday evenings in that city are of particular interest. The contrast between Friday mornings and evenings is striking. For the first time since leaving my home in Europe I felt sure, in Safed, that "come Shabbat, come relaxation...."

---

[1] "The Prepared Table," a monumental compendium of precepts of the Torah.

The bustle of late Friday afternoons was like that of a big city. The people were moving hurriedly around, the shops were crowded, there was intense bus and automobile traffic, and people were buying flowers, fruits, and other gifts for their families.

With the approach of the Sabbath, peace and silence descended on the roads. They seemed cleansed and embellished, as if by their own means; one could sense the coming of the day of repose.

Suddenly the silence was broken. Along highways and byways, unhurriedly, the people were on the move. There was something majestic about their gestures, as befits the Sabbath, a day on which every Jew is a prince. A colorful multitude was moving toward the synagogues; there was a glitter of high hats (*shtraimlen*) and of silk frock coats. There were also young Sabras in white shirts with open collars, mingling with soldiers, with fathers leading their little ones by the hand and with tourists from various countries. All greeted one another with a warm and friendly "*Shabbat Shalom*" and there was great joy and happiness in their faces.

In Safed there are many ritual bath houses (*mikvot*) some of which are two hundred to five hundred years old. In the old Jewish quarter are two synagogues, one Ashkenazic and one Sephardic; the latter is named after Ari the Saint, who prayed there only. There is also a synagogue in honor of Rabbi Isaac Aboab, author of *Menorat Hamaor*. Another synagogue, honoring Rabbi Joseph Ranay, contains the Scroll of the Torah that is traditionally borne at the festival of Lag Ba'Omer to the town of Meron, where the mortal remains of Rabbi Simon Bar Yohai lie buried.

Down a narrow byroad I reached the Synagogue of the Ari at the very moment evening prayers were beginning. I was deeply moved as I crossed the threshold of the synagogue. Along the eastern side a number of venerable Jews were seated. They were the *Yekireh Tzfat* (Beloved of Safed) God-fearing men who devoted themselves to the Kabbalah and to preserving the sacred character of Safed. There was a small recess in the wall where only the Ari used to pray; candles are lit there and the Zohar is studied.

Suddenly there came to the pulpit an elderly Kabbalist of Safed,

Rabbi Shlomo David Cohen, whose figure seemed surrounded by a spiritual halo, as if he had recently descended from Heaven. In a soft, pleasant voice, he began to receive the Shabbat. The congregation was profoundly affected by his prayers, the culmination of which was the *Lecha Dodi*, which engendered feelings of ecstasy in all those present.

The congregants included people from very different social strata; many must have been accustomed to different rites of divine service. But here we all felt indissolubly united, and we could feel how the air was pervaded by the spirit of many generations of holy men. In this sanctuary, prayers were offered up differently; here the words of the psalmist seemed to come true: "Out of the depths have I cried unto thee, O Lord" (130:1). Only one who has been in this place during prayers can realize the full magnitude of the Jews' feelings in these moments. I stayed rooted to the spot and wished to prolong indefinitely this *Kabbalat Shabbat*, but I had to return, much against my will, through the narrow lanes of the venerable city.

The image of those rites or reception of the Sabbath, and the memories of that evening, without detracting from the merits of other impressions I received during my stay in Israel, will remain indelibly graven in my heart.

Rabbi Yehuda, the Hasid of Regensburg: A Revered Figure of Jewish History

He was one of the most revered personalities of Jewish history: a deservedly famous sage, Kabbalist, and a man of profound moral rectitude. He lived in the late 12th century in Germany, mainly in the city of Regensburg (Ratisbonne).

His actual birthplace is still unknown. Legend recounts that at the age of eighteen he was still an ignorant youth, but that he set himself to study zealously, quickly becoming a scholar who astounded the whole Jewish world with his knowledge.

His generation believed that only an envoy of Heaven could have taught him so much in so short a time. Besides being a Talmudic scholar, he was a noted mystic who organized in Germany a Hasidic movement with a character of its own, whose adherents were known as Ashkenaz Hasids. He dedicated himself to study of the Kabbalah and of the secrets of the Torah, and led a life of great rectitude, marked by strict abstinence. He used to fast for a whole week, eating a modest meal only in honor of the Sabbath.

He observed Yom Kippur for two days. Jewish scholars of the time said of Rabbi Yehuda: "If he had lived in the time of the Tannaim, he would have been one of them; if he had lived in the times of the prophets, he would have been a prophet."

He was head of an important yeshiva (Talmudic seminary) whose students became well-known Kabbalists, among whom such figures as Rabbi Eliezer of Worms (author of the *Book of Rokeach*), Rabbi Isaac (author of *Or Zarua*), and Rabbi Baruch of Mainz (Mayence).

His life was enveloped in a halo of mystery and legend, like that of a saint who worked miracles and marvels. He also devoted himself to medicine and, at a time when the elders of his generation were concerned with the study of *Halacha* (Talmudic legislation) and of the Gemara (the Halachic part of the Talmud), Rabbi Yehuda dedicated himself to the Kabbalah, to ethics and the virtues, winning a deserved reputation as a mystic and Hasid for his prayers full of sincere faith and laws of God. That, together with his habit of delving deeply into the secrets of the Torah and Kabbalah, which he held to be above study itself, caused the people to regard him as a saint.

A legend recounts that his father, Rabbi Samuel, who was head of a yeshiva, was studying Torah with Yehuda and his brother Abraham. Suddenly, as he pronounced a certain sacred word of the Kabbalah, the whole yeshiva was lit by holy fire. Abraham was gripped by fear and began to weep and tremble; Yehuda, however, was unshaken. Then Rabbi Samuel, who had noticed the reaction of his two sons, said: "Abraham, my son, all your life you will be a student of the Torah, but your brother Yehuda will know the secrets of Heaven and Earth, and no secret of the Torah will remain hidden from him."

For Rabbi Yehuda the Hasid, the main thing was to delve into divine secrets, the hidden teachings of God, and to pray fervently. With him arose Ashkenazi Kabbalah, which eventually merged with Sephardi Kabbalah.

Rabbi Yehuda held that men should serve God with love and respect and glorify His Name by always doing good deeds. Studying the Torah was very important, provided it went hand in hand with virtuous conduct, since God is especially interested in men's hearts and in their good intentions. He liked to illustrate his sermons with a variety of stories; here is one of them:

> There was once a Jewish shepherd who everyday prayed to God as follows: "Lord of the Universe, you know the truth; if you have a herd and give it to me to look after, I will carry out your wish wholeheartedly, since I long for you." One day a wise man passed that spot. On hearing the shepherd's simple prayer he said to him angrily: "Fool, you must not pray in that way." Then he taught him a number of prayers and benedictions that the shepherd soon forgot, as well as his own prayer. In the meantime the wise man had a dream: he dreamed that in Heaven he was severely reprimanded for having estranged the shepherd from his own way of serving the Almighty. Then he realized his error and, returning to the place where he had met the shepherd, told him that he should resume praying as he had done before.

Rabbi Yehuda ended his story with the following explanation: although the shepherd had not studied the Torah, his heart was pure, he was God-fearing and well-intentioned, which was more important. The same ideas appeared later in the teachings of the Baal Shem Tov and of many other Hasidic Rabbis.

Rabbi Yehuda wrote many books, most of them of a mystical character and dedicated to revealing the secret messages of the Torah, besides prayers and benedictions. His most important work was the *Sefer Hasidim*, which considers a Jew's duties, customs and traditions, relationships with fellow men, how to treat servants, and even cattle husbandry. The book overflows with wisdom and is replete with mystical teachings on subjects of daily life and co-existence.

The *Sefer Hasidim* became the most popular book of its time, having been written during the period of the Crusades, when religious fanaticism and irrational hatred reigned supreme and thousands of Jews offered up their lives on the altar of their faith. The terrible situation of the Jews raised a multitude of personal and ethical problems that daily called for urgent practical solutions. In those times the *Sefer Hasidim* filled an enormous void and became a genuine guide for religious Jews of those and later times. Many were the generations that drank from this source, whose lifegiving waters also nourished the Hasidic movement, which took up many of its opinions and ideas.

The book taught that people should be treated with love and kindness regardless of race and of social, intellectual, or spiritual allegiance. All human beings are equal; no humiliations should be imposed even on servants. Not only human beings should be treated affectionately and spared distress, but so should animals: they must not be harmed, for instance, through burdening with excessive weights. Every human being would have to render account of his actions in the other world. One should not beat dogs or any other animal even if they bite, nor throw scalding water over them. Animals should not be maimed, for God created them according to what is good for them. To animals of the ox family He gave horns for defense against predators and a tail to drive away the insects that sting them; when man shortens their tails, he first causes them pain and later suffering, since they can no longer protect themselves. It is also sinful to pull a cat's ears in order to hear it meow. It is utterly wrong to do injustice to either Jew or Gentile; God hears the complaints of both equally. If a Gentile asks counsel of a Jew on whether it is advisable to negotiate with another Jew, he should act honorably and tell him the whole truth.

A very special place in *Sefer Hasidim* is held by the warning to keep away from evil deeds, false reports and empty talk, hypocritical affection, lies and fraud. The Jew should be honest whatever the circumstances. One interesting piece of advice is not to plead in favor of one person, when this harms another person. A father should not kiss his son in a public place, since this might offend and sadden Jewish onlookers who are childless, or those orphaned of their fathers.

The *Sefer Hasidim* is among the most important, wonderful, and original works of the Jewish cultural heritage. It serves as a guide for going through life worthily, with dignity. Many generations of studious and God-fearing Kabbalists were educated by its teachings, and to this day it remains one of the fundamental works for the education of honest Jews, devoted to God and their fellow men.

Rabbi Yehuda the Hasid was a true saint; that is why his memory has endured in the hearts of the Jewish people to this day.

Eliezer Ben Yehuda Rokeach: Kabbalist Known for His Book Rokeach, *a Guide to Righteousness*

A glance at outstanding figures of the period of the Crusades—men who set the fundamental principles of Jewish national and ethical ideology—brings into striking relief the dominant figure of that great Jewish spiritual leader, *posek* (post-Talmudic commentator) and Kabbalist Eliezer Ben Yehuda (1165-1243), of the German city of Worms.

In those times the German people, as in the 20th century, had set out to exterminate the Jewish people. The Jews, in their dangerous situation, had to face up to many serious socio-ethical problems that called for quick solutions. Those solutions were put forward by Rabbi Eliezer, and as a result his moral influence on Jewish life became very marked.

In his times, ruthless persecution and massacres of the Jews were the order of the day. He himself describes those years of mindless Christian religious fanaticism, paying tribute to the Jews' heroic stand in defense of their belief when in the year 1196 King Henry issued the decree compelling them to convert to Catholicism. Those who refused were expelled without mercy and

52 THE KABBALAH AND JEWISH MYSTICISM

exposed to prolonged hardship as a result of this cruel persecution.

Rabbi Eliezer was inspired by this tremendous distress to write his *Slihot* (prayers of penitence), saying: "They slander us and deliver us like booty. One disaster follows the other; every day is worse than the day before it. The oppressor demands that we replace our God with an idol."

Rabbi Eliezer was a student of Rabbi Yehuda the Hasid and joint author of *Sefer Hasidim*, the most popular ethical work of those times, which faithfully reflected the socio-ethical thinking of the most prominent religious personalities of the period and was, as one might say, "consecrated" by the Jewish people as a guide in solving innumerable problems of a moral character.

Although Rabbi Eliezer Rokeach was a post-Talmudic commentator, he dedicated himself to unraveling the secrets of the Torah and even of the Kabbalah. His home did not escape the horrors of the Crusades: the killers mowed down his wife Dultze, who was the family breadwinner, and Rabbi Eliezer poured out his sorrow in moving prayers of penitence and lamentations (*slihot* and *kinot*) which have been preserved to this day.

His principal work, the *Sefer Rokeach*, embodied both Halachic (Talmudic law) and Kabbalistic elements. The Jew's finest crown, he wrote, is the crown of humility. The most acceptable sacrifice is a humble heart; the major virtue is modesty. Man should be extremely humble, have compassion for all creatures, and walk the path that leads to eternity.

When during days of annihilation your enemies rise against you, he wrote, to compel you to renege your faith, offer up your life and do not protest on seeing how evil men prosper and become rich and powerful, for the way of God leads to redemption, his designs are shrouded in mystery, and it is not given to us to understand them.

Love your neighbor as yourself, he went on; that is the one moral rule, the true and only yardstick for measuring and evaluating the deeds and lives of human beings. How should a person who is given authority behave? To that question, the *Rokeach* answers: let such a person reflect and think how he would like to be treated when he finds himself on another man's property.

Significance of the Kabbalah, the Zohar and the Great Jewish Mystics

Men must not covet something for their own advantage, if this harms their neighbor.

The old hatred of the Jews was brought about by their own faults. All the persecution at the hands of their oppressors should therefore be considered punishment for the evil the Jews have done to one another.

Do not defraud anyone, whether he be Jew or Gentile. No prejudice should be directed toward the Gentiles, nor advantage taken of their errors; they should be treated with honor as much as or more than the Jews.

If a Gentile comes to a foreign city and inquires of a Jew of his acquaintance, asking with whom among the local Jews he should do business and with whom not, the Jew must deal uprightly with him and tell the truth, warning him not to do business with this or that person.

Rabbi Eliezer enjoined men to serve God without fear but with love; this would naturally lead them to become God-fearing. He counselled them to preserve their humility and the other virtues that adorn the heart of man and purify his thoughts. Those were the foundations that should serve to guide the Jew's life, in any place.

He held that the pleasures of life are nonsense, because they led nowhere, since this world is transitory. Man's days are few and much hardship awaits him. Due to their innumerable faults and misfortunes, men's hearts were failing. He warned the Jews that "there is no crown so splendid as that of honesty, rectitude and a good name, nor sacrifice equal to a humble heart before God, nor wisdom that exceeds that of the Torah, nor virtues like decency and modesty. If you have been blessed with wealth and honors, let not your heart wax proud over that of your brother, for you do not know what tomorrow may bring, nor what will come after you. You were both born naked from your mother's womb and on leaving this world, you will return to dust."

Rabbi Eliezer said of penitence: "If you have sinned a little, it should be in your eyes as if you had sinned much. Man must balance pain and pleasure and measure joy, besides making confession daily with weeping and sighs, in pain and torment."

Rabbi Eliezer's teaching on penitence (*teshuva*) eventually became the foundation of the last Kabbalists' doctrine of self-chastisement and strongly influenced the system of the Ari and his disciple, Rabbi Chaim Vital, and even the Gaon of Vilna and his adepts. The first to depart from this teaching was the Baal Shem Tov, who urged the Jews to serve God happily, even if they were sinners.

Initially, Rabbi Eliezer studied with his father, a well-known scholar. Thereafter, he studied Talmud with Rabbi Moses Hacohen in Mainz and later under the guidance of the famous Rabbi Yehuda the Hasid, notable for his knowledge of the Talmud and as a mystic. While sharpening his talents in Halachic questions, he became engrossed in the profundities of Jewish mysticism and its worlds without beginning or end.

He inherited all this from his father, Rabbi Meshulam the Hasid, principal of the Talmudic Academy of Speyer and author of two ethical-religious books, *Sefer Hairah* and *Sefer Hatshuva*, in which he described and analyzed the foundations of prayers and morals. Virtues, purity of thought, and generosity of feeling were the foundations of Judaism, and men's souls and lives should be devoted to cultivating them.

Rabbi Yehuda passed on this mystical teaching to his disciple Rabbi Eliezer, who set the foundations of the Kabbalah in Germany, where it was completely unknown. And when Yehuda the Hasid wrote his *Sefer Hasidim*, Rabbi Eliezer set himself to revise and complete it.

Rabbi Eliezer's erudition was strongly apparent in his *Sefer Rokeach*. Many of his conclusions were thereafter incorporated in the *tosafot* (annexes) of the *Bavah Kamah* Talmudic tractate, and elsewhere. He was immersed in mystical doctrine; this was reflected in his writings, which revealed hidden meanings gleaned from almost every word of Holy Scripture.

His book *Yayin Harokeach*, a commenting on the Five Scrolls and the Haftarot, is also well-known. His other work, a commentary on the Torah, is replete with mystical teachings and holds a privileged place among Jewish Kabbalists.

Due to the cruel persecution unleashed against the Jews, Rabbi Eliezer left Mainz and finally settled in Worms. He recounts how,

Significance of the Kabbalah, the Zohar and the Great Jewish Mystics

when that city was besieged by the Crusaders, the Jews fought heroically so as not to be suspected of siding with the enemy, and he authorized his congregation to fight even on the Sabbath.

The calamity that befell the Jews of Germany in those disastrous days did not spare Rabbi Eliezer. He lost his entire family, whom he mourned for the remainder of his life.

As a chronicler of that period wrote: "Rabbi Eliezer threw light on all the secrets of the Torah and became a guide of generations."

Ari the Saint:
A Star That Shone With a Light of Its Own

After the disappearance of Rabbi Joseph Caro, a new star appeared in the firmament of Safed that shone with a dazzling light of its own: the *Ari*.

Until then, logic had been the predominant element in Judaism. The Tannaim as well as the Amoraim and subsequent Jewish scholars and thinkers, up to Rabbi Joseph Caro, held that knowledge and fulfillment of *Halacha* (Talmudic laws) was of primary importance.

The personality that arose in Safed after the author of the *Shulhan Arukh* adopted a completely different approach. Of an exalted and mystical disposition, he believed in supernatural power, in miracles and in things that transcend logic and human understanding. This was Rabbi Isaac Ben Shlomo Luria, known as the Ari, a name derived from his anagram (Ashkenazi Rabbi Isaac) and held to be the foremost Jewish authority of his time.

The Ari was born in Jerusalem in 1534, of Ashkenazi parents. His father died while he was still a boy. His mother lapsed into

Significance of the Kabbalah, the Zohar and the Great Jewish Mystics

penury and appealed to a wealthy brother, Rabbi Mordecai Francis of Egypt, for assistance. Rabbi Mordecai, who was a tax collector, took them into his house in Cairo.

In the land of the pyramids, young Isaac studied with the Geonim Rabbi Bezalel Ashkenazi (whose name he later adopted) and Rabbi David Ben Zimrah (Radbaz). The Ari was such a fine student that his uncle Mordecai made him his son-in-law.

Under the influence of the Radbaz, a noted mystic, young Isaac dedicated himself entirely to study of the Kabbalah. Gradually he began to move away from his home; he would spend the whole week in solitude in a house that his father-in-law owned on a bank of the Nile, returning to his home only on Sabbath evenings to be with his wife, with whom he conversed only in the holy language—Hebrew. Late on the Sabbath he would return to his retreat to immerse himself anew in the secrets of the Kabbalah.

In his extreme isolation, there occurred the *Gilui Eliyahu*: the prophet Elijah appeared before him. The prophet had come to study with him and pass on to him secrets of the Torah that no human being had ever heard before. On one of his Sabbath visits to his home, he told his wife that Eliyahu Ha-Navi had appeared before him to ask that he settle immediately in the city of Safed, in Israel, in order to make known the practical Kabbalah that he had developed, since he had only two years to live. This occurred in the year 1570.

The Ari then settled with his wife in Safed, where he was received with great respect.

Those were hard times, when people believed in angels, demons and other supernatural beings. To know the secrets of Divinity and Creation was not enough. The Ari and his adepts sought to apply that knowledge in practice, in order, perhaps, to speed up the coming of the Messiah, to win mastery over evil spirits, or to exorcise the possessed.

There is a story that before the Ari came to Safed, a certain woman was showing signs of insanity. She became delirious and behaved very strangely. When she was taken to a group of practical Kabbalists, they diagnosed that she was possessed by a *dybbuk* (a lost soul or devil, in search of salvation), which should be expelled from the unhappy woman's body for her to recover sanity.

A party of three distinguished Kabbalists was then appointed to exorcise the evil spirit: Rabbi Abraham Lachmi, Rabbi Elyahu Falkon, and Rabbi Solomon Alkabetz. The Rabbis first talked to the evil spirit, who told them that in life he had been an unbeliever; he had been moving from place to place for thirty-three years, until he finally found rest in the body of the possessed. The devil, asked if he wished them to intercede with the Almighty, answered in the affirmative; the Kabbalists then repeated an appropriate prayer three times and sounded the *shofar* (ram's horn). On being next asked if he wished to be administered a *tikun* (remedy), he replied that there was no solution to his case. Finally, after persistent shouts of "Out, evil spirit!" in the sacred language, the *dybbuk* was forced to leave the unhappy woman, who was covered with protective amulets. Having ascertained that the possessed was better, the Kabbalists withdrew.

Soon afterward they were recalled: the evil spirit had regained possession of the woman. The exorcists studied the case and concluded that the evil spirit had returned because the amulets were ineffective and did not prevent its re-entry. They decided to wait for a time and to return later to drive it out for good, but within eight days the woman died, being unable to withstand further torment.

Another case of possession during that period in Safed was also well-authenticated. Exorcism was performed by Rabbi Elyahu Falkon, who drove out the evil spirit and recorded the event. The protocol was also signed by Solomon Alkabetz, Abraham Lachmi, Samuel Biyani, and Abraham Avrothi, and reports were sent to all the Jewish communities.

Ari the Saint thereafter found in Safed propitious ground for his teachings on practical Kabbalah in the service of the loftiest ideals, in an ambiance of supernatural things and occurrences, and of knowledge of divine secrets and powers that could not be used to destroy evil and restore the rule of righteousness. Belief in evil spirits was strengthened at that time and persisted among Hasidic

Rabbis for several centuries, together with faith in the efficacy of exorcism through Kabbalistic practices. This phenomenon is strikingly reflected in a work of Yiddish literature; we refer to the play *The Dybbuk—Between Two Worlds* by Samuel An-ski.

Rabbi Isaac Luria came to believe, with time, that he was the *Ben Joseph* messiah, forerunner and annunciation of the *Ben David* messiah; he won many adherents.

At the start of his residence in Safed he did not make himself known and engaged in trade, counting on the material support of his uncle and father-in-law, as reported in the *Ari Noem* of the Mahari of Modena, in the name of Rabbi Jacob Abulafia.

Soon, however, the Kabbalists of that holy city became aware of the presence of such an outstanding personality, began to visit him, and became his devoted disciples and adherents. The Ari wrote many mystical works in Safed, but the end announced by the prophet Elijah was inexorably fulfilled: he died in 1572, two years after settling in that city.

Rabbi Chaim Vital: The Faithful Disciple of the Ari Hakadosh

The expulsion of the Jews from Spain and other countries had an enormous impact on the Jews of Europe, the Middle East and Asia. The example set by Spain engendered a state of turmoil in the minds of Jews the world over. They began to realize the dangers that threatened them, since in whatever country they settled, bringing to it economic and cultural development, they might suddenly be compelled to take the road of exile, for they could be expelled without redress, prevented from taking with them even a small portion of their belongings.

All this persecution and misery aroused longing for the Messiah, who would redeem them. This feeling was strongest among the Jews of Western Europe, owing to the sufferings they had to endure.

The messianic movement was based on the practical Kabbalah of the venerated Ari and won many adepts; it eventually became a popular movement headed by Rabbi Chaim Vital, a faithful disciple of the venerated Ari the Saint; he was similarly known for his erudition and piety and as the co-initiator of the Kabbalah of his revered master.

Rabbi Chaim Vital was born in the city of Safed. He studied revealed Kabbalah with Rabbi Moses Alsheikh and secret Kabbalah with Rabbi Isaac Luria, also known as Ari the Saint.

His father, who was a native of Italy, where he worked as a scribe, settled in Israel; he was a Kabbalah scholar. In the Holy Land he took up *tefillin* inscription, for which there was a big demand.

Two years after his arrival in Israel, a son was born to him, who he named Chaim, in honor of the Kabbalist Rabbi Chaim Ashkenazi.

Besides the education that he received from his father, he also attended the *yeshiva* of the Kabbalist Rabbi Moses Alshech, who noticed young Chaim's qualities, remarking that he possessed a heart and mind that would one day shed light on the world.

His name became known in the Jewish world, and the Ari took an interest in him, making him one of his favorite disciples.

The extraordinary Ari, who mostly remained aloof from the world, told his secrets to nobody. To Rabbi Chaim alone he taught hidden truths of the Torah and of the human soul and other secrets—for instance, how to drive out an evil spirit that had taken possession of a person. At that time a widow was afflicted with a visitation of that kind, and the Ari sent Rabbi Chaim Vital to exorcise the demon, which he did successfully.

The Ari did not write books: nor did he leave anything in writing. The great spiritual leaders of the time did not consider this necessary; to them the main thing was the spoken word—fiery, full of life and fervor, according to the words of the prophet: "The spirit of the Lord speaks to me, and His words are on my tongue."

Nor did the Ari want others to write down his teachings, fearing that his words might not be recorded correctly. Rabbi Chaim Vital was the only person he allowed to do this, making him his acknowledged successor. Rabbi Chaim wrote an autobiography, titled *The Book of Visions*, but it was published under the title of *Shivchei Rabbi Chaim Vital*.

In his books, in which he amplified his teacher's system, Rabbi Chaim Vital described the personality of the Ari, whom he considered a celestial being. He asserted that since the times of Rabbi

Simon Bar Yohai and the ancient Tannaim there had not been so many miracles as were performed by his teacher, who not only had profound knowledge of the Mishna, the Talmud, Aggadah, and Midrash, but discovered the secret knowledge based on the mysteries of *Maaseh Bereshit*, the creation of the world.

He understood the language of the birds, the rustling of the trees, and listened to the conversation of the angels; he talked with both good and evil spirits. He could appraise a person by observing his face and forehead, and he knew graphology.

Shortly before his death, Rabbi Vital gave instructions that all his writings on the Ari should be deposited in his grave. But as Rabbi Chaim Joseph Azulai reported in his book *Shem Hagdolim*, soon after his death Rabbi Vital appeared before his friends in dreams and gave them permission to edit and publish his writings.

His most important work was *Etz Hachaim* (Tree of Life); it contained his commentaries on his teacher's Kabbalah system. It also included interpretations of the Zohar.

In *Shaarei Kedusha* (Gates of Sanctity) he showed how men could attain to sanctity through practice of the virtues. In Rabbi Chaim Vital's writings, the Ari's ideas were approached from two angles: practical Kabbalah and theoretical Kabbalah.

Practical Kabbalah was concerned with the influences of secret divine forces of the world and in daily life, as they appeared from miracles that could be performed by means of sacred words.

According to the Ari, the souls of this world could be amended by means of torment, flagellation, fasting, mastery over the passion, and renunciation of pleasures; through atonement for sins committed; through isolation for closer communication with God; through the ritual bath for purification from sin; and by means of prayer according to certain forms of the Ari's rite.

Likewise all the precepts and laws should be observed, and that applied to the Written Law (Torah) as well as the Oral Law (Talmud).

The foregoing offers practical means of setting one's soul to rights, as well as speeding the coming of the Messiah and attaining total redemption.

Theoretical Kabbalah is concerned with the essence of Divinity, the existence of the world and the influence exerted upon it by the Torah and the *mitzvot* (precepts).

The guiding idea is that our world does not lie outside Divinity but forms part of it, so that all existing things and happenings in the world are part of God.

However, some things and events belong to a lower level, others to a higher level.

The "practical result" of those theories leads to the idea that man also forms part of Divinity and can unite with the same through a life of sanctity, study and observance of the precepts, meditation on Divinity and the material world.

According to the Ari, the world is composed of souls. Likewise the desert, the waters, trees, plants, animals and birds are part of God's mystery.

The Ari believed in the reincarnation of the soul—of the wicked as well as of the just, which if they had sinned in the previous life would be reincarnated to atone for their sins.

In his "Reincarnations" book, Rabbi Chaim Vital revealed a list of leading Jewish sages who had recently returned to this world.

His books are held in high regard to this day, especially in Sephardic communities, within which they are studied with respect and devotion.

Rabbi Yeshayahu Halevi Horowitz: Shela the Saint

The expulsion of the Jews from Spain and from other countries was also a harrowing experience for their brothers around the world, in whom distress was combined with feelings of helplessness. The conclusions they drew from those events were disturbing: having settled in a country and contributed to its economic and cultural development through their labor and ability, they could be expelled without ceremony.

The Jewish people were disheartened by this unjust treatment, which awakened in them a deep-seated longing for Redemption and the coming of the Messiah. This feeling was particularly strong among Polish Jews, who were exposed to continuous harassment at the hands of both the governing powers and the people. For this reason the messianic movement founded on the teachings of Ari the Saint's practical Kabbalah quickly won the hearts of the oppressed Jews, developing into a mass movement headed by Rabbi Yeshayahu Halevi Horowitz (known as the Shela)[1] a renowned scholar, mystic, and master. He was a Rabbi in

---

[1] The anagram of his principal work *Shneh Luchot Habrit* (Two Tables of the Covenant).

various Polish cities and also in Frankfurt and Prague, and the creation of Lurianic Kabbalah (by Rabbi Isaac Luria, the Ari) in Poland is attributed to him.

The Shela was born in Prague in 1565. His father, Rabbi Abraham, was his first teacher. Thereafter he continued his Torah studies with the noted scholar the Maharam (Morenu Harav Rabbi Meir) of Lublin. From an early age he had won fame as a Talmudic sage and scholar of such distinction that he was expressly invited by the Four Nations Council to confirm by his signature a provision prohibiting purchase of the position of Rabbi.

In 1597 he published in Cracow a work of his father's, *Emek Bracha* (Blessed Valley), to which he contributed commentaries. In the prologue he wrote: "I realize that I am an ignorant person, without clear understanding of men.... I am insufficiently versed in the Torah and in science. But what can I do if my father, blessed be his memory, ordered that I devote myself to his book?" Those words speak of the stature of the future author of *Shneh Luchot Habrit*, the Kabbalist book that went to the hearts of the Jewish masses, winning their veneration and that of the following generations.

As a Rabbi in various cities in Poland, in which oppression of the Jews was well-nigh intolerable, he knew how to bring to his brothers counsel and hope as well as wise teachings. Later he was a Rabbi in Frankfurt, and when the Jews were expelled from that city he accompanied them in exile. Thereafter, he held the position of Rabbi in the historic city of Prague, where he mistakenly thought he would find peace and happiness. His hopes, however, were frustrated, and he eventually left that city.

He felt a deep affection for the Promised Land and traveled to the Land of Israel, where be began preparations for his well-known book *Shneh Luchot Habrit*. It is a mystical, Halachic, and ethical encyclopedia, a genuine guide to prepare men for life in the other world, which they should reach in a state of purity and sanctity. It explains in a mystical tone the significance of the precepts of the Torah and the traditions of Judaism. This book introduces new ideas and concepts that reflect the enriching influence of Ari the Saint and of his disciple Chaim Vital. It was written in the form of a will dedicated to his sons, affording them guidance in matters of everyday deportment. Written in clear and accessible Hebrew, it won such favor among Jewish readers that it was reprinted thirty times.

In this work, the author holds that the Kabbalah is the key that opens the gates of wisdom. He writes:

> Know the God of your fathers, His Uniqueness be blessed; learn His Names and the secret of His Essence, which is achieved through study of mystical science, which brings wisdom to the ignorant. He who has seen this light of knowledge will know that it is the true light. He will then discover and understand the secret of His blessed uniqueness and the mystery of His help and protection together with that of His attributes, which are mentioned in the Torah and are revealed by the philosophers. Blessed is the eye that has seen all this. And he who departs from it (from the Kabbalah) departs from eternal spiritual life.

The Kabbalah became the basis of his preaching and guided his writings to such extent that he came to interpret the Three Principles of the Rambam (Maimonides) "according to the truth that is subjacent in secret knowledge...." As a mystic he held that the secrets of the Torah could be more significant than the readily apparent; if the latter was the body, the secret part was the soul.

His maestros in matters of Kabbalah were Rabbi Moses of Córdoba and the Ari, representatives of Sephardi theoretical mysticism and Ashkenazi practical mysticism, respectively. The ideas of both, with a few addenda of his own, are interlaced in his works, especially in *Shneh Luchot Habrit*. Thus he writes unambiguously: "I come only to reveal part of the little that I picked up from the Zohar and from subsequent works."

He was among the first who set out to conciliate both systems through an eclectic approach. Thus in referring to theoretical subjects like God and the Creation, or Israel and the Torah, he made use of Sephardi Kabbalah, citing whole chapters from Rabbi Moses of Córdoba; and in dealing with practical subjects, like worship of God and its objectives, he availed himself of Lurianic

Significance of the Kabbalah, the Zohar and the Great Jewish Mystics 67

Ashkenazi Kabbalah. Rabbi Yeshayahu Halevi Horowitz showed an inclination toward this practical mysticism. Worshiping God, doing good, and complying with the precepts are the foundations of human living. Knowledge is not enough; it must be completed and crowned by deeds, which are the principal virtue. By fulfilling the precepts of the Torah, man comes nearer to God, to whom he should seek a likeness. "They [the precepts] are the outer form, the mediators between those who fulfill them and the Almighty." Thus, that passage of the Zohar that reads: "Three in number are those interlinked among one another: God, the Torah, and Israel." Nevertheless, deeds cannot be perfect unless they are based on good intentions. Only he who serves God with fervor and with appropriate purpose, through the spirituality and secrets that underlie such purpose, will walk joyfully along the path of life.

Rabbi Yeshayahu longed for a life of sanctity for the Jews. "Repentance for sins committed is the first step toward *teshuvah* (return to the path of righteousness).... Blessed is he who puts on sackcloth, sits on ashes, weeps for his sins and confesses himself with lamentations, bowed head and reclined body, until all the muscles of his body move, thus fulfilling that which is meant by the word *teshuvah* (the letters of which are initials of the Hebrew words T, *taanit*: fasting; S, *sak*: sackcloth; V, *ve'epher*: ashes; B, *bekhi*: weeping; H, *hesped*: lamentation).

Aware of the pernicious influence that is exerted on man's thoughts and actions by the environment amid which he develops, Rabbi Yeshayahu advised withdrawal into isolation from tumultuous surrounding life. "Isolation," he asserted, "is more profitable for him who studies... It is a great and lofty virtue, through which one can ascend many steps..." Such a man was therefore in duty bound to "remain solitary in his Halachic world, seek seclusion and not abandon his sacred recess. He should not mix with people, to ensure that he is safe from any kind of sin against his neighbor; then his thoughts and his deeds will be pure, he will be safe from temptation and excesses and able to dedicate himself fully to the Torah...and God will give him His blessing."

To Rabbi Yeshayahu Halevi Horowitz, acts of penitence are only valid provided they are the product of sincere repentance. He knew the human heart, holding it to be sinful and an easy prey to temptation, and he therefore advised that every night, before going to bed, "a man should seek solitude, lie down on the ground, strike a balance of his deeds and revise them. And if he finds anything evil, he should cast it out...to be able to return with heart uplifted and not downcast.... God will not make him feel ashamed." The *teshuvah*, then, is the foundation of salvation.

"He who longs for eternal life must seek daily self-correction.... Though he may have committed all the sins in the world, he can repent and return... But the *teshuvah* must be the fruit of love and not the product of fear."

Rabbi Solomon Alkabetz: Kabbalist and Religious Poet

Rabbi Solomon Alkabetz was one of the luminaries of the Diaspora who lit up the Jewish firmament with his writings, erudition, and wisdom and is venerated to this day by the Jewish people. The world-renowned Kabbalist and religious poet is remembered for his liturgical poem *Lecha Dodi*, which became a popular prayer in the temple of Jewish liturgical music.

Rabbi Solomon Ben Moshe Halevi Alkabetz lived in the 16th century and settled successively in Salonika, Adrianopolis and Safed. In Safed he was the leader and guide of the Kabbalist group known as the Sukat Shalom, whose ranks included mystical divines such as Rabbi Joseph Caro, Rabbi Moses of Córdoba, the Ari, Yeshayahu Halevi Horowitz, and Rabbi Chaim Vital. In Salonika he was a disciple of the mystic Joseph Taitatzak, who was said to have fasted for 40 years to accelerate the coming of redemption.

Solomon Alkabetz was a *tzadik* (righteous man), a man of the highest moral standing and a brilliantly inspired religious poet, whose works were received in his lifetime with enormous enthusiasm as popular prayers throughout the Jewish world. His prayer *Lecha Dodi* (Come, My Love) instilled a new spirit into the Jewish people and turned the idea of the sabbath into a universal concept, kindling and captivating the hearts of poets round the world, who translated it into their own languages and assigned it a place of special distinction in world literature.

Since ancient times, Jews have rejoiced in the Shabbat. It has long been a custom to receive the Shabbat with music (*Sefer K'vod Hachamim*). In the synagogues of Prague the Shabbat was received with great joy, and the *Lecha Dodi* was sung with instrumental accompaniment. In Safed, too, with the advent of the mystics, the Jews received the Shabbat with great rejoicing. Rabbi Isaac Luria (the Ari) introduced the custom of setting out with his disciples, late on the eve of the Sabbath, toward the mountains, far from the city, there to receive the Shabbat with rejoicing and song. A number of fine Sabbath poems were written in those times; in Safed, the Ari wrote songs for the three Sabbath meals: *Azamer Bishvakhin*, *Asader Liseudatah*, and *Benei Heichalah*.

Safed, the ancient historic city of Upper Galilee, was the center of secret knowledge (Kabbalah). It is one of the four holy cities of Israel (the others are Jerusalem, Hebron and Tiberias) and it was the cradle of the Kabbalah. The Ari, Rabbi Chaim Vital, and others lived there. It was the home of prominent Jewish Rabbis and scholars, famous as mystics, and the center of *Halacha* (Talmudic law) at that period. In Safed, Rabbi Joseph Caro created his *Shulhan Arukh* and other works.

Outstanding Hasidic leaders such as Rabbi Mendel of Vitebsk, Rabbi Abraham of Kalisk, the disciples of the Maggid of Mezericz and others rose to prominence in Safed, which became the center of Jewish mysticism, of Hasidism, and of men of action. In that propitious atmosphere Rabbi Solomon Alkabetz created his *Lecha Dodi*, his religious poem that is a song of Redemption. In that prayer, the author emphasizes the sanctity of the sufferings of the Jewish people through the ages, from the "ten martyrs of the faith" to the crypto-Jews of Spain, and arouses hopes in soon-to-come redemption.

The Jewish mystics considered the Shabbat a ceremonial circumstance—a day that foretold and hinted at Redemption. Each *kabbalat Shabbat* (receiving of Shabbat) was a harbinger of Redemp-

Significance of the Kabbalah, the Zohar and the Great Jewish Mystics

tion. No wonder, therefore, that this poem went straight to Jewish hearts; it should be stressed that it was composed in times in which high hopes had been raised.

Daily tidings were arriving of the notable achievements of Joseph Nassi, to whom the Sultan had conceded control over seven territories on which to set up a Jewish state; it was also rumored that the idea of the Jewish state was supported by the wealthy and influential Grace Mendes, who had made her wealth available for the rebuilding of Tiberias as a Jewish city.

Within a single year Tiberias was rebuilt, thus fulfilling the wish of the Jews of those times expressed in the verses of *Lecha Dodi*:

Shrine of the King, royal city,
Arise, come forth from thy ruins.
The end of your exile has arrived
And God will show you abundant mercy.

Shake off your dust, arise,
Put on your glorious garments, O my people,
Restore the dynasty of David
And be near to my soul to redeem it.

This admirable poem became the spiritual foundation of the messianic movement and of the immigration of Jews to Israel.

Rabbi Alkabetz was also a renowned Kabbalist. As principal of the Talmudic seminary of Safed he instructed his students in the teachings of the Zohar (Book of Splendor). He became increasingly well known, so that such a prestigious personality as Rabbi Joseph Caro consulted him on problems of interpretation of secrets of the Kabbalah.

He used to assemble his students and hearers at his home for round-table discussions, under his supervision, on the secrets of the Kabbalah. At times he would suddenly interrupt the debate to ask the students to accompany him to the tomb of the holy Tanna Rabbi Simon Bar Yohai, to whom Jewish tradition attributes authorship of the Zohar.

His soul soared ever upward to the heights. Moses Ben Chaim Alsheikh wrote of him: "Solomon Alkabetz is a saint; his words and thoughts are holy." On the subject of his disappearance, the same legend is told as that which surrounded the passing of Rabbi Solomon Ibn Gabirol, the famous Jewish poet of Spain: a certain Arab envied Rabbi Alkabetz's profound wisdom and learning, killed him, and buried his body under a fig tree. The tree began to arouse the admiration of passersby for the marvelous fruit it yielded; the people began to investigate the cause of this wonder and discovered the Rabbi's lifeless body. The king ordered an inquiry; the Arab criminal was apprehended and sentenced to death by hanging ("Baal Shallshelet Hacabala").

Some historians maintain that this legend was born of the people's great affection for the author of the *Lecha Dodi*. The Jews of those times could not resign themselves to the idea that their beloved poet and Rabbi had passed away like any mortal, so they embellished his death with that legend.

Alkabetz wrote many other poems that made a deep impression on the Jewish people. Likewise his books *Manot Halevi*, *Beth Hashem*, and *Apiriyon Shlomo* were justly famous.

Blessed be the memory of the Just Man.

Rabbi Chaim Ben Atar (Or Hachayim): Sage and Kabbalist

The great scholar and Kabbalist Rabbi Chaim Ben Atar, known through the title of his best-known work as *Or Hachayim* (Light of Life) was among the most prominent Jewish personalities for his intelligence, erudition, and teachings.

Or Hachayim was born in the small town of Tali, Morocco, in 1696. That place is known and considered holy by all the Jews of North Africa. It adjoins the city of Rabat, which under French rule was the capital and residence of the European governor.

Rabat had an ancient and very important Jewish community. The Moroccan and North African Jews took pride in their prominent personalities, who had earned worldwide recognition. Such noted Sephardic scholars as Rabbi Moses Ben Maimon (Rambam), Rabbi Isaac Alfasi (Rif), Rabbi Isaac Bar Shesheth (Ribash), and Rabbi Menachem Ben Saruk, the famous Hebrew grammarian and poet, lived there.

Rabbi Chaim Ben Atar came of a very well-known and widely ramified North African family that had arrived there from Spain as a result of 15th century persecution. His thirst for learning and the knowledge he acquired had been outstanding since childhood.

His teachers sensed in him the soul of a saint and predicted a great future for him.

From boyhood he dedicated himself to the Kabbalah and research in the principles of this secret fount of learning.

In Morocco the Or Hachayim had to face many difficulties, for the official authorities persecuted him under accusations of engaging in witchcraft. He was finally imprisoned, and it was only by dint of much effort and payment of a heavy ransom that his release was secured. He was, however, forbidden to reside in his birthplace and he traveled to Livorno, Italy.

His fame as a scholar had preceded him, and he was received with great honor by the representatives of the local Jewish community, who offered him the position of Rabbi.

Although his final objective had been to settle in Jerusalem, he agreed to stay in Italy for some time, being weary with much travel from one place to another. He opened a yeshiva in Italy, where he conducted Torah studies among Jews who were keen to receive instruction from such a great scholar. He was deeply appreciated by all, but nevertheless nobody could make him forget his beloved Land of Israel and the holy city of Jerusalem, where he ultimately managed to settle. For some time he lived in Safed, center of the leading mystics, in order to immerse himself even more fully into the secrets of the Kabbalah. There he visited the graves of the leading Kabbalists, bowing in admiration, respect, and communication. Thereafter he returned to Jerusalem to set up a yeshiva, which was attended by many students from all countries, eager to hear his lectures.

According to Rabbi Ben Atar, Talmud and Kabbalah studies were not contradictory, but complementary. His most widespread work is the *Or Hachayim*, a commentary on the Torah. His text deserves study with almost the same assiduity as the Pentateuch with Rashi (the most popular Torah commentary). The *Or Hachayim* interpretation combines simple with mystical elements in an understandable, agreeable, yet profound form, which accounts for its widespread popularity.

His prophetic vision of the future of the Jewish people and its redemption is worth knowing:

Significance of the Kabbalah, the Zohar and the Great Jewish Mystics

When the Congregation of Israel shall rise for the first time to repel the onslaughts of the enemy, it will display amazing heroism and its triumph will be so crushing that the peoples of the world will be filled with admiration.... Despite the Jews' prolonged stay in the Dispersion, where they endured persecution and oppression and had to fight many battles on different fronts, they will not be weakened but on the contrary they will be strengthened and their image among the peoples will continue to grow, and they will win the praise and respect of the whole world.

(*Or Hachayim*, chapter "Balak").

Rabbi Ben Atar firmly opposed the false messianic movement of Sabbatai Zevi, which had spread dangerously in the East and threatened to lead to catastrophe among the Jews. The movement had also succeeded in penetrating Africa, where many adherents had begun to depart from the right path, but the Or Hachayim's timely and resolute intervention, getting the African Jews to understand that Sabbatai Zevi and his followers were nothing more than the product of the unbridled imagination of sick minds, put things back in proper perspective.

In those days Rabbi Israel Baal Shem Tov emerged in Poland to drive away from the Jewish firmament the black clouds that had obscured it and to breathe new life into the people. Rabbi Israel strongly opposed the unreasonably ascetic practices of the false messiahs—various forms of penitence, fasting, and others; he taught that God should be served joyously. That was the fundamental principle of the creator of Hasidism, who extricated the people from the darkness in which they had been plunged.

Hasidic writings relate that the Baal Shem Tov sent his brother-in-law Rabbi Gershom of Kitev to the Land of Israel for fuller Kabbalah study in the Or Hachayim's yeshiva. Rabbi Gershom went to Jerusalem, but he met with many difficulties in attempting to enter that high-study institute. He complained to Rabbi Ben Atar who, learning of Rabbi Gershom's identity, embraced him. He then told Rabbi Gershom that he had received tidings from on high that he would shortly be visited by an emissary of the holy father, Rabbi Israel Baal Shem Tov, who had descended to Earth with the mission of bringing light and hope to the Jewish people.

Thenceforth Rabbi Ben Atar concerned himself personally with the Kabbalistic studies of his distinguished student.

Another Hasidic legend recounts that before the Or Hachayim arrived in Jerusalem, the Baal Shem Tov had tidings from on high that within less than nine months there would arrive in the holy city a great and God-fearing sage who would be the messenger of the Messiah. The creator of Hasidism then understood that the Or Hachayim had risen to a position that no one had succeeded in attaining before.

Rabbi Israel did all he could to rise to the level attained by Rabbi Chaim Ben Atar, but his efforts were in vain. Then he admitted that Chaim was a great man, righteous and God-fearing, who through the Kabbalah had risen to the highest position possible for a human being. Rabbi Israel's brother-in-law Rabbi Gershom wrote and told him that his master's godliness was such that no man could look directly into his face and that his piety and intelligence were limitless. In the last years of his life it was impossible to reach him, for he seemed girt by a protective ring of fire.

Rabbi Ben Atar died in 1743, at the age of forty-seven. He had no children and was buried in the cemetery of the Mount of Olives, beside his wife's grave.

The Arabs destroyed that cemetery, and after the Six-Day War of 1967 the historic spot in Jerusalem disappeared almost completely. Only one grave remained intact in the old Sephardic cemetery: that of the Kabbalist Rabbi Chaim Ben Atar.

Rabbi Yehuda Liwa Ben Bezalel,
The Grand Kabbalist: The Maharal of Prague

Among the luminaries of the Dispersion, one whose knowledge, intelligence, and wisdom shed a dazzling light in the Jewish sky and whom the Jewish people venerate to this day is the famous Gaon (sage) Rabbi Yehuda Liwa (Loew) Ben Bezalel, known as the Maharal of Prague.

His knowledge of the secret as well as the declared aspects of the Torah amounted to genius, as did his knowledge of languages, mathematics, physics, history, philosophy, and even alchemy.

He was an authority on the Kabbalah and a master and teacher of the Torah. The masses held him in added veneration through attributing to him the creation of the legendary Golem by means of sacred names. The Golem carried out all the orders it was given and also various missions; on becoming aware of the unhappy situation of the Jews, it succeeded in rescuing them from persecution at the hands of Catholic fanatics. The Golem was the first "robot," created centuries before modern science created its own mechanical servants.

His multitudinous and eternal legacy is bound up with the Jewish people, who revere him to this day; it has become legendary. He was listened to with veneration, and his name is pronounced with deep respect by thousands of Jews.

The Maharal's times were rich in outstanding Jewish personalities—notable figures, including many wise men who brightened the Jewish skies of those times.

The Maharal was born in 1515 in Posen (Poznan) to a distinguished Rabbinical family that descended from King David. From an early age he was noted for his prodigious memory, mental sharpness, and knowledge. In reaching his *bar mitzva* (age 13) he already knew by heart a complete tractate from among the six that form the Mishna. His knowledge made him famous in the Jewish world, and the leader of the Prague community chose him as bridegroom for his daughter Pearl.

After his marriage he was invited to take charge of the Rabbinate of Prague, a city with a distinguished record of Torah studies and for the scholars who lived there. For generations no other city in Europe was so closely bound up with Jewish history, with its sages, scholars, and masters. Every stone was a record of past generations—of happy periods as well as medieval obscurantism.

Jewish history in Europe during the last millennium has been marked by progress alternating with decadence, flowering with destruction, and brilliant periods with persecution, but the interest it aroused was particularly due to the famous Maharal, who for many years held the position of Chief Rabbi of Prague.

At the popular level the story is accepted of the creation of a human figure, a Golem in whose mouth a card was placed under the tongue with God's name written on it, which gave it life and enabled it to carry out various tasks. The Golem was amazingly fearless and terrorized the Gentiles of Prague who persecuted the Jews.

In those times, persecutions by the Catholic Church were serious. Charges of the utmost gravity were brought against the Jews, and the inflamed and unbridled masses, believing those accusations, eagerly seized upon the Jews as their victims. The "ritual murder" charge became increasingly frequent; that was

Significance of the Kabbalah, the Zohar and the Great Jewish Mystics 79

why the Maharal resorted to the Golem to bring help to his persecuted brethren. According to the legend, the Golem appeared when the Christians plotted to accuse the Jews of ritual murder; on such occasions, they would put a dead child or bottles of blood outside Jewish houses or synagogues, thereafter to accuse the Jews of murder; then the Golem would appear and wreak vengeance on the real killers.

Rabbi Meyer Perle in his *History of My Family* wrote:

> My grandfather the Maharal was much loved and revered for his greatness in the Torah and his great piety, and the Jews loved him like a father. He looked after them and protected them from a variety of calamities, with God's help. Repeatedly he used his wits to save them from the murderous schemes of their Christian enemies, but his right hand on such occasions was his creature the Golem. Once on the night of Pesach, when the Maharal, together with his sons and grandsons, was covered during the *seder* with a white *kitel* in the likeness of an angel, the Golem suddenly came in and warned them that during the night the Christians had placed bottlefuls of blood next to the synagogue's Sacred Chest (*Aron Hakodesh*).
>
> The Maharal went to the spot and took them away. The next day, while the Jews were praying in the synagogue, a battalion of armed soldiers accompanied by the bishop and other priests surrounded the spot and began a furious search for the blood of Christian children murdered by the Jews; but with faces red with shame before the authorities whom they had assured that a corpse would be found in the Jewish temple, the Christian prelates had to admit that they were mistaken.

The Maharal always kept the Golem under control and late on the Sabbath he removed the card bearing God's name from under his tongue, depriving the Golem of his life-force, so that he became a mere clay figure. Since the Maharal's time and to this day, it has been the custom in the Old-New Prague Synagogue to recite twice on Friday evenings the chapter *Mizmor shir leyom hashabbat*. In that respect, as the Jews of Prague explain, one Friday night, when the Maharal was praying in the synagogue and the cantor had begun to read out the *Mizmor shir leyom hashabbat*, someone burst in upon them from the street, shouting that the Golem created by the Maharal was going berserk in the streets of Prague, destroying everything in his path. The Maharal at once left the synagogue and set out on the Golem's trail. When he caught up with him, he removed the card; immediately the *homunculus* went limp, losing his "life-force." On returning to the synagogue, the Maharal ordered the cantor to read out the *Mizmor shir leyom hashabbat* again, and ever since then the same text has been in that Prague synagogue read twice every Friday evening.

The people thought that the clay figure was hidden in the attic of the old synagogue, but the Maharal, in order to put a stop to growing curiosity and forestall a demand to see the Golem, announced that anyone who went up to the attic to see the clay figure would die in the act. He thereby prevented intrusion; the attic door was bolted and sealed for all time.

The word *golem* means "a body without a soul"—an inanimate form made by God, but without power of comprehension. In the Mishna and *Pirkeh Avot* V, the Tanna sets forth the characteristics of a sage, and his opposite is a golem. The Midrash Leviticus (*Vaykrah* XXIX) says that in the beginning God created the first man as a golem and thereafter breathed a soul into him. Jewish legends abound in accounts of a variety of characters who created a golem, that is, put certain materials into bodies and with the help of God's name instilled life into them and made them obey their orders.

The Gemara (*Sanhedrin* and *Hulin* CVIII) mentions Amorites who created living beings. There are similar reports of certain Kabbalists who utilized the mystical text of the *Sefer Hayetzirah* (Book of Creation)—which was composed during the Talmudic period—and with its help created living beings. It is also accepted that Rabbi Solomon Ibn Gabirol, the greatest Jewish poet and philosopher produced by European Judaism during the Golden Age, created a golem.

The founder of the yeshiva of the town of Voloshin, Rabbi Chaim Voloshin, who was a student of the Gaon of Vilna, wrote in the prologue to the Gaon's book *Sfirat Hagrah*: "My teacher the Gaon of Vilna himself told me that when he was about to create a golem, he foresaw the prejudice it might cause and decided to destroy and bury the clay body."

The Old-New Synagogue of Prague is bound up with the name of the Maharal and will henceforth be called the Synagogue of the Maharal. It is the oldest European synagogue, built more than a thousand years ago and later destroyed; it was rebuilt in the 13th century in the Gothic style. The parishioners there celebrate Pesach for nine days. This is attributed to an incident that occurred in the Maharal's time. There lived in the Jewish ghetto a baker who was a great Jew-hater. He once planned to poison all the Jews of Prague, knowing that at the end of Pesach the Jews would come to buy bread. That day he put poison in the bread he had baked for them, but the Maharal got wind of the intended villainy and instructed the Jews of Prague to eat matzot one day longer—a custom that the small community observes to this day.

The famous Prague synagogue miraculously escaped destruction by the Nazis, who were dazzled by its beauty and fine architecture. As the end approached, the Nazis hastily evacuated the city, pursued by the Russian Army. The monument of the Maharal, raised by the inhabitants in the last year of the Austrian empire, luckily escaped destruction. The statue had been hidden during the German occupation, and after the liberation it was restored to its original site beside the old synagogue.

Jewish history abounds in beautiful stories about the famous Maharal of Prague, revered by Jews of all generations. He was held to be of divine essence—a righteous man who strengthened and uplifted the Jewish life of his time and of following generations.

Teachings of the Kabbalists on Sin, Repentance, and Penitence

There has always been sharp controversy between the literalists and the mystics in the matter of repentance and acts of penitence for sins committed. The literalists held that the main thing was mortification in spirit and not in body, which was mere matter. The mystics, on the other hand, taught that the body should be purified and totally mortified even for a minor sin.

At that time the literalists taught that "when the sinner repents in his heart he becomes a righteous man [see Talmudic tractate *Kiddushin* XLIX, 72]. Since it is the heart and the mind that incite one to commit sins, it is enough if man reflects on his estrangement from God and the sinner renounces his sin and banishes it from his thoughts, firmly resolving from the bottom of his heart not to repeat it" (*Yad Hazaka*, "On Repentance," LXXXII, 2).

The mystics, conversely, put forward the idea that not only the mind and the heart had sinned, but also the 248 bones and 365 blood vessels of the body. Therefore, if a person had sinned, he should torture his whole body.

This idea was born of a complicated system of acts of penitence and contrition. Thus the Kabbalists taught, for example, that men should expiate certain sins through daytime fasting. At night they could have bread and water. For other sins, they had to fast on three consecutive days (*Rokeach*, "On Repentance"). More serious sins could require fasting of not less than forty days, or of seventy-two, or of eighty-four, and for even more serious guilt, up to one hundred and sixty-four days of abstention (*Rokeach*, "On Repentance," letter *zayin*). The mystics, however, did not hold that fasting was adequate and conceived various forms of castigation to which the sinner should submit himself: sleeping on the ground, give up washing, sit on snow or ice an hour a day in winter and, in summer, sit naked on the ground among flies, ants, and bees. They prescribed for each person a different act of penitence according to the sin committed, the suffering, on occasion being weighted to equal the pleasure obtained when committing the fault. This type of atonement was known as *teshuvat hamishkal*; another form was *teshuvat hakatuv* (penitence according to Holy Scripture). According to the latter, if a sin was punishable by death according to the Bible, the sinner should torture himself to such an extent and for so long until he felt suffering as great as that of death.

As the Jews of Eastern Europe were subjected to increasing political, social, moral, and economic pressures and a succession of disasters befell them—pogroms multiplying and whole communities being wiped out—their asceticism grew in proportion with the mystics inciting them to increasingly terrible tortures. This attitude re-emerged during the period of widespread Cossack vandalism (1648-1649) and during that of Sabbatai Zevi, when the Jews came to believe that the disasters which befell them "heralded redemption" and they prepared to receive the Messiah.

Rabbi Solomon Maimon writes in his autobiography:

> ...in the town of Lochwitz there lived a well-known Jewish scholar, Rabbi Simon, whose only aim in life was to purify his soul by means of acts of severe penitence. He had managed to complete the *teshuvat hakaneh*—that is, self-chastisement consisting in fasting by

day for six years with "defasting" by night but without eating anything derived from a living being! Moreover, he went into voluntary exile in token of atonement, moving from place to place without settling anywhere for longer than one day, wearing a rough sackcloth over his naked body. Rabbi Simon believed that he had not yet atoned for his supposed sins; he therefore next decided to undertake the *teshuvat hamishkal*. But on weighing his sins he concluded that they were far too grave for atonement through penitence, so he decided to die of hunger. After a long fast he continued his weary exile until he came to my father's house, and without a word to anyone there, he entered the barn and collapsed. My father, happening to enter the barn, found Rabbi Simon, whom he had known for a long time, stretched out on the ground half dead—with a Zohar in his hand.

Since my father knew him well, he hastened to bring some wine...but Rabbi Simon would not taste it. My father begged him to drink a little to recover his senses, but he did not. With my father busy in the house with much work, Rabbi Simon took the opportunity to resume his exile: he managed to rise to his feet, leave the barn, and set off toward the village. When my father returned to the barn, he found Rabbi Simon had gone. He decided to follow and trace him and finally found him lying on the ground on the other side of the village—he was dead. News of that incident quickly spread among all the Jewish communities and Rabbi Simon was held to be a genuine saint.

Occurrences of this kind were relatively frequent in that period. The Jews largely derived this theory of sin and atonement from a book by Rabbi Isaac Aboab the Sephardi, *Menorat Hamaor* (Chandelier of Light), which was considered one of the authoritative works on ethics.

Rabbi Isaac Aboab lived in Spain in the late 14th century, and his book was and is still widely read. It has been reedited many times, including a Yiddish translation, and became a means of disseminating strict moral rules among the Jewish masses for centuries.

The author maintains that this world is nothing more than a bridge of transition. Therefore, a wise and sensible Jew should keep away from the pleasures of this world and concern himself only with saving his soul.

The world we know is full of falsehood and vanity, hatred, envy, and unnatural passions. In his book Rabbi Aboab developed many ideas on morals, respect, and virtue enumerated in the Gemara and the Midrash, as also in earlier works, but his mystical thoughts, which were new for that period, were the main feature.

Menorat Hamaor is divided into seven sections, like the traditional seven-arm Jewish chandelier. Each section is entitled *Ner* (light, candle). In the first section the author quotes a number of passages from Talmudic and post-Talmudic literature, enjoining men not to seek the lights and vanities of this life. In the second part he sets forth the evil consequences of dissipation, of lies and flattery, of slander, of quarreling with people and doing them injustice, and the like. The third section gives advice on how to fulfill duties and obligations such as observances of the Sabbath and of feast days; to treat parents with due respect; to give children a proper education; to observe the rules of hospitality and family life. The fourth analyzes the importance of Torah study and the fifth deals with the subject of sin and atonement. The sixth, in exchange, extols the merits of peace, of coexistence, of respect and love of one's neighbors. The final section is devoted to the subject of humility, from which no man should ever depart, whatever his condition.

The work enjoyed much prestige and was widely circulated among the Jewish masses. One result was a movement toward penitence and asceticism that lasted for several centuries. A change came in comparatively recent times—in the 18th century—through the Baal Shem Tov, the founder of Hasidism, who set out to combat the old teaching in all its forms, including opposition—in that respect at least—to the great mystic the Ari of Safed, who had also urged self-mortification.

The Rabbi of the Good Name said that "it is better to serve God without mortification of the flesh" (*Baal Shem Tov's Testament*) "because fasting weakens the body too much for it to serve God, so it is preferable that man's effort expended in fasting be dedicated to study of the Torah and to prayer and that he prays with all his strength and all his heart" (*Torah Or*, "Tehillim," in the name of the Besht).

The Baal Shem Tov taught his students to renounce fasting and prevailed on them not to fast.

The Besht maintained that if the flesh was weakened, men's souls would also be weakened. Therefore man should take proper care of his body, "since one of the tricks of the instinct of evil is to dazzle a man's eyes and make him believe that he has achieved righteousness by inciting him to mortify his body" (*Baal Shem Tov's Testament*).

The Rabbi of the Good Name held that not all was bad in this world and that one could find good things. He used to say: "Whoever thinks that this world is unsubstantial is mistaken; this world is beautiful for him who knows what to take from it and how to enjoy it."

That doctrine was taken up by his followers, the standard-bearers of Hasidism. For examples, consider these aphorisms of leading Hasidic Rabbis:

Joseph Hacohen said that "once a person accepts to do penitence for his sins, he becomes a genuine *tzadik*" (just man) (*Toldot Ya'akov Yosef*) and "good intentions may even underlie the act of eating, such as when a man purposes to serve the Almighty." "Man should seek to eat all kinds of food, for he needs them all" (*Midrash Pinhas*). Moreover, "salvation of the body precedes that of the soul" (*Sefer Hamidoth*, by Rabbi Nahman Bratzlever).

It is interesting to record the penitence that one of the adherents of the Maggid of Mezericz imposed on a Jewish woman for a grave sin. Here is the story:

The woman had stifled her child in its sleep, having put it in her own bed. The unhappy woman visited many Rabbis, who ordered penitence through eighty-four days of fasting, on all Mondays and Thursdays.

A well-known Rabbi, an adherent of the Maggid of Mezericz, once visited the town where the unfortunate woman lived. On inquiring as to what punishment the local Rabbis had imposed, he not only ordered her to stop fasting, but to eat more than usual:

that would be her penitence. The Rabbi explained his ruling as follows:

> The best penitence is known to be the *teshuvat hamishkal* (penitence according to the gravity of the sin committed). Now, what sin has this woman committed? She had killed a Jewish child; therefore, she should bring another Jewish child into the world. She can only do this by eating and drinking in order to be healthy and beautiful and thus find favor in her husband's eyes; she will then become pregnant and give birth to a child. If, on the contrary, she fasts, she will become thin and displease her husband. How, then, can she atone for her sin? (*sifte tzadikim*).

Thus we should not wonder that the disciples of the Baal Shem Tov taught that if a man ate only enough to have sufficient strength to serve God, that service would be deficient, since eating and drinking in themselves were ways of serving God (*Ma'ayan hahochma*).

And when the Hasidim wanted to ridicule those who tortured themselves by fasting—the moralists who claimed that one should lead an ascetic life—they would tell the story of the Besht horses:

One day the last-named horses had to make a long journey. As usual, according to Hasidic accounts, the Baal Shem Tov miraculously shortened the route (*kefitzat haderech*) and the horses raced like arrows. In an hour they covered hundreds of miles. When the noble animals passed inns and taverns without stopping at any, they were extremely suprised; one asked the other:

"Why don't we stop to eat? We're so hungry!"

"What a strange animal you are!" answered the other. "Perhaps you think we are ordinary horses? We are the Baal Shem Tov's horses, so we are like men and do not have to stop at every inn for food."

The first horse was silent and both continued their rapid journey. They passed several more inns and taverns. The first horse protested again:

"Listen! D'you see those people in the coach? They are eating. Don't we get anything?"

"What does that matter?" answered the second horse. "You know that we are men, so you should remember that we are traveling to fulfill a very important mission; thus we are 'like angels.'"

"Is that so?" asked the first horse in amazement, his ears drooping. "I never imagined such a thing."

And the Hasidic story ends with the noble animals continuing their journey for several days without stopping to eat or drink anywhere. "They were then genuine angels, but as soon as the Baal Shem Tov had stopped the coach at its destination and the horses went to the eating-trough, they were no longer angels, but reverted to what they really were: just horses."

The Hasidim told that story to show that even the greatest ascetics, so long as they indulged in self-chastisement and fasting, were like angels, but they stopped being angels at the first opportunity, eating greedily like ordinary human beings.

There was a story that a certain *mitnaged* (opponent of Hasidism) came to Rabbi Elimelech of Lizensk, sadly confessing that he had committed a grave sin in his youth and asking for the imposition of a severe penitence. The Rabbi listened as the man poured out his sorrow and finally said:

"A sin as serious as yours can only be atoned for by drinking a spoonful of boiling lead!"

The man was determined to do this penitence, but Rabbi Elimelech signified to him that the spoonful of lead was not in itself sufficient to cleanse his errant soul. For that, he should first seek contrition in heart and mind.

To that purpose, the Rabbi gave him daily instruction in various Hasidic works, fully preparing him to drink the spoonful of molten lead.

The day finally arrived when the Rabbi considered that the sinner was worthy to atone for his fault by drinking boiling lead. Then he called a gathering of Hasidim, had the metal melted, and described to all those present what sin the penitent had committed, concluding that there was no other way he could atone for his guilt than by drinking a spoonful of molten metal.

The sinner in great fear and trembling opened his mouth,

though he felt sure he could not survive such a trial. And Rabbi Elimelech poured out for him...a spoonful of jam.

That, Rabbi Elimelech maintained, was how a man should cleanse himself of sin and do penitence. What mattered was genuine repentance for sins committed; the remainder was not of major importance, though it was certainly preferable to swallow a spoonful of jam than a spoonful of molten lead.

One day the Rabbi of Rapschitz was shown a Jewish ascetic who fasted much of the time and wore a rough sack over his unprotected body. The Rabbi stared at him for a time and then sadly remarked: "The evil spirit has deluded him, putting him in a sack!"

It was said of Rabbi Elimelech that when he was told of a Jew in that town who fasted a great deal and lived in isolation, he wished to have nothing to do with him.

Rabbi Jacob Emden (Ya'abetz): Influential Scholar

It is now more than two hundred years since the disappearance of the world-famous scholar Rabbi Jacob Emden, known under the name of Jacob Ben Zevi. This genius, a many-sided personality about whom more has been written than about any other celebrity of his time, is worth knowing.

Rabbi Jacob Emden is closely bound up with a major controversy that went on for thirty years with another prominent figure of his time, Rabbi Jonathan Eybenschütz, of blessed memory.

Rabbi Emden was born in Altona in 5458 (1697) as the son of the *hacham* (sage) Zevi and the grandson of the noted scholar and author of *Shaar Ephraim*. Gifted with unusual wisdom and learning, he was appointed spiritual leader of the Jewish community of his native town and given permission to open a printing shop to publish his writings. The first work to come to light was a *Siddur Hatefillah* (Order of Prayer) which contained advice on how Jews should behave in everyday life; he published many other books on religious subjects, precepts, legends and other subjects. Jews from all parts of the world came to him for advice on a variety of religious questions.

It fell to Rabbi Jacob Emden to live in deeply troubled times for the Jews. The terrible slaughter in the times of Bogdan Khmelnitsky was followed by the movements of the false messiahs Sabbatai Zevi and Jacob Frank. Those movements claimed to be based on the secrets of the Kabbalah. Jacob Emden led a number of important religious personalities in opposing those false redeemers, who had arisen as a result of demented distortion of the elements of Jewish mysticism.

It is a well-known fact that the principal book of the Kabbalah is the Zohar, attributed to the illustrious Tanna Rabbi Simon Bar Yohai. It contains innumerable secrets and clues that are accessible only to a few persons. It is therefore dangerous to penetrate into that mysterious world without thorough knowledge of the Torah and without being truly God-fearing. Unfortunately the Kabbalah was studied by persons who lacked understanding of the profundity and sanctity of the Zohar and who by false, faulty reasoning processes concluded that they themselves were prophets or messiahs, invoking Jewish mysticism. Such was the case with Sabbatai Zevi and Jacob Frank, artful deceivers who succeeded in winning many adherents, who believed blindly in them, giving rise to violent disputes that did grave harm to Jewish life.

In this convulsed period, prominent personalities among the People of Israel sought to restrict study of the Kabbalah in order to prevent deviations through erroneous reasoning and interpretations.

One of the outstanding leaders of this trend was Rabbi Jacob Emden; the dispute was between him and Rabbi Jonathan Eybenschütz. The two famous leaders of German Judaism roused to fever pitch the spirits of people of their generation.

Rabbi Jonathan Eybenschütz (1690-1764) was born in Cracow. His father, the Rabbi of Eybenschütz, was a well-known Kabbalist. Jonathan was a remarkably talented speaker, capable of gripping the attention of large audiences. He was also outstanding as a philosopher, mathematician, and astronomer, which is why he was invited to hold the position of Chief Rabbi for the Altona, Hamburg, and Wandsbeck (AHW) communities, where his intense activity in the spiritual field won him many friends and followers.

He wrote many commentaries on Rabbinical law such as *Karteh Uphalteh* and *Urim Vethummim*, apart from his *Yaarot Dvash* collection of sermons. As a believer in practical Kabbalah, Rabbi Eybenschütz believed in talismans and oaths. He also made amulets as a safeguard against serious infirmities.

In those times there was an epidemic in his community, and many people came to him asking for talismans. But when some of them were shown to Rabbi Emden, who also lived in the city of Altona, he found in them alleged references to Sabbatai Zevi, which meant that Rabbi Eybenschütz cured disease in the name of the false messiah.

Rabbi Eybenschütz was indignant at this accusation, strongly rejecting it. This further aroused the anger of his opponent, who began to pursue him relentlessly and excommunicated him.

The furious dispute went on for a long time and led to a split between the two famous Talmudic scholars. The local community rose in defense of its renowned Rabbi and attacked the accuser, issuing a quantity of pamphlets that called on people for support in the quarrel. Two parties were formed. In the meantime the dispute had spread to many other communities in several countries, and means were being sought everywhere to restore peace.

The matter was brought before the Four Nations' Council (Poland, Podolia, Galicia, and Volhynia) which stepped in to calm things down, and today nobody in the Jewish world casts doubt on the sanctity of both personalities, who wrote a splendid page in the history of the People of Israel.

With the same fervor that Rabbi Emden opposed Rabbi Eybenschütz and therewith a rebirth of the Sabbatai Zevi movement, Rabbi Eybenschütz fought against Illuminism and the false messianic movements.

In his *Siddur Beth Yaakov*, Rabbi Emden warned against following the luxurious way of life that had spread among the Jews of that period. It was there, he maintained, that the evil was rooted. The Jewish masses wanted to resemble the Gentiles, which was also apparent in their wish to assimilate. They learned from them and dressed according to the dictates of their fashion. He also warned of excessive enthusiasm for teaching Jewish children world philosophy and secular subjects, a custom that had become general practice in Jewish homes.

The Kabbalah and mysticism, with time, were supplanted by Hasidism, which saved a majority of the Jewish people from the path of decline.

The Paths of Heaven and Their Mysteries

The Talmudic scholar who asserted that he could see the paths of the stars with full clarity was Samuel Bar Abba, better known as Samuel Yarhinai. He was one of the first Amorites in Babylon and principal of the yeshiva of Nahardeah. What he said was: "I know the paths of the Sky as well as those of Nahardeah." This chapter appeared in the tractate *Brachot* LVIII. Those words did not mean that he knew the designs of God, but that he could see and understand the movements of the stars and planets. This paragraph occurs frequently in somewhat changed form, such as when the word *shmayah* is replaced by *rakiyah*; there is little difference between the two, since both mean Heaven.

The Talmud says in *Hagigah* XII, in the name of Rabbi Simon Ben Lakish, that there are seven heavens, each with a name of its own. *Shamayim* would seem to be a term to designate them all. It says in Genesis I: "And God called the firmament *rakiyah* (Heaven)." The Gemara says that all the stars and the signs of the zodiac are in *rakiyah*. In the Pentateuch too it is written that God put the luminaries, the sun and the stars, into the *rakiyah* of the sky.

This, therefore, seems to be the reason why some scholars changed the name *shmayah* into *rakiyah* in Samuel's passage, since *rakiyah* means sky (firmament) and contains most stars.

Samuel Bar Abba was a noted scholar. Apart from his knowledge of the Bible, he was an expert in the secular sciences. He studied mathematics, natural science, and medicine, but his favorite subject was astronomy; he elaborated the Jewish calendar, including leap years, for a period of 100 years.

Samuel Bar Abba, also known as Samuel Yarhinai, was highly intelligent and had profound knowledge of the Torah. He won recognition as a sage in all centers of Jewish life. No other scholar won so many honors; although his father, too, was an important personality, he was referred to as the "Father of Samuel": the family's claim to distinction came from the son.

Samuel was a friend of the famous "Rabbi," and both shed the light of the Torah over the whole Jewish center of Babylon. Samuel asserted that, just as one should not go from Jerusalem to Babylon, one should similarly not go from Babylon to other countries (*Ktuvot III*).

In addition to his knowledge of the Torah, Samuel Bar Abba was well versed in medicine and practiced it. He traveled to the Land of Israel to cure Rabbi Yehuda Hanassi, who had eye trouble. He won much recognition for his dedication to experimental medicine and tried out many of his discoveries on his own body. The tractate *Nedarim* reported that he personally tried out a medicament to cure stomach trouble and that it gave him a fainting fit.

He knew the laws of Babylon and other countries well, but his knowledge of astronomy and astrology exceeded all else. In these two subjects he was the leading expert of his time, as he himself said: "I see the paths of the sky as clearly as I see those of Nahardeah."

He was a distinguished member of the Royal Academy of Sciences that met in the palace, and where noted scientists from a number of countries gathered to analyze scientific problems and religious writings. It was there that his learning and his intelligence shone forth, in such manner that the monarch ordered that a seat of honor be set up for the Jewish scholar. He granted him a title of nobility, which led to Samuel meeting King Shadur of Persia. The king consulted him on a wide variety of affairs, including how to wage his wars; Samuel took advantage of the opportunity to influence the king in favor of the Jews, which led the king to point out that he had never killed a Jew.

Fuller details of the foregoing can be found in the tractates *Shabat CXLVIII*, *Sucah LIII*, *Berachot LVIII*, and *Bavah Bathrah VII*.

The Jewish View of Astrology

Astrology is not an exact science; the ancients used to argue about how much of it was science and how much superstition. It is widespread in the United States where the horoscope trade produces profits estimated to run into many millions of dollars.

Astrology was first studied in Babylon, whose inhabitants called the astrologers "Chaldeans" or "Kasdim." Among the Romans too they were known as "Chaldeans." In the Bible the astrologers are referred to as *hevreh shamayim* (friends of the firmament). Astrology is mentioned in the Talmud, which asserts that Abraham was an astrologer. The patriarch Abraham, born and raised in Ur Kasdim, was versed in astrology. The Talmud tells that he used a rare crystal which he studied with great care and that from it he could tell the future and the fate of the individual person. The tractate *Bavah Bathrah* gives the interpretation of the verse of Genesis 24: "and the Lord had blessed Abraham in all things." The sages' explanation of the foregoing was that God blessed Abraham with everything and delivered to him a rare stone in which he could read a man's destiny. He carried it hanging from his chest and the kings of east and west came to Abraham that he might predict their destiny.

In another part of the Talmud, the tractates *Shabbat* and *Nedarim* tell that Abraham turned to God, saying: "Lord: I have looked through my crystal to see the stars and I saw that I cannot generate sons and that I shall die without leaving descendants." God replied: "Abraham, do not seek to determine your destiny from that crystal alone, for I have decided that the stars of the firmament shall not have power to control and decide your destiny, nor that of your people."

The scholars explain Genesis 20:7 saying that God appeared before the King in a dream and said to him: "Restore Abraham's wife to him, for he is not only an astrologer, but much more: he is a divine prophet."

As to whether it is forbidden to seek the advice of astrologers as it is forbidden to consult sorcerers and necromancers, the sages declare in tractate *Pessahim XIII*: "One should not seek advice from astrologers about the future," but there is not the same prohibition as with necromancers.

In the Middle Ages, some of those with profound knowledge of the Pentateuch believed in astrology, among them Ibn Ezra, the famous commentator. Rabbi Abraham Bar Hai Hanasi, in the 11th century, also believed in it, as did Rabbi Abraham Zakuto, who was a great astronomer. Conversely, the Rambam rejected it, considering it superstition. Not one of the Gaonim believed in it. The opinion of the great European sages was divided: hundreds of them did not believe in astrology: on the other hand, there were many bogus astrologers who set up in the trade without a license—they were mere frauds.

We know the story about Rabbi Akiba's daughter who was afraid of getting married because an astrologer had predicted that she would die on the day of her wedding. Her wise father, however, convinced her that she should not believe in astrology because the stars had no influence over the Jews, who were under the direct protection of God, their guardian.

Then something unusual happened. On the night of her wedding the young woman went into the garden for some fresh air, sat down on a bench, took off her nuptial diadem, and fell asleep.

When, some time later, people came to lead her to the canopy, they found that the point of the diadem that hung on the tree had pierced the head of a snake, which of course was dead. Rabbi Akiba asked her: "Tell me, dear daughter, what good deed have you done today that caused God to perform the miracle of saving your life?" His daughter answered: "In the wedding hall today I noticed that all were busying themselves to attend to the prominent guests and that simple people were neglected and left hungry. So I went to the kitchen and fetched food, and distributed it among the humble people." Rabbi Akiba exclaimed: "My daughter is a God-fearing woman and in her the saying has been fulfilled that 'charity saves man from death.'"

The Sages' Attitudes toward Magic, Spiritualism, and Sleight-of-Hand

The Pentateuch contains several warnings to keep away from magic. According to Deuteronomy 18: "There shall not be found among you any one that useth divination, or an enchanter, or a witch."

There are different kinds of sorcerers: some kill people; others can provoke such hallucinations, or apply hypnotism in such manner, that one is sure of really seeing what they say. The Mishna and Gemara contain frequent warnings against sorcery.

The Rambam, great Jewish sages and religious authorities held that sorcery arose out of the superstition, widespread among the Jews of those times. Deuteronomy 18 prohibits the presence among the Jews of diviners, enchanters, or "persons that interrogate the dead"—that is, who invoke the spirits of the dead to rise from their graves in order to converse with them. One gathers that they have certain powers, but that they may not exert them.

Much later, in the times of King Saul, we find in the first Book of Samuel, that the king consulted a witch who caused the dead prophet Samuel to appear before him, and that the king conversed with him. Rabbi Hai Gaon and Rabbi Saadya Gaon explained that it was not the witch who caused the apparition, but that the spirit of Samuel had risen up from the ground by divine will, to warn Saul of coming disasters.

The learned commentator Ralbag treads more carefully. He maintains that Saul did not speak with Samuel, but that the conversation was the product of his sick imagination and state of depression ever since Samuel had explained to him that he would perish, and his kingdom with him. The Rambam voiced a similar opinion, assuring that the incident was the product of the king's sick imagination.

Abravanel did not agree; he pointed out that those assertions contradicted the meaning of the verse. He held that a specter donned Samuel's clothing and spoke with Saul.

The Gaon Rabbi Samuel Ben Hafni maintained that nothing of the kind occurred, but that it was a trick of the witch's, who deceived Saul by speaking to him from a distance in a masculine voice, supposedly that of Samuel, and that Saul, downcast and ill, thought it was real and effectively believed that he had seen Samuel and spoken to him.

In the time of the Second Temple and later in the times of the Mishna and Gemara, various forms of witchcraft spread among the Jews. In the Mishna (*Shabbat*) it is forbidden to use as amulets against sickness a fox's tooth, or a hook from which the figure of a hanged person is suspended, both of which were used by sorcerers. The sages said that such amulets were worthless, but there were also Jewish sages who believed in the power of amulets and specters and in exorcising the evil eye. Holy books of the time, especially those of adepts of the Kabbalah, attributed great value to talismans, exorcism, and omens.

In the Pentateuch there is a passage that strictly forbids the practice of magic, belief in it, or belief in other superstitions. Deuteronomy 18 says: "There shall not be found among you sorcerers, nor anyone that useth divination, or exorcists, or a necromancer." These are described as "abominations of those nations." The book also declares that a wrong and errant belief leads to idolatry.

The Talmud held that the sages of the Sanhedrin surely understood magic, for they were often called on to judge sorcerers and therefore had to know whether those on trial really possessed powers. They also had to be careful to avoid being harmed by the sorcerers. The sages of the Sanhedrin did not resort to the forces of evil but used only sacred means—the help of the angels.

The Talmud also mentions that Simon Ben Shetah, president of the Sanhedrin, captured eighty witches who were sheltering in a cave at Ashkelon.

The Rambam maintained that all those beliefs were superstition and it was not right that the Jews, sons of a scholarly and intelligent people, should believe such nonsense. Anyone who believed in fraud, even if he believed in God, would be severely punished.

The Rambam explained clearly the nature of sleight-of-hand and why it should not be practiced. He gave examples. If someone kept a rope in one of his pockets and suddenly took out from it a grass snake, or if someone threw in a ring into the air and then took it out of his mouth, it was trickery and should be punished by whipping.

It should be pointed out that although this sort of activity was prohibited among the Jews, some outstanding masters of sleight-of-hand were Jews. They included Professor Herman and Harry Houdini, who displayed their skills before thousands of people, including kings, sultans, princes and noblemen, who generously rewarded them with money, diamonds and jewels.

The Czar of Russia used to invite Herman to give private performances in his palace in St. Petersburg to provide entertainment for his guests and on one occasion presented him with a watch set with diamonds.

Herman used to do wonderful things with his hands, from which he produced coins, flowers, fruit, sweets. In New York he pushed a knife down his throat, and gold coins came tumbling out of it. In the Sultan of Turkey's palace he cut off a pigeon's head and stuck another head onto it, and the pigeon remained alive.

Houdini, son of a Rabbi, performed marvelous feats thanks to the dexterity of his fingers and his bodily agility. Bound hand and foot, he allowed himself to be locked in a trunk that was sunk in deep water; after a time, he would emerge safe and sound, free of his shackles. One day, however, he did not reappear and when the trunk was raised he was found dead. Doctors held that he died of a cerebral hemorrhage brought on by sudden immersion or by an unusually violent blow.

Dreams as Explained in the Talmud and the Kabbalah

Dreams held a very important place in the Bible, in the Talmud and among scholars of the Middle Ages. There were great differences of opinion as regards their significance, as well as their content and importance.

Dreams have a lift as intense as that of the human being. A Latin proverb says: "I dream, therefore I am alive." Dreams are often mentioned in the Bible, and many of them are considered prophetic. We read in Exodus 12:6: "In a dream I spoke to Him." There is a passage in the Talmud which confirms that dreams contain important predictions. Maimonides, too, asserted that many prophets perceived their prophecies through dreams.

The first prophecy through a dream was that which came to the patriarch Abraham when he made his covenant with God and the Lord assured him that he would be the father of a numerous people. At that moment Abraham was asleep, and in a dream he heard the voice of the Lord, who predicted to him the future of his descendants, his sufferings in exile, and his reward.

The second prophetic dream came to the patriarch Jacob, when he fled from his brother Esau and saw the ladder that led to Heaven, with angels ascending and descending. Then God spoke to him from the top of the ladder, promising him protection and the multiplication of his seed, and assured him that the land would belong to his descendants.

The third prophetic dream appeared before Joseph, when the sheaves in the field, the sun, the moon, and eleven stars bowed down before him. There followed Joseph's interpretation of the dreams of the Pharaoh's cup-bearer and baker, and his interpretation of the Pharaoh's own dreams, which were duly fulfilled. Also recalled are Joseph's words that God makes known the future of people and countries through dreams, which eventually become reality, as related in the Bible.

But the dreams of an ordinary man are different: most of them are meaningless, "vain dreams," as the prophet Zacharias said.

The tractate *Berahot* mentions different types of dreams, giving opinions on them at some length. Rabbi Jonathan said that people dream only about things that preoccupy them in their waking hours.

The Talmud also speaks of the need to interpret dreams, in particular if they seem of bad augury. A bad dream may be changed into a good one; this was called "improving the dream." *Berahot LV* says that "dreams follow in the wake of words"; that is, if a dream is interpreted in a favorable sense, something good will happen, and if in the bad sense, misfortune will follow. The kings of antiquity included interpreters of dreams among their counselors. There were Jewish scholars who dedicated themselves to this subject; the Talmud mentions twenty-four expert interpreters of dreams who lived in Jerusalem and were well paid for their services. The sage Abai used to pay for interpretation of his dreams, but Rabah never did; he held that the interpretation of a dream was a matter of ethics, like every human being's duty to do good deeds.

There were times when it was customary to fast and pray after a bad dream, and this was allowed even to on the Sabbath (*Berahot XXXI*). This depended on how much distress and suffering had been caused by the dream.

But not all Talmudic scholars were in favor of interpreting dreams. The Amorite Samuel used to comfort himself after a bad dream by saying that dreams were meaningless. If, conversely, the dream had been a pleasant one, he would ask: "Are all dreams really meaningless? Surely this one will come true."

The Gemara reported that the Amorites Amimar, Zutra and Ashi were discussing dreams and that one of them asserted: "When one has a dream of ill portent, one should go to the house of prayer, where the priests raise their arms and bless the people, stand before them, and say in a loud voice: 'Lord, I have had a bad dream and I do not know what it portends. So let it be Your will that all my dreams portend good fortune.' " That prayer was introduced into the *mahzor* and the *siddur*.

According to the Talmud, if a person has had a bad dream, he should fast for a whole day, the "fast of the dream." That fast may take place on the Sabbath. One who has had a bad dream should resort to three persons who have "improved" their own bad dreams, should describe his dream to them and they will interpret it in the favorable sense.

The scholars who dedicated special attention to study of the Kabbalah were closely concerned with the interpretation of dreams. In their writings they tell of visions and meetings with angels who clarified unintelligible problems for them, indicating to them what path to follow. One of the notables of the Kabbalah, Ari the Saint, tells that his aims in those studies were sent from Heaven through a dream, and that in the same way he fathomed the secrets of the Zohar.

Maimonides held that many dreams were founded on reality. But he distinguished between those that were true and those that were false; that is, there were false prophets who in interpreting dreams gave them a false ideological slant, and many of those dreams never even occurred.

The Evil Eye: Belief and Exorcism

Our sages almost always fought against superstition because they realized the need to bar the path toward idolatry. Certain superstitious practices, however, had become deeply rooted in the people and were so difficult to eradicate that they had to be tolerated—especially in cases when they brought relief to those who believed in them. This was the ruling of the Rambam, who pointed out that if a person fell ill of snake-bite, the victim's exorcising practices could be tolerated even on the Sabbath, though they would serve no useful purpose (Rambam, *Hilchot Akum*, chapter 11).

One of the oldest beliefs is that the glance of a malignant person could harm another. In the Talmud this is described as "the evil eye" (*Sanhedrin*, XCIII). It was customary in such cases to add the word "without" or "no": ("no evil eye"; *bli ayin harah* or *kein ain horeh*) and to spit three times.

To exorcise an evil eye or a plague was a widespread practice in olden times; the Jews may have taken over this superstitious beliefs from other peoples. The evil spell could be exorcised in different ways. Some used to spit three times in the sick person's face and pronounce words of exorcism; others spat three times to the right of the sick person and once on his forehead, then uttered oaths and murmured certain words to drive out the evil spirits that afflicted him. Whether the sages accepted these practices is not known; the Talmud notes that some Tannaim believed in the evil eye but it does not mention that the sages believed in exorcism.

The story that the Tanna Rabbi Meyer sent for a woman to exorcise an evil eye does not prove that he really believed in it, because he was known to have done so with the intention of helping the woman who performed the exorcism. His purpose was to restore peace in her house and this could be done by receiving spittle from the woman. It is a deeply moving story:

The Tanna Rabbi Meyer was known to be a remarkably fine preacher apart from his profound knowledge of the Torah. Great crowds used to attend his sermons; people stood tirelessly for hours to listen to his wise words. One Friday night, Rabbi Meyer's sermon lasted longer than usual. A certain woman, listening to him with rapt attention, forgot that her husband had asked her to return home early. When she came home, the lights were out and her husband was sitting in darkness and very angry. The woman tried to placate him, telling him that she had been at the *Beth Hamidrash* (House of Study) listening intently to Rabbi Meyer's sermon and words of wisdom and had been so impressed that she had not realized the lateness of the hour. This angered her husband still more. "I order you to leave this house," he exclaimed, "unless you go to Rabbi Meyer and spit in his face."

The woman of course could not do that and sadly left the house. When Rabbi Meyer was informed of the affair, he was both saddened and annoyed with himself, since this unhappy woman's sufferings were his fault. He decided to help her and sent for her; when she arrived, the sage feigned illness and asked: "Perhaps there is among you someone who can exorcise an evil eye?" The neighbors said to the woman: "This is a God-given opportunity. Go and exorcise his evil eye. You have to spit into his eye; then his complaint will disappear, and your husband will make peace with you."

The woman agreed, but for fear she was unable to move her tongue and remained silent. "Why do you not exorcise the evil eye?" asked Rabbi Meyer. "Perhaps you do not wish to cure me?" In a tremulous voice the woman replied: "Rabbi, I have forgotten how to do it." "Daughter," said the Rabbi, "it is a simple matter. Just spit on me seven times and I shall get well." The woman felt encouraged and obeyed. Then Rabbi Meyer said to her: "Now go to your home and say to your husband, 'You ordered me to spit on Rabbi Meyer once and I spat seven times.' "

The woman was ashamed, but she was happy at the outcome, for her husband made peace with her.

The students asked Rabbi Meyer: "Rabbi, should a sage submit to such an indignity?" The sage replied: "Yes, for the sake of peace in the home a man may suffer indignity, since if the Almighty allowed His Name to be erased by the Bitter Waters (Numbers 5) for a deviation, then I also, in order to restore peace between husband and wife, may submit to an indignity."

Belief in Demons and Evil Spirits

In the Talmud, Midrash, and Kabbalah, the term *shed* is used to define a devil, demon, evil spirit, apparition, or figure that seeks to do harm to men. In the tractate *Hagigah XVII* we read that devils are like angels. They have wings and fly from one end of the world to the other; they know what will happen in the future, according to what is decided in Heaven. In some ways they are like men: they eat and drink, are born and die like them. The Kabbalah also tells of demons who married human beings and had children with them.

The word *shedim* occurs in the Bible, but its meaning is not wholly clear. It would seem to refer to an idol. A verse in Deuteronomy says: "They sacrificed unto idols" (32:17). From the Biblical passage one may conclude that the *shedim* were considered idols, gods to which the people offered sacrifices: "God said to Moses: 'It is better you bring me sacrifices to the altar, before you sacrifice to the idols'" (Leviticus, *Vaikrah XIII*, 7).

In the Gemara, the Midrash and many other books from later

Significance of the Kabbalah, the Zohar and the Great Jewish Mystics 111

periods, the *shedim* are considered "evil spirits," that seek to do harm to men. In the tractate *Eruvim XVII* and elsewhere they are given other names: *mazikim* (devils), *malakheh habalah* (destroying angels) and the like.

In the Gemara and Midrashim there are many reports on demons and evil spirits, especially about the king of demons, Ashmadai. *Pesachim* CX and *Gitin LXVIII* tell how King Solomon took Ashmadai prisoner and made him tell where to find the famous earthworm Shamir, which could cut stones and would be used in building the Temple. The same books narrate that Ashmadai, on the way to the palace, told Solomon's military leader, Benayahu Ben Jehoiada, many things about coming events concerning different persons whom they met on the road. They also tell how Ashmadai succeeded in freeing himself from his chains, on which the name of God was engraved, manacled King Solomon, and flew with him to a distant country, where he abandoned him. He then disguised himself as King Solomon, returned to Jerusalem, occupied the throne, and reigned over the country. But one day people noticed that his feet were not human; they were cock's feet. Then the people realized that he was not the real King Solomon but a demon. Ashmadai succeeded in escaping and changed back into king of the demons. Solomon wandered for a long time through an unknown country, crying aloud: "I am Solomon, King of Jerusalem!" but nobody believed him.

In the tractate *Shabbat CLI*, it is said that Lilith is the name of the queen of the demons and that she rules in the darkness of night. The name Lilith may be derived from the word *lailah* (night) since she reigns only by night. On the other hand, the passage of the Gemara says that a person who sleeps alone in a house at night is under Lilith's influence. On the cards with the words of *Shir Hama'alot* (Songs of the Steps) that are hung above the bed of a woman in childbirth, there is written a prayer that both she and her newborn baby may be protected from Lilith. The work *Kav Hayashar* contains a number of stories about Lilith, who is said to appear in the guise of a beautiful woman to attract men and turn their heads. This belief was widespread among the Jewish masses. Also Jewish books from later periods contain legends of demons that married human beings and had children with them, including the notion that Adam and Eve lived for a certain time with demons.

The Jewish sages of the Middle Ages differed in the matter of belief in demons. The Rambam did not believe in their existence, nor in that of any other evil being or spirit.

The Golem and Its Creator, the Maharal of Prague

The original meaning of the Hebrew word *golem* is "formless body." Later it was a human figure, or species of homunculus, but without the faculty of comprehension. In the tractate of the Fathers (*Pirke Avot V*) the virtues of a wise and intelligent man are contrasted with the faults of the *Golem*. The Midrash of Leviticus (*Vaikrah XXIX*) asserts that in principle God created the first man in the form of a *golem*, but later breathed a soul into him.

There are innumerable Jewish legends of prominent personalities that created homunculi and gave them life with the help of the Almighty. The homunculi blindly obeyed their creators.

The Talmud (*Sanhedrin LXIII*; *Hulin CV*) tells of Amoaim, who, like the Kabbalists later, created living beings, using formulas contained in the *Sefer Hayetzirah* (Book of Creation), a work that Jewish tradition attributes to the patriarch Abraham but that according to researchers belongs to the Talmudic period.

The tractate *Sanhedrin LXVII* tells that Rabbi Hananiah and Rav, with the help of the Book of Creation just mentioned, created living beings, but that book is referred to as *Hilhot Yetzirah* (Laws of Creation).

The Maharal wrote important books, among which are *Gur Aryeh*, an interpretation of Rashi's famous commentary on the Torah; *Derech Hachaim*, a commentary on the tractate of the Fathers (*Pirke Avot*); *Nethivoth Olam*, a tractate on morals and precepts; and *Be'er Hagolah*, on Talmudic legends.

His sons too were noted scholars. The elder, Rabbi Chaim, was a friend of the prominent legal expert Rabbi Moses Isserles (Rema).

Rabbi Yehuda Loew died in 1609 at the age of ninety-four and was buried in Prague. His statue by the sculptor L. Saloun was set up before the Prague City Hall; oddly, the Nazis did not destroy it.

The old Prague synagogue is visited to this day by many tourists, both Jewish and Gentile, for a look at the statue that reproduces the effigy of the Maharal.

The legend of the Golem has been told and retold by world-famous writers and poets, both Jewish and non-Jewish; never has it failed to arouse interest in the world of the stage and screen through its profundity and human content, as full of drama as life itself.

Dybbuk and Gilgul in the Light of the Kabbalah

Dybbuk and *gilgul* are Hebrew words that refer to two distinct beliefs that originated during a post-Biblical period.

The term *dybbuk* (union or bond) is based on the three-letter Hebrew root *dbk* found, for example, in Genesis 2:24: "A man shall cleave unto his wife and they shall be one flesh." It refers to the tortured soul of one who, having been a great sinner in life, is unable to find a place of repose and penetrates forcibly into another person, taking possession of his body and control of his will.

The human being thus invaded is no longer himself; he becomes a different person. He acts, speaks, and thinks like the dead man. Such a situation is described as the "(forced) entrance of a *dybbuk*" or of an evil spirit.

Already the Talmud refers to a Rabbi and a *dybbuk* who on one occasion acted together, by mutual agreement: Rabbi Simon Bar Yohai was on his way to Rome to petition the emperor to nullify a decree that would have been extremely harmful to the Jewish population of the Land of Israel. A demon named Ben Temalion met him on the way and told him that he had been ordered to help him accomplish his mission. The demon proposed to enter the body of the emperor's daughter and cause her to fall ill, after which the Rabbi would arrive and restore her to health.

The Tanna wept bitterly at not being granted the privilege of acting with an angel, and being forced to act with a demon. He nevertheless accepted the proposition, since it was a matter of saving the People of Israel from calamity.

The demon took possession of the princess's body. She fell seriously ill and began to demand with increasing vehemence: "Bring me the Jewish saint, Rabbi Simon Bar Yohai. Only he can cure me." The emperor of Rome sent for the Tanna, and when he arrived at the palace, the emperor at once received him and begged him to save his daughter.

Rabbi Bar Yohai expelled the *dybbuk* from the body of the young woman, who was immediately made well. The emperor, deeply grateful, granted the Tanna's petition, and nullified the harmful decree.

The belief that the tortured soul of a dead person, or a demon, can enter the body of a living person and take possession of it was spread through the books of the Kabbalah. One of them, the 16th century *Shivchei Rabbi Chaim Vital* (Praise of Rabbi Chaim Vital) contains a wealth of narration about different *dybbukim* and acts of exorcism performed by God-fearing men, who, using combinations of sacred names and oaths, blowing the *shofar* (ram's horn), and other means, succeeded in driving the evil spirits out of the live bodies. Likewise, the *dybbuk* could be given corrective means to atone for his multiple grave sins, mend his ways, and thus find eternal rest.

The expression "a *dybbuk* has entered into him" first appeared in the *Sefer Hakanauth* by Rabbi Jacob Emden. It records that a certain Rabbi Tzadock, a none-too-erudite member of the Sabbatai Zevi sect, began to prophesy that the Messiah would come in the year 5408. Of Rabbi Tzadock, the distinguished author noted that "surely some *dybbuk* or evil spirit has taken possession of him." Ever since then, that expression has been current in both Hebrew and Yiddish.

The term *gilgul* (meaning "transmigration") refers to the mutation of a human soul, which leaves the body of the dead to begin a new cycle in the body of the newborn. According to that belief, the soul may transmigrate as often as may be necessary.

The *gilgul* is said to be a form of punishment imposed on a human soul for failing to fulfill its obligations in this world, or for sins committed. In extreme cases the soul may enter into a nonhuman, which means that the behavior of the deceased had been animal-like.

This belief was deeply rooted among the people and was disseminated by the Kabbalists, who insisted that not only the souls of sinners were transmigrated but that the same process might occur in just men whose souls had not completed their purification.

The *gilgul* is not mentioned in the Bible, nor in the Talmud. Nor did medieval scholars believe in transmigration of the soul, for instance Rabbi Saadya Gaon flatly rejected the belief in his famous work *Emunot ve-Deot*. The Zohar, however, mentions it in its commentary on the Biblical book *Mishpatim* (Judges). Ari the Saint and his disciples also believed in the transmigration of souls. One of them, Rabbi Chaim Vital, wrote the *Sefer Hagilgulim* (The Book of Transmigrations), which names prominent Jewish sages whose souls transmigrated to compensate for neglected obligations, even indicating into what other personalities they had passed.

It is a curious and notable fact that Maimonides, in his commentary on the book of Job, supported belief in the *gilgul*. The writings of Philo of Alexandria (which date from the time of the Second Temple) also contain vestiges of this belief, which leads to the inference that even in those times it had begun to spread among certain Jewish sects and that with the passing of time it gained increasing credibility.

The Jewish People and Their Eternal Longing for Redemption

The prayers of the Jewish people express the hope that their redeemer, the Messiah, may come at any moment to lead them from exile to their ancient home: the Land of Israel. That is why they say day by day: "I fully believe in the coming of the Messiah." According to Maimonides, this is one of the Jew's principal beliefs, and he who rejects it is forsaking the Jewish religion.

This messianic faith brought comfort to the Jews whenever their plight in the Dispersion reached the limit of what was humanly bearable, as occurred for instance under Nazi rule in the concentration camps, where they sang with especial fervor the traditional *Ani Maamin* (I Believe) creed.

Under the hardships of wars, in times of slaughter, pogroms and exile, the Jews immersed themselves in study of Holy Writ—Bible verses, the aphorisms of the Torah and Kabbalistic works—in the search for a ray of light, a sign of redemption, the approaching steps of the Messiah. It is therefore easy to understand why the Jews expelled from Spain fervently believed that salvation of the People of Israel was close at hand.

Significance of the Kabbalah, the Zohar and the Great Jewish Mystics 119

At the same time they nevertheless sensed that they themselves had to do something for their wishes to be fulfilled. They had to prepare the ground for the coming of the Messiah, since he would not come unless they repented sincerely, did penitence, fasted, and deepened their studies of the Torah and the Kabbalah—these being necessarily conditions of redemption.

The millenary, sublime messianic idea originated in the times of the prophets, and became deeply rooted in the People of Israel; it accompanied and comforted them throughout their history of suffering.

The expulsion of the Jews from Spain drove them to the very limits of despair and had a profound impact on their brethren worldwide, reviving the old messianic dream.

But how could it be realized? On whom did it depend? They soon understood that they themselves had to be the architects of their own destiny. Only their own good actions could convert the dream into reality. The Talmud provided the answer: "If they deserved it—it would come sooner. If not—it would come at the appointed time." That meant that the people's return to the path of righteousness could accelerate the coming of the Messiah.

The Talmud recounts that Rabbi Isaiah Ben Levi once asked Elijah, the announcer of the Messiah, when the redeemer would come, to which the prophet replied: "Today." Seeing Rabbi Isaiah's amazement, Elijah added the clarification "Today, if you heed My voice." That meant that perfect fulfillment of God's commandments could bring immediate salvation.

The Jews expelled from Spain began to prepare for it. They carefully studied the Kabbalah and sought in the Zohar hidden signs and pointers to messianic times. This attitude spread among the masses and, according to Rabbi Moses Isserles (Rema), "not only scholars studied the Kabbalah, but also many ordinary Jewish people, even those who could not distinguish between right and left." Similarly, the eminent Rabbi Solomon Luria (Maharshal) said that "the Jews began to confess to contrition and to fast."

In those times, Salonika and Adrianopolis, in Turkey, were the two principal havens of refuge for the Jews expelled from Spain. Both communities were headed by the eminent Rabbi Joseph

Taitatzak, a great scholar and Kabbalist, of whom Rabbi Joseph Caro, author of the *Shulhan Arukh*, wrote: "He was the light and the sanctuary of the Jews, the crown of those persecuted."

The great scholar did penitence. He slept in a bed only on Saturdays; on other days he slept on a hard box, rising for midnight prayers (*Reshit Hokhmah*, VII). His pupil the distinguished Kabbalist Rabbi Solomon Alkabetz (author of the Sabbath poem *Lecha Dodi*) did likewise. Describing Jewish life in Turkey, he wrote in his book *Berith Halevi*: "Here I met scholars who are strong as lions and swift as eagles. They sanctify themselves like the angels, serve God day and night and are like dwellers in Heaven."

The great scholar and Kabbalist Rabbi Joseph Caro also belonged to this period. Working for many years on his notable book *Beth Yoseph* he enhanced his knowledge of the Mishna and immersed himself in the secrets of the Kabbalah. According to legend, he was visited every Friday by a preacher from Heaven who revealed secrets and prophecies to him. That preacher was the Mishna.

In those same years of hope and longing, the Jews suffered a calamitous disillusion through the messianic movements of David Haruveni and Solomon Molho. The first, a dreamy politician, appeared as a wanderer from distant Arabia, telling wonderful stories about the ten lost tribes of Israel. The second, a convert to Judaism, began to have visions and to announce redemption.

Soon afterward the messianic movement passed from Turkey into Israel, in as much as Israel was held to be nearer than any other to the Dispersion for the purposes of preparing the coming of the Messiah, and because *Shehinah* (Divine Providence) resided there.

Thus the Land of Israel became the center of that movement, supported and encouraged by the most distinguished Kabbalists and scholars, the great majority of whom elected to settle in the holy city of Safed (*Tzfat*) believing that they would be more successful there in understanding and revealing the mysteries contained in Holy Scripture. Among those notable figures were Rabbi Joseph Caro, Rabbi Solomon Alkabetz, Rabbi Moses of Córdoba, Rabbi Moses Alsheikh, Rabbi Elazar Askari and Ari the Saint. All intensified their efforts to hasten the coming of the Messiah.

Significance of the Kabbalah, the Zohar and the Great Jewish Mystics

Similar feelings and longings were the lot of the Jews in 1648. The pogroms had become steadily worse, leading to the massacres of 1648-1649, in which some 500,000 Jews lost their lives; they died as martyrs on the altars of their faith.

The Jewish Kabbalists interpreted these disasters as announcing redemption, referring to Leviticus 16:3: "Thus shall Aaron come into the holy place." This was interpreted as a sign of the coming of the Messiah in the year 1648, since the numerical value of the Hebrew word *zot* (this) is equivalent to the year 5408 of the Hebrew calendar, which coincided with the year just mentioned of the present era.

Jewish blood flowed on Polish soil in a ceaseless stream, and fresh hopes were kindled by this "deluge of the red element." The sufferings were interpreted as "pains of childbirth" heralding redemption; the Jewish Kabbalists of Poland found in the Torah and the Zohar evermore frequent signs that seemed to confirm their messianic longings.

Real life undertook to destroy those fine theories, and the Jewish masses lapsed into despair. It was then that Rabbi Sabbatai Hacohen sent out the following message to the people of Israel: "'This' comes from God. 'This' is the year 5408 (1648) and was set by the Supreme Maker. But we did not deserve His mercy, for we are sinners. First and foremost, we should have repented and done penitence. Sadly, we have not done so."

Today as in the past, the Jews believe in the coming of the Messiah and they say every morning in their prayers: "And even if it is delayed, I hope for it day by day."

The Significance of Jewish Prayers

One of the most important commandments—which indeed accounts for the major part of our religious life—is mentioned in Deuteronomy 10:12: "Thou shalt serve thy God with all thy heart." Hence the obligation to pray that is laid down in the Torah.

The Rambam (Rabbi Moses Ben Maimon) held that prayer is an obligation that is laid down in the Torah.

The Ramban (Rabbi Moses Ben Nahman), however, held that it figures in the Torah only for a case of emergency.

Prayer has always performed an important role in the life of the Jewish people. It is the way a human being speaks to his Maker, as a child speak to his father. Throughout two thousand years of persecution and suffering in the Diaspora, prayer was an important part of Jewish life—the spiritual communion that kept the Jews alive and gave them strength to survive.

Our sages held that prayer was the Jew's praise to God for His mercies granted to men. The essential was "to establish an order in praise of the Lord, blessed be His name."

The Kabbalists gave a different explanation, maintaining that the main thing in prayer was the intention-understanding of the meaning of the words contained in prayers; they held that if a man failed to understand the meaning of his prayer, it was as if he had not prayed.

The Besht (Baal Shem Tov) said that God was everywhere and very close to man, and that He could be reached by prayer, providing it was honest and sincere.

It was thus that the prayers of very simple, often illiterate people were listened to in Heaven. The Besht (founder of Hasidism) and his disciple allowed parishioners to pray in Yiddish because it gave them added spontaneity and feeling.

Some spiritual leaders of Hasidism, such as Rabbi Levi Isaac of Berdichev and Rabbi Nahman of Bratzlev, conversed with God in Yiddish. The well-known prayer that begins with the words: "God of Abraham..." said by women during the *Havdalah* (ceremony marking the end of the Sabbath and the beginning of the week) was written in Yiddish by Rabbi Levi Isaac of Berdichev. It is a moving prayer that religious women, our mothers and grandmothers, say on the Sabbath night when the first stars come out. When a group of Jews asked Hafetz Chaim to give them the "children, good health and nourishment" blessing, he replied: "Pray yourselves to the Eternal Father who is your Maker as He is mine, and do not seek the words of formal prayer. Speak in Yiddish, the language closest to your own emotions. The Lord demands that prayer be spoken and offered up in the language of the heart, mingled with tears."

The Bible makes frequent mention of the prayers that our ancestors offered up to the Lord. Abraham implored God on behalf of Sodom; Isaac prayed that Rebecca be no longer sterile; Jacob prayed to be saved from the brutality of his brother Esau. Moses implored the Lord to pardon the rebellion of the Jews against Him and also for the safety of his sister Miriam, who had fallen gravely ill because of her blasphemy against Moses. Joshua prayed for victory over his enemies, and the prophet Samuel offered up prayers for the unity of the tribes. King David composed beautiful prayers: the Book of Psalms is full of prayers to the Lord. King Solomon uttered beautiful prayers at the inauguration of the Great Temple; so did Jonas from the belly of the whale. King

Hezekiah prayed during his sickness, beseeching the Lord to let him live, and Daniel prayed for redemption of the Jews from captivity in Babylon. Ezra and Nehemiah also offered up prayers when they set out from Babylon toward Israel.

To serve God with your whole heart and strength: that is prayer.

Rabbi Israel Salanter, founder of the *Musar* (moral) movement, used to say: "In the Torah, God is speaking to man; in prayer, it is man speaking to God."

Later the Hasidim asserted that the main thing in prayer is communion with God and a state of ecstasy, and to attain that, they prayed in isolation, thus the Hasidim of Kotzk were seen walking from one end of the synagogue to the other in the attempt to purify their thoughts, and the Rabbi of Kotzk frequently said his regular prayers at irregular hours.

Conversely, the Hasidim of Belz held that the best way to drive out evil thoughts was to say one's prayers quickly so that one's thoughts would not wander. They were therefore said to pray with the speed of an express train.

When did it become customary to pray three times a day—*Shaharit*, *Minha*, and *Maariv*? Some say that the members of the Great Assembly introduced the custom during the period of the Second Temple and that they also set the prayers. According to the Talmud, however, the three daily prayers were set by the Patriarchs: Abraham composed the prayers of *Shaharit*, Isaac the *Minha*, and Jacob the *Arvit*. That does not mean that those prayers were the same as those we say today, but that the Patriarchs set the custom of saying prayers three times a day. Later, during the period of the Second Temple, these prayers became better established, and after the destruction of the Temple they were amplified and used in replacement of sacrifices.

The *Shmoneh Esreh* was introduced in Yavneh by the Nassi Rabbi Gamliel after the destruction of the Second Temple.

The Ramban maintained that in olden times it was the rule to pray just once a day, but the members of the Grand Assembly ruled that prayers should be offered up to the Lord three times a day.

Significance of the Kabbalah, the Zohar and the Great Jewish Mystics

As time went on, prayers proliferated: the worse life became in the Dispersion, the more prayers were composed. Each generation added something to the prayer book. The Jews prayed to God for redemption, hoping that their prayers would be heard in Heaven. This continued until the appearance of Rabbi Amram Gaon, principal of a yeshiva in Babylon, who introduced a more settled order of prayer. He chose the most important ones and included them in a special book. It was actually Rabbi Amram Gaon who compiled the first prayer book under the title *Seder Hatefilot*.

A collection by Rabbi Natronai Gaon, of Pumbedita, Babylon, who lived fifty years before Rabbi Amram Gaon (roughly in the early century) was found not long ago. That collection was not entitled *siddur*, but "One Hundred Prayers." There is also a *siddur*, dating from about 940, by Rabbi Saadya Gaon: a *siddur* by Rashi and a *mahzor* by one of Rashi's disciples, Rabbi Solomon Vitri.

In olden times, each personality felt obligated to publish a collection of known prayers, with new ones added.

A *siddur* by the Rambam appears in his *Mishneh Torah*. Many collections of prayers appeared thereafter. The *siddurim* are distinguished by the different styles and by the populations and countries of their origin. There are Sephardi, Ashkenazi, Polish, Romanian, and many other styles.

When the Kabbalah appeared, new *siddurim* were compelled that included it. Among them was the Ari's version, which contained different litanies and blessings.

Siddurim appeared that contained all the psalms, chapters, and *hosannas*, and others with readings from the Torah. Still others included commentaries and laws. Among them were the *siddurim* of Rabbi Jacob Emden, of Rabbi Jacob Lisser, of the Gaon of Vilna, that of Lyubavich, of the Rambam and the far-famed book of prayers for women, the *Korban Minha*.

Attitude of the Polish Geonim toward the Kabbalah

The Kabbalah, which aims to unravel the secrets of the universe, dates from ancient times when man already took a deep-seated interest in the mysteries of Creation and the works of God. According to Jewish tradition, the author of the Zohar, the principal work of the Kabbalah, was the Tanna Rabbi Simon Bar Yohai, who lived in the 2nd century of the Common Era.

But it was in the 7th century in Spain that the Kabbalah was revealed to the Jewish world through Rabbi Abraham Abulafia, Rabbi Isaac Sageh Nahor and Rabbi Moses Ben Nahman (Nahmanides). The Kabbalah was rediscovered as a source of study by the Ashkenazi Hasidim: Rabbi Yehuda, the Hasid of Regensburg; Rabbi Eliezer of Worms, author of the *Rokeach*, and Rabbi Isaac of Vienna, author of *Or Zaruah*. It was Rabbi Moses de León who in the 13th century in Spain discovered and disseminated the Zohar, the backbone of Jewish mystical teaching bearing on the Torah. It is a difficult work to understand; its secrets were passed from

Significance of the Kabbalah, the Zohar and the Great Jewish Mystics

generation to generation only to respected scholars of lofty spiritual standing.

Even in those times, it was apparent that the Kabbalah was divided into two distinct systems: theoretical Kabbalah and practical Kabbalah. The first seeks to discover the essence of divinity and the influence of the Torah and its precepts on the universe. The second, conversely, is concerned with practical application of secret divine forces in the world and in life, such as the performance of miracles through appropriate utilization of the names of God.

The title of Zohar (Splendor) is derived from Daniel 12:3: "And they that be wise shall shine as the brightness of the firmament." The Book of Splendor tells how on one occasion, while Rabbi Simon Bar Yohai and his disciples were studying the secrets of the Torah, they were enveloped by a sheet of flame that came from Heaven.

Theoretical Kabbalah was aimed at penetrating the complex and secret world of spiritual matter. How does one explain, for instance, that a material world emerged from immaterial divinity, or that things material and finite were formed from infinite spirit? The mystics maintain that ten spheres emanated from divinity, and that they are like intermediate stages between the two extremes.

Man must aspire to unite with Divinity, following a path that passes through profound meditation on the Torah and its precepts.

The Kabbalah came to Poland by a roundabout route (through semi-Hispanicized Italy) in the practical version of the Ari and of his disciple Chaim Vital.

The Ari developed the idea of *tzimtzum* (contraction) according to which infinite divinity contracts, in various stages, to form the material world, in which celestial particles, remnants of divinity, descend to the lowest levels. Every Jew is duty-bound to rise to his original sanctity; this can be done only by fasting, prayer, acts of penitence and similar means.

The introduction of practical Kabbalah in Poland was by no means easy. It met with opponents and detractors, both avowed and unavowed, and many difficulties had to be overcome.

The classical initiator of rabbinical literature in Poland, Rabbi Moses Isserles (1520-1572, known as Rema from the acronym of his initials), was distinguished for his facility in unraveling the most difficult passages concerning things prohibited and things permitted. His researches were based on rational deduction in the best style of Maimonides, intermingled with mystical elements of a transcendent nature. In his work *Torah Haolah* he put forward the idea that the architecture of the Holy Temple, as well as the articles of cult, had been fashioned in response to secrets of Creation.

The Rema was a consistent follower of the Rambam, whose basic principle was the predominance of reason, which rejected illogical ideas. One who believed that every problem should be elucidated through research would naturally be expected to seek a logical foundation for most things. Nevertheless, the Rema did not reject the Kabbalah; rather, he openly expressed his unconditional recognition: "All that the Kabbalists say is true." He also accepted the custom of jumping during the New Moon ceremony (*Hiddush* or *Kiddush Levanah*) to which he attributed great value. He further asserted that all emanations from Heaven came from the sphere *Keter*, which possessed a luminosity one thousand times greater than that of the sun. He believed in acrostics, combinations of letters, sacred numbers and the transmigration of souls, finally affirming that the Kabbalah was the true Tree of Life.

But the Rema knew that the path of mysticism was fraught with considerable danger. In a reply to Rabbi Solomon Luria (Maharshal), he wrote: "If there is something I wish to avoid, it is study of the Kabbalah, since one has to be always on guard not to commit errors."

The Maharshal's approach to the Kabbalah is not entirely clear. He dedicated himself to his studies in silence, but inwardly he believed that his innovations were born of divine revelation. On the other hand, he openly expressed his opposition to the Rabbis' intepretation of the Zohar, which they attributed to inspiration from the Holy Spirit: "The Torah is not in Heaven and is not the concern of the 'echo.'" The opposition to the Rema's opinion, he held that jumping during the New Moon ceremony was "a custom of fools."

Rabbi Mordecai Yaffe, a disciple of the Rema and the Maharshal, was a fervent supporter of the Rambam. Despite that, he did not disdain mystical teachings and believed in miracles, transmigration, evil spirits and the power of sacred names. He was initiated in mystical doctrine by the Kabbalist Matatiyahu Ben Solomon during his ten-year stay in Italy. Rabbi Yaffe set out to interpret the precepts of the Torah in the light of the Kabbalah. He held that many customs could reveal profound mystical secrets. Thus he asserted, for example, that to recite the psalms before prayers was an effective way of silencing the judges of the heavenly court of justice, or that in the benediction lay the secret of wealth.

In a commentary on the mystical works of Rabbi Menachem Ben Benjamin Recanati of Italy, he dealt with fundamental problems. He maintained that the ten spheres risen out of Divinity were united with God as fire with coal, and could not be separated. At the highest level, the emanations could be considered branches of the same tree.

Rabbi Mordecai held that study of the Kabbalah should not be generalized but should be reserved to a minority of the truly elect.

Nor did Rabbi Samuel Eliezer Eidelis (*Maharsha*) fully commit himself in favor of the Kabbalah. The author of *Hidushe Halachoth* also wrote *Hidushe Aggadah* which reveals a strong mystical influence. He believed in transmigration (*gilgul*) and in the sanctity of study of the Kabbalah, but he held that dedication to its study should be sporadic and not daily, to avoid falling into grave error.

Rabbi Joel Sirkis (known as *Bach*) propounded similar ideas in his principal work *Bait Hadash* (New House). To an inquiry from the Jewish community of Amsterdam about a physician who was dedicated to philosophy and derided the Kabbalah, he replied that he should be excommunicated, for the Kabbalah was genuine science and not philosophy. King Solomon had warned against the Kabbalah, pointing out that it caused men to err and led them to transgress a peremptory interdiction contained in the Torah:

"Thou shalt not put a stumbling-block before the blind" (Leviticus 19:14). Nevertheless, Rabbi Sirkis did not permit the precepts to be interpreted through Kabbalistic formulas.

The step from the *pilpul*[1] to the Kabbalah was gradual. The Jewish scholars in Poland found it difficult to emerge from the circumscribed world of Bible verse and penetrate into the fantastic world of the mystics. An instance of that was the Rabbi of Cracow, the *rosh yeshiva* (principal of a rabbinical seminary) and Kabbalist Rabbi Nathan Ben Solomon Shapira, who hesitated between the rational and the mystical. The "science of the occult" had a profoundly disturbing effect on him. In every word of the Torah he sought a secret path leading to redemption, for which he prepared daily. He felt deeply distressed before midnight prayers; he wept bitterly over the destruction of the Holy Temple and the exile. On one occasion, during *hatzot* (midnight prayers) he had a vision of angels singing the very melody he used to sing himself.

Nevertheless, Rabbi Shapira was unable to shake off the *pilpul*, which he mingled with the wonder world of the Kabbalah to put together an unusual sort of dialectic mystique. An inscription on a stone tells that "the prophet Elijah spoke with him."

In one of his works, 252 interpretations by the Ari's system are interwoven in mingled symbolic concepts. As *rosh yeshiva* he trained a whole generation of accomplished Kabbalists.

Rabbi Yeshayahu Halevi Horowitz of Cracow was a fervent mystic, noted for having dedicated himself in his youth to publishing his father's book *Emek Bracha*, fulfilling a wish expressed by his father before his death. He asserted that whoever enters the *pardess* (study of the occult) discovers the secrets locked in the Torah.

In his book *Shneh Luchot Habrit* (Two Tables of the Law) he merged the mystical world with the rational world in order to adapt the mystical to the ways of thinking of Polish Jews, who years later, after the persecution and massacres of 1648, found comfort and hope in the Kabbalah.

The year 1648 raised great hopes of redemption. Most Kabbal-

---

[1] A subtle dialectical method used in study of the Torah.

ists believed that "the day of the Lord" was at hand. The end of the Diaspora had been expected for 1600. Later calculations set the fateful year as 1635, 1638, and finally 1648, when the Jews from all over the world would return to their land, never to leave it again. The calculations were based on an interpretation contained in the Zohar of a verse of the Torah that read: "In *that* jubilee year every man shall return to his plot of land." The numerical value of the word *that* in Hebrew is 1648.

Rabbi Malbim: Interpreter of Holy Writ and Kabbalah

The Jewish world remembers one of the leading Talmudic personalities of the 19th century, a man of unimpeachable ethical standing, who had a manysided social life: Rabbi Meyer Libush Malbim. His true name was Meyer Libush Michel Halperin. Born in Volochisk (Podolia) in 1809, he won fame for his Bible commentary, which explained Holy Writ in such a manner as to put it within reach of all levels of the Jewish people, who recognized him as a great scholar and interpreter of Scripture. He was, moreover, well versed in Hebrew, a master of grammar and a Talmudic scholar. His attainments in the fields of study aroused much interest in the intellectual world of his time.

A noted scholar in philosophy and Kabbalah, he was gifted with a penchant for poetry and rich fantasy. In addition, he was a man of lofty ideals and enlightened piety. He was a God-fearing Jewish sage who dedicated his life to helping the poor and the destitute. An authority in the world of Bible study and commentary, he won esteem throughout the Jewish world. Nevertheless this remarkable ethical and spiritual personality endured much suffering in his life—he trod a trail of want and fear, wandering from place to place.

He held positions as a Rabbi in numerous towns of Western and

Significance of the Kabbalah, the Zohar and the Great Jewish Mystics   133

Eastern European countries, but due to his combative attitude on behalf of human rights and a better life he was unable to hold his positions for long. Everywhere he raised up enemies who persecuted him. He was denounced, arrested, expelled, persecuted, and tortured. He seldom found rest from harassment, but like all great and good men he willingly accepted his fate and never gave up his ideal of struggle for justice, for a better Jewish world, and of helping to train genuine Jews and turn them into "a kingdom of priests of a sacred people."

His first Rabbinical post was Wreszno in the Poznan region, where he was served from 1839 to 1845. Thereafter he was the Rabbi in the little town of Kempen, Prussia, where he won fame among scholars. His name began to be quoted as unquestionable authority in scholarly matters. From Kempen he was called to take charge of the rabbinate in Bucharest, Romania. This position marked the start of his tenacious struggle against the reformists, who accused him of being disloyal to the Romanian government. He was arrested and, after a prolonged detention, was released when the philanthropist and statesman Moses Montefiore intervened with the Romanian government. Montefiore also secured for him a new position as the rabbi of Lenczyca (Poland) where he lived between 1861 and 1877. Here, too, a dispute arose between *Hasidim* and *Mitnagdim* (opponents), and the Rabbi was transferred to Kherson, in the Ukraine. But, due to his close links with the impoverished masses of manual workers and his indictment of wealthy people and intellectuals, whom he rebuked for not granting assistance to their poverty-stricken Jewish brethren, the city community leaders brought accusations against him before the government and he was again compelled to leave the city and move elsewhere. His plight was now lamentable.

After spending five years in Bucharest, weary and abandoned, offended and persecuted, he was feeling well-nigh hopeless when he received a letter from his wife's two brothers, calling him to return for his share of the legacy that his father-in-law had left them on his death in Lestchitz. To his surprise, he found that their father-in-law had left them ten thousand rubles, a house and a business.

After the bad times he had been through in Bucharest, the gates of happiness now opened before him, since he could dedicate himself to study. But these happier times failed to last. He had entrusted all his money and his business to an administrator, who was said to be reliable, but the man tricked him and got away with all his possessions. The Malbim was left penniless. Not wishing to remain in that town, he renewed his wandering ways. Nevertheless, he never ceased to create; he wrote book after book, leaving a notable legacy to the Jewish people. Interpretation refreshing for its acuity, erudition, and easy style characterized his writings. His innovations in commentary had a marked emotional impact on the scholarly world; they saw in him a sage whose brilliant intellect and fine work overshadowed many others of his time. That grandeur was apparent in his book *Artzot Hachaim* and in his commentary on the *Shulhan Arukh*, in which his erudition shone with astonishing power and brilliance.

Artzot Hachaim is a classical work: it brings out his merits as a researcher, as well as his profound knowledge. His explanations of the Bible and Pentateuch—*Hatora Vehamitzvah* and *Mikra Kodesh*—show that all the laws (*Halachot*) taught on the basis of the Pentateuch and its verses are logical. His working method and interpretations created a new approach to Holy Writ never previously used by any scholar and brought new light to all the Jewish scholars of that period.

The Malbim traveled extensively. He visited many countries and learned German, French and English. He felt a special inclination toward the Bible; in that respect he followed the teachings of the Gaon of Vilna, who remarked that in order to understand the Gemara properly, one first must know the Torah.

His life story contained many wonderful chapters. The Malbim (whose name consists of the initials of his own name and that of his father, Meyer Libush Ben Yehiel Michael Halperin) was orphaned at the age of six. His father had been a noted scholar. His mother remarried, and young Meyer was educated by his stepfather, Rabbi Yehuda Leib, who was well versed in the Torah and took a deep interest in his education. He entered him in a *heder* and personally taught him Torah and Gemara, to the age of twelve. He had realized early that the boy would develop into a great scholar, since at the age of eleven he already knew not only the Talmud and Bible commentary, but also Kabbalah. Rabbi Yehuda's entourage realized that here was an outstanding spiritual personality.

In those times it was the custom among Jews to marry at a very young age, and his father arranged a marriage to the daughter of a rich Jew of the city. The marriage was not a happy one, however, and was dissolved; the Malbim went to Warsaw, where he was received with great honor. In Warsaw he was married for the second time, to a daughter of Rabbi Chaim Auerbach. He studied Torah for a few years and then began moving from one community to the other, where at first he was welcomed with honors and respect and won general esteem and affection. After a time, however, he began to make enemies among members of the community who could not tolerate his sermons directed against them, his stand in favor of the poor and oppressed, the fact that he spoke the plain truth and demanded that the communities provide assistance for the homeless poor, for people living in isolation, for the oppressed.

The established scholarly Hasidic world was not originally receptive to his explanations, since with him the main thing was not the Bible but rather the Gemara and the *pilpul*. To him, Bible was a matter for teachers, not for scholars and Rabbis.

Nobody, however, ventured to say anything against a scholar like the Malbim, though the Jewish luminaries and intelligentsia were not enthusiastic about him because he was too religious for their liking. In time he came to be accepted at all Jewish social levels. He won full recognition as a sage of lofty moral and ethical standing, for his knowledge and spiritual grandeur.

The Malbim was the symbol of justice and truth. His whole life was a story of righteousness, service to God, erudition, and preoccupation with the cause of the oppressed. He truly implemented the great Jewish idea of "love of the Torah and love of Israel."

His name will remain graven in the hearts of the Jewish people and shine there forever.

Hasidic Leaders
Who Were Also Outstanding
Exponents of the Kabbalah

The Kabbalah and Hasidism

In the first half of the 16th century, after the expulsion of the Jews from Spain, an important Jewish community was constituted in Safed in what is now Israel. That community became a famous center of Torah and Kabbalah.

Among the mystics that rose to prominence in that holy city, Rabbi Moses of Córdoba and Rabbi Isaac Luria, known as Ari the Saint, must be singled out. The first stood out as the most profound thinker of the Sephardi Kabbalah; the second was the leader of Ashkenazi Kabbalah.

Rabbi Moses of Córdoba developed lofty concepts of an abstract nature on God and the Creation, on the spirit and on matter. Ari, conversely, concentrated on man and his deeds, on atonement, and on of controlling the demands of the flesh.

Theoretical Kabbalah centered its attention on problems that referred to the essence of the Divinity, on the influence of the Torah, and on concepts of the world and other things. Practical Kabbalah, on the other hand, sought to make use of occult divine forces, perform miracles, and enact things supernatural with the help of Holy Writ, combinations of letters, and other similar means.

Development of Jewish spiritual life in the 17th century was strongly influenced by the Ari's mystical teachings. For the first time, the Kabbalah ceased to be a doctrine for the elect to spread among the masses, becoming a decisive factor in the social and spiritual life of the Jewish people.

The master idea of Luria's mystique was the *tikun*, the doctrine of world restoration and salvation. According to *tikun*, man is the center of Creation; on him, even the destiny of the universe depends. His actions could be decisive for salvation.

Any generation is able to win redemption; it only has to wish for it with all its heart and back up its wish with action. Generally speaking, this idea was not entirely new, but the fact of establishing that world salvation depended entirely on man's action certainly was new.

And what could human beings do to achieve redemption? The Ari's answer to that question was: Repent and return to the path of righteousness (*teshuvah*). And *teshuvah* must consist of fasting, of acts of penitence, of the mastering of instincts, of abstaining from eating meat or drinking wine during week days, of serving God starting from midnight, putting sackcloth and ashes on one's head, weeping bitterly over the destruction of the Holy Temple, studying and praying with unction. It was indispensable to renounce worldly pleasures in order to serve God fully and establish total communion with the Supreme Maker.

This ascetic concept of life differed totally from that created by the founder of Hasidism, Rabbi Israel Baal Shem Tov (1700-1760), for whom Divinity was not confined to Heaven, but was also everywhere on earth, within reach of men. As he alone taught, "there is practically no place in the world that is not occupied by His Presence."

God, said the Baal Shem Tov, occupies the whole universe to the limits of all levels and this is the occult meaning of the words "And Thou preservest them all" (Nehemiah 9:6). Divine Providence encompasses the whole world and everything without exception; the good, like the bad, forms part of Creation.

God is generous to all, and He can be reached from any place. It is written: "The Lord is thy keeper" (Psalms 121:5), meaning that He is present everywhere: at work, in the field and the workshop, in the home, wherever you are, provided your thoughts are honest and your heart pure and you long for the roots of righteousness.

A man should not sadden nor torture himself with fasting or other ascetic means, but be content to enjoy life, since only through joy can he aspire to attain to the loftiest spheres of love of God and his neighbor.

The Jewish mystics taught that salvation could come only through *teshuva* (which consists in imposing penitence on oneself) and drew up a series of rules, such as fasting by day and taking only bread and water by night two or three times a week, sleeping on the floor, sitting on snow, and other things. The Baal Shem Tov, however, opposed asceticism, teaching that it is in every way better to serve God without torturing oneself, since fasting weakens the body and prevents man from serving the Almighty. It is better that the strength lost in fasting be dedicated to study of the Torah and to prayer, so that one can pray with all one's heart and all one's strength and in the right frame of mind (*Torah Or* on Psalms, in the name of the Baal Shem Tov).

The teachings of the Baal Shem Tov (also known as Besht from his initials) penetrated deeply into people's minds, and his followers gave up the ascetic life and fasting, "since weakening the body also weakens the soul. Men should seek good health, for the evil spirit was lying in wait to seize upon the moment of weakness."

According to the Besht, it was enough for a man to decide to return to the path of righteousness for him to be considered a just man. He based this on the tractate *Kiddushin* XLIX of the Talmud, which asserts that if a person does *teshuvah* in thought only, he becomes a *tzadik*. On the other hand, already Maimonides, in his work *Yad Hazaka* (the chapter "*Hilhot Teshuvah*") held that the fundamental objective of *teshuvah* was that a man should renounce sin and return to the path of Judaism. Thus the Baal Shem Tov ushered in a new and happier way of serving one's Maker.

Even if the Besht did not invalidate the sanctity of the Ari's teachings, he maintained that the path to God was much simpler.

Everyone, even the most ignorant, could associate with the Almighty. For that, he needed only a clean heart, belief in the Supreme Maker, and to tread in His paths with joy and not with fasting or sadness, and God would be with him. To know His greatness it was enough to look at a tree, at the grass, or at any of His creatures, without bringing in complex reasoning.

The Baal Shem Tov had profound knowledge of the soul of man, infinite love of his fellow men and of all Creation. He liked simple people, kept in close touch with them and was deeply involved in their lives, speaking their language, comforting them and encouraging them with simple stories and parables based on everyday affairs, and acting as a father, brother, and friend to his followers. His unfailing message of love of God, of the Torah, and of man struck deep roots in Judaism and became the foundation of the Hasidic movement.

Rabbi Leib Sores:
One of the Thirty-six Just Men

The luminous figure of Rabbi Leib Sores has been venerated for generations throughout the Jewish world as a true saint. His life was shrouded in mystery. To many, his spiritual personality was like a sealed book and remains an enigma that human intelligence is unable to solve. As one of the most popular figures of the Jewish world, he was known as "he who sees without being seen" (one of the attributes of God) and was also held to be one of the Thirty-six Just Men.

According to the Gemara, there are Thirty-six Just Men in each generation, and through their merits the world goes on. Hasidism deepened and amplified this idea, creating admirable stories about them. They were said to avoid people in the towns, living secretly in chosen places in the woods and fields; they usually were dressed in worn clothing and on meeting their fellow men, nobody knew who they were, for they seemed ordinary people.

Rabbi Leib Sores was considered one of the most mysterious and most holy among the Just Men. The Jews knew, saw, and heard little of him, but he was known to dwell in a secret place and was believed to be dedicated to carrying out sacred missions of the utmost importance for the Jews, from both the spiritual and the material points of view. Strange stories were told about him during his lifetime and since his disappearance.

As a lad of barely sixteen he went to see the Baal Shem Tov, who attested that he could walk on the cutting edge of a sword. He was said to fast from Sabbath to Sabbath—not to forego the pleasure of eating but in order to forget about it, so close was his communion with God. The Maggid (preacher) of Mezricz used to say that the world existed thanks to Rabbi Leib Sores, who fulfilled precepts and did good deeds whose meaning no one could understand.

He will endure in the memory of the Jewish people for his sanctity and purity and for his readiness to sacrifice himself for any Jew. His dominant trait was a limitless, divine kindness. Generations of Jewish children have borne his name—a custom that endures to this day.

His revelation occurred through an incident in a village inn, at which many Jews used to stop. One night the innkeeper's wife went up to the attic with a lighted candle to fetch something and accidentally set fire to the thatched roof, causing a blaze that began to spread throughout the inn. A panic ensued; people rushed to extinguish the fire, but it continued to spread. Rabbi Leib Sores, who had been seated in a corner immersed in his thoughts, suddenly stood up and said: "Bring me a bottle of water." He sprinkled a few drops onto the flames and immediately the big fire died down. According to Hasidic tradition, that was his first revelation. Like the Baal Shem Tov, he too revealed himself in a village inn.

Ever since that event, everyone knew that Rabbi Leib Sores was a great divine. He did not issue teachings, hold banquets, or accept written petitions from adherents, like the other Hasidic Rabbis, but the people were fully convinced that he performed miracles.

At that time, in the mid-18th century, the Jews were in a critical situation. Poland had been divided and occupied by several countries, including Russia and Austria. The invaders set themselves to assimilate the Jews forcibly. Czar Nicholas I issued a savage decree, ordering the obligatory recruitment of boys between the ages of six and twelve to serve twenty-five years in the army.

The children were snatched from their homes and sent to villages of White Russia, where they were tortured to force them to renounce Judaism and to convert to the Russian Orthodox religion, which they had to learn. The edict prohibited the children from speaking Yiddish and from praying by Jewish rite and compelled them to eat pork, go to church daily, and so forth. The least offense was punished by fifty lashes. Most of the recruits died at the hands of their jailers. Only a few boys managed to escape that inferno and return to their homes; they knew nothing of Judaism and remembered only the Hebrew alphabet and the *Shema Israel*, but it was enough to preserve their Jewish faith.

The civilized world remained silent—an attitude that was repeated during the 20th century when the Nazi criminals carried out genocide against the Jewish population.

The other invaders, the Austrians, were no better than the Russians. They, too, issued anti-Semitic decrees. They closed the Jewish schools and compelled the children to learn German in state schools, receive a Gentile education, dress according to non-Jewish custom, and demonstrate their support of the invaders.

One of Moses Mendelsohn's adherents, Herz Homberg, was put in charge of carrying out the reform. With the help of the Austrian government he devoted himself wholeheartedly to the task of "transforming" the Jewish children.

The Hasidim considered this the equivalent of compulsory religious conversion. Other prejudicial edicts followed: the Jews had their innkeeping licenses withdrawn, and many families were left without means of subsistence. Fear, despair and bitterness gripped the Jewish population, who looked to their spiritual guides for help.

According to Hasidic writ, Rabbi Sores, who knew how to work miracles, could see without being seen and had power to shorten distances, traveled on each occasion to the capital of Austria, entered the palace of Emperor Franz Josef II unseen and, undetected by the palace guard, accused and attacked him physically until the iniquitous decrees had been annulled.

The emperor was angry with his servants: "Why did you allow this stranger to enter and torment me?" But as they had not seen anyone they were unable to detain him. In vain they searched the whole palace and its grounds. The emperor pointed a finger and shouted: "This raged Jew stood here, raised his hand, and threatened to hit me!" Next he complained of pain caused by blows and shouted: "Haven't you anything to say? Why don't you protect me?" But the guards had not seen or heard anything; they thought that the emperor was becoming insane.

Franz Josef was compelled to rescind the decrees; by similar methods, the Russian edicts too were cancelled.

In the year 1791 Rabbi Sores said to his adepts: "I must prepare for a journey, since it has thus been decided in Heaven. I ask that I be given a very simple burial, without ostentatious inscriptions on the coffin, just: 'Rabbi Moshe Leib, who loved Israel.'"

And thus the name has been remembered in the Hasidic world to the present day. Blessed be the memory of the Just Man.

The Baal Shem Tov, Creator of Hasidism: His Relation to the Kabbalah

In recent years, the Hasidic movement attracted widespread attention. Hasidism became the central subject of much research. Scores of books and tractates, some of great value and significance, have been dedicated to the history of Hasidism, its leaders, and its detractors.

Hasidic literature covers a period of over two hundred years; not only its quantitative wealth but also its colorful content and its frankness are remarkable. It encompasses many fields of creation and thought, gives explanations and interpretations of the writ of our sages as well as sermons, speeches, moral object-lessons, discussions, poems and legends. Hasidic books are disseminated worldwide.

The appearance of the Baal Shem Tov in the arena of Jewish life at the outset of the 18th century cannot be considered anything but a miracle. It amounted to salvation of the Jewish people, whose situation was most disturbing. The Jews had fallen into a state of depression after two major catastrophes, one physical and the other spiritual: the Khmelnitsky massacres (1648-1649) and the unfortunate Sabbatai Zevi episode. Most people were so dejected, both physically and spiritually, that their very existence was threatened.

Then came the Baal Shem, who revolutionized Jewish life. He revived the people and instilled a new spirit into them. He fulfilled Ezekiel's prophecy of the dry bones that gained new life. He raised his downcast brethren's spirits and awakened hope; through the power of his profound yet simple approach, his moving humanism, he showed the Jews the way to reach out to God, giving them spiritual strength and faith and showing that they, too, simple people, could approach and associate with God.

The creator of Hasidism, Rabbi Israel Baal Shem Tov, did not leave any written work except for a few letters to his brother-in-law Rabbi Gershom of Kitev. Not all the great religious leaders believed in the written word; for them, the main thing was the spoken word—vital, live, and full of fire according to the words of the prophet: "The spirit of God is in me and His word is on my tongue."

Nor did the Baal Shem Tov want others to write down his teachings, for fear they might not be correctly transmitted; but one of his principal adepts, Rabbi Jacob Joseph of Polna, transcribed the stories, fables, and proverbs that he heard from the maestro; they appeared in his book *Toldoth Ya'acov Yosef*.

Later, other students and his disciples recopied the Baal Shem Tov's teachings and arranged them in a definite sequence. Thus the Baal Shem Tov's teachings appeared: *Keter Shem Tov* and *Tzavaoth De Baal Shem*, as well as a series of stories about the Baal Shem.

Those books set forth the Baal Shem Tov's philosophy.

People are much dedicated to study, said the Besht, and this is in most cases the work of *yetzer harah* (the instinct of evil). Every man who aspires to be more important than his fellow men must seek the path of learning. The instinct of evil is so dominant in man that he cannot study that which concerns morals and fears of God, or knowledge of a law, but only Gemara and its interpretation, merely of the sake of study. Among believing men, the evil instinct has its own ways of working: it convinces a man that he is a sinner, although he takes care not to sin, or his transgression is a minor one that cannot be considered sin. Thus the spirit of evil frequently transforms men so that they lapse into depravity and are punished and forsaken by God. Yet God is close to man, in such manner that there is practically no separation between the Creator and his creatures. At first sight it would seem that the Highest is concealed behind iron walls, but those who understand know that walls of iron, like any attire or disguise, are part of Divinity, for there is no place empty of Him. All is one single unit, because all was created and issued from His essence.

God is in the highest, said the Besht, but He descends to the lowest step. That is the secret of the verse "And You revive all" (*Veata mehayeh et kulam*) because Divinity is with man even when he commits a sin. Without Divinity, man would be powerless to move his limbs. The Highest is in all the world, also where sins are committed. And God is present not only in what man does but also in men's thoughts, although thought is usually poor, according to the verse "Behold here, Your enemies" (*ki hineh oivecha, Hashem*) which means that among the enemies of God, Satan and evil instincts, is Divinity.

It is therefore right that man should always aspire to good and pure thoughts; thought is the principal thing in man's life, for he can only attain a certain level according to his level of thought. It is the principal element of the soul of man; a good thought is like a "holy spirit." Man can correct an evil thought and raise it higher; but if the idea of how to correct it does not come, it should be cast aside.

All the elements and creatures of the world, minerals, plants, animals and men, both the good and the bad, are contained in God. How is it possible that God should contain such contradictory elements as the good and the bad? The answer is that the bad is as a support for the good. Nor does absolute evil exist, since evil can usually produce good; then everything turns to good, like an elimination of the "shell," as it will be in future. Thus the law is limited by the principle of justice. The harshest law can be converted into justice; the same thing happens with man's sins of pride or avarice. Pride may appear only as one-eighth of the total; as regards avarice, man may squander no more than one-fifth of his fortune. The same applies to unhappy love and false modesty, which should be used as a step to aspire to righteousness; they should be eradicated, in the search for things higher and sacred. It is the same with *sichot hulin* (profane talk)—people's simple talk and ideas, with which vestments for the Torah can be made.

Since everything consists of letters and everyone depends on the twenty-two letters of the Torah, their union brings change; the profane may turn into the sacred.

We therefore deduce that there is no wicked action or conduct, because any evil human action or conduct can change into good action or conduct. In every evil there is a grain of good, just as every lie contains a grain of truth, and the acts and behavior of the evildoer find a parallel in the spirituality of the just. The evildoer is not satisfied with what he possesses, but always wants more; the righteous, conversely, is not content with the good deeds he performs, but always wants to do more.

The world of the Highest, says the Besht, is full of wonderful secrets and heavenly light, but the small hand of man covers the eyes and the great light goes unseen. A clear eye can see God everywhere, and also hear His voice. But there are people who cannot and will not see, or who cover their ears and cannot and will not hear, like the blind who cannot see the beauties of the world or the deaf who are unable to hear music.

It should be realized that all that is on high, like all that is below, is one single great unity; when one takes part in that unity, one has it totally in one's hand. Man is part of Divinity and is intimately bound up with the lofty worlds that receive the influence of men, whether good or bad. Men gifted with sanctity and spirituality exert influence on the lofty world, in the same way as those that do the contrary through the profane and the material.

A man's being is contained in the words that he speaks and, as his being comes from the Highest, man's clean and pure words rise and exert influence from on high for greater spirituality and a better nature. When a man walks on the street and speaks simple words to others, they are so pure that they seem an offering to the Highest, since man's speech and hearing come from the soul and the soul is part of Divinity.

In the Baal Shem Tov's opinion, the influence of man on the higher worlds is perhaps greater than the influence of those worlds on man. The Mishna says: *"Da ma lemala mimecha"* (Know what is above you). The Besht explained this, saying that man should know *"shekol ma shelemala, hakol mimecha"* (All that is on high is yours). The Besht said the same thing about the verse *"Hashem tzelecha"* (God is your shadow): like the shadow that does everything a man does, similarly the Almighty does what man does, even when he eats, drinks, or dresses himself. Man can proceed knowing that all is for God and the Highest will accept his actions as prayer.

And when man acts in this way, spirituality awakens to arouse in him the sacred fires of his material being, raising them to the loftiest spiritual level, to unify the divine part of his being with God in a complete union. Therefore all should be done joyfully, without weeping and without prostration, not like a slave obeying his master's will, not like a second class human being doing the will of one above him in station, not like a sinner before a judge, but cheerfully and happily, like a son beside his father.

Men should not be sad, for when a man is cheerful and good-humored he rises out of his littleness to unite with his Maker. For the same reason it is wrong for a man to weep, for he should serve God cheerfully. Therefore one should not be so particular about everything people do, because that is what the evil spirit wants—to strike fear into men's hearts, making them believe that nothing will satisfy God and thus sadden them. Sadness is a great drawback in worship of the Creator. When someone has fallen into sin, it is sufficient if he sincerely repents; thereafter he should be of good cheer for he has earned the right to serve God.

Through his opposition to sadness the Besht lashed out at fasting and self-chastisement, for they weaken the human body and engender sadness. A weakened body contains a weakened soul; a man with a weakened soul does not have strength to pray as he should, even if he is free of sin. A weakened soul produces a state of panic, and a man in a panic could never ascend the three high ladders to which a Jew should aspire: love of God, love of Israel, and love of the Torah.

Not everything the Besht said was new to Jews. But he knew how to express his opinions vigorously on every subject in such manner that people felt attracted body and soul.

Charity, he used to say, is the most important human action and rates higher than other *mitzvot*. Any of the other *mitzvot*, if carried out with another purpose in mind, could invoke the remark that it is better not to fulfill the precept in that way. This is not the case with charity, for charity practiced with another intention is the same as if practiced for its own sake; through it, souls are revived. One should not expect the poor man to hold out his hand, for this diminishes the *mitzva*.

Next to charity, modesty is the foundation and the root of man's deportment. An immodest man, though he does only good deeds, is relying on a weak foundation. And when that foundation is rotten, the whole edifice falls down. Modesty should not be superficial but deeply rooted in one's heart, but it should be balanced, for if it becomes too strong, the evil spirit may use it as a means of estranging a man from the Highest.

Another virtue that the Besht preached was *devekuth* (coming nearer to God) to which every person should aspire. This can be attained by wholeheartedly deepening of study and prayer, leading to union of thought with interior spirituality that lies in sacred letters, for each letter possesses part of a man's soul, which is bound to and unified with God. This relationship with letters must be sacred and pure in possibility and reality—in speech and thought. Uniting heart and soul with the sanctity of the precept and the Torah brings enlightenment and truth.

The intention behind every act, said the Besht, is the soul of every act, which with its help may lead to union between God and his people, and man can attain the stage of its realization when the soul is denuded, separated from the body and clothed in sacred ideas of which man will talk, so that he cannot feel any earthly sentiment or have any relationship with his surroundings. And since the Torah and the precepts come from the Highest alone, one may say that when man fulfills a precept and does so with love, it is as if there was total communion with the Highest and all the precepts had been fulfilled and there would be genuine integration of the Maker with His world.

One often meets men who pray and study much, but they lack the necessary fervor and their efforts are in vain, because they lack "soul." Fervor is an element for which one should pray much, so that the Highest kindles from the Torah and the *mitzvot*. A man should also know that in fulfilling a precept, it is not the precept that is the most important but the intention behind it. That is why one should beguile the evil spirit in fulfilling each precept.

Man is accompanied wherever he goes, said the Besht, by outside forces that point out his errors and his virtues. He should therefore conduct himself worthily, in such manner that it does not matter to him when he is praised or condemned by other men. The principal thing is prayer, in which a man should be punctilious, for praying feeds the angels. Prayer should be so ardent that in preparing for it, a man should appear to be preparing to die. And when he finished praying, he should thank God for his goodness in giving him strength to finish his prayer alive and for not extinguishing his soul through the fervor of prayer.

Prayer should flow like smoke from a fire, and the fervor put into the act should contain all the force, uniting with the Highest, that rests between the sacred letters. That fervor may weaken the forces of the body. One should not laugh at a man who sways back and forth in praying, no more that at a person who falls into a river and moves his arms and legs to keep afloat: the reason is that swaying and moving the arms and legs in the act of praying helps to protect his soul against evil thoughts and thus reach the haven of clear thinking.

At the same time one should take into account that the tongue is the pen that writes what is dictated by the heart; thus it speaks that which the tongue wishes to record. One should therefore be more careful with one's tongue than with other limbs and not speak ill of anyone, not even of an evil person. One can only speak ill of wicked conduct, but not of the person. In the words of the Besht:

> When someone speaks ill of others, other people will do the same to you, though you do not know it, because a man cannot see his own faults and those of persons close to him. Even the worst offender must be given the benefit of the doubt, for his wickedness

is due to the fact that he was created of coarse material, but he may turn from his wickedness; and when a man must be punished for his wicked deeds, this should be done with mildness and not in anger. But if anger is ever shown, it should be an exception, for the heart of every man should be full of goodness and kindness.

In addition to those virtues, the Besht taught of the need for the *tzadik*, who for the people is the same as the soul for the body. He represents complete integrity, the "loftiest man," who must show the rest of the people the way toward God. The *tzadik* finds in the Torah the light that he needs, and by it he sees from one end of the world to the other. The core of his soul consists of isolated sparks that correct his actions, and when a man is united with a *tzadik*, he is protected by him and is saved in moments of danger and other situations. Recounting the praises of a *tzadik* is like studying *ma'aseh merkavah* (the secrets of the ascension of the prophet Elijah in a chariot of fire). The power of the *tzadik* is so great that all in Heaven tremble at the sound of his voice and the Highest is happy to do everything the *tzadik* asks.

Rabbi Nahum of Tchernobyl:
Kabbalist and Defender of the Meek

Outstanding among the primary founders and architects of Hasidism was the just and God-fearing Kabbalist Rabbi Nahum of Tchernobyl, known also as the Grand Rabbi Nahum, who was born in the town of Novorinsk, Volin province.

He developed and disseminated the teachings of the Baal Shem Tov and was a prominent mystic. He created a synthesis between the Kabbalah and *Hasidism*, instilling into Hasidism a new breath of life that met the needs of every Jew, including the humbler strata of the population.

Through his sermons and prayers he taught the people his approach to Hasidism. He very ably explained the teachings of that doctrine and traveled extensively to spread it in a number of population centers.

Through his extraordinary charisma he attracted adepts on a mass scale; among those who listened in rapt attention to his sermons were leading Torah scholars.

Rabbi Nahum was orphaned at an early age; he was educated in the home of his father's brother. In *heder* (primary school) he showed a variety of talents and a knack of perseverance, and his teachers predicted a brilliant future for him.

Immediately after his marriage he became a primary-school teacher. All the great Hasidic leaders—the Baal Shem Tov, the Maggid of Mezricz, and others—began in the same way. In order to reach the people, they began with the children and later established contact with the adult population.

Rabbi Nahum's salary as a teacher hardly provided him with enough to eat and he remained poor and weak all his life, but he bore it willingly. He used to say: "He who seeks worldly pleasures is worthless." He taught until late in the day and studied the Torah at night—not in the way he was taught in the yeshiva but through study of the Kabbalah and of the mystical teachings of Ari the Saint.

He adopted the Ari's system, based on fasting, weeping and contrition, as his way of life; he fasted twice a week, donning worn sackcloth, and regularly at midnight he arose for *hatzot*[1] service, strewing ashes on his head and weeping bitterly.

At its beginnings, Hasidism had to take stands against ways of life and customs that had taken root in Judaism concerning the relationship between man and his fellow men as well as between man and his Maker.

There was sharp controversy among the old spiritual leaders in the matter of penitence. Conflicts arose between those who preached that the essential thing in penitence was not in afflicting the body, which was mere matter, but the heart and soul, and those who taught that the body should be fully purified and chastised for every transgression committed.

The former group contended that when someone repented in thought, he became a just man, according to Gemara (*Kiddushin* XLIX, b).[1] They further asserted that the principal organs that induced sin were the heart and the brain. It was therefore sufficient if a man meditated on how he had departed from God in

---

[1] The midnight prayer, mourning the destruction of the Holy Temple of Jerusalem.

sinning, corrected his faults, and decided inwardly not to repeat them (according to the Rambam, *Hilhot Teshuvah* LXXXII).

Against that, the Kabbalists, including Ari the Saint, maintained that not only the heart and brain sinned, but also the 248 parts of the body and its 365 tendons. Therefore, when a man committed a sin, he should afflict his whole body. For example, he should not eat by day, but by night, only bread and water, and fast twice a week.

The Kabbalists did not restrict themselves to fasting, but demanded a variety of sacrifices such as sleeping on the ground, abstaining from washing, sitting on each side of the body on snow or ice for an hour, in general prescribing atonement for each person according to his transgression. They usually prescribed a "balanced act of contrition," that is, the penitence should be weighed as to equal the pleasure obtained by the transgression. It should, moreover, be an "act of contrition according to Scripture," that is, penitence according to the Torah. For instance, if death was the appropriate penalty for the sin committed, the sinner should torment himself until the pain was as great as that of death itself. Rabbi Nahum believed in this system and practiced it daily. At that time the Baal Shem Tov's Hasidism began to spread among the Jews of the Ukraine, reports of his miracles were heard everywhere, and there was much talk of his views on the right way to approach God. Rabbi Nahum decided to meet the Baal Shem Tov to learn something of his new system.

Hasidic legends tell that the Baal Shem Tov knew he was coming and told his wife to prepare the choicest food, because a very important guest would be arriving for Shabbat. Rabbi Nahum stayed at their house for a time and won the deep respect of the Besht and his disciples for his honesty and humility. He became known as a genuine saint, whose life was pure spirituality.

Rabbi Nahum maintained, like his hosts, that the more widely Hasidism was spread among the people, the sooner the Messiah would come. Like the Baal Shem Tov, he visited the towns and villages, speaking to humble folk in their own language, in simple and affectionate terms, until they understood his ideas.

Hasidism uplifted the humble, who formed a high proportion of the Jewish population, and defended the humiliated and downtrodden Jews of the villages against frequent affronts on the part of the rich. His sermons convinced simple Jewish folk that they were participants in Hasidism.

What money Rabbi Nahum made from his sermons he spent for charitable purposes, including marriages of poor young women and the release of prisoners. He was especially dedicated to aiding prisoners, many of whom impoverished Jews who were incarcerated simply because they could not pay their rent on time.

Legend tells that on one occasion, while trying to rescue a prisoner, he fell into a trap and was himself imprisoned. One of his disciples, Rabbi Velvl of Zhitomir, obtained permission to stay with his teacher in the cell. In the cell, he seemed to see a woman wrapped in a silk mantle who asked Rabbi Nahum: "Is this your reward for your sacrifice on behalf of the Jews? Is this the Torah and the happiness it brings?" When the woman disappeared he asked Rabbi Nahum for an explanation of that strange conversation. The reply was: "It was Mother Rachel who asked me if that was the reward for the precept to save those imprisoned, to which I answered that it was from Heaven that I was brought here, to appreciate better the vital importance of the precept to rescue those in distress and concern myself more wholeheartedly with it." He sought ceaselessly, by every possible means, to alleviate the sufferings of the Jews wherever they were.

One of the Baal Shem Tov's disciples, Rabbi Jacob Joseph Falger, said of Rabbi Nahum: "People think that he is a Just Man. Actually he is as good as ten Just Men." All who knew him considered him a genuine saint and some called him "the little Baal Shem Tov." When the daughter of the Chief Rabbi of Lyubavich, Rabbi Shneer Zalmen, fell gravely ill, her father sent a special messenger to Rabbi Nahum, asking him to pray for her.

Despite his renown he always lived in humble circumstances and endured hardship. He despised money and wealth and spent all he had for charitable purposes.

Visited by a rich and a poor Hasid, he received the poor man first, conversed with him at length and then interviewed his wealthy visitor more briefly. When the rich man offered him payment he refused, saying: "Go in that direction, there you will meet a poor man; give it to him."

His Hasidim recount the following incident: "On one occasion Rabbi Nahum noticed that in his son's home they were cooking fish in midweek.... He then put on his Sabbath attire, went to his son's house and ironically remarked: 'I wish you a Good Sabbath, my son, since you have converted the weekdays into the Sabbath and you cook on those days as on the Sabbath.'"

Rabbi Nahum wrote a number of important books, with which his disciples Rabbi Elihau Katz was concerned. One of them, under the title *Maor Einayim* (Splendor of the Eyes), contains sermons based on weekly readings from the Torah, together with a collection of legends. That book created a deep impression in the Hasidic world. His fellow disciple Chief Rabbi Levi Isaac of Berdichev wrote of it: "His words are the words of God and have power to arouse the spirit of man to unite with the Lord, as also to kindle a man's heart to serve his Maker. The book is like the cool water that slakes a man's thirst."

The Rabbi of Sheptovl also wrote: "His words are serene and clear as shining metal and have power to purify the hearts of the Jews in order to guide them along the right path to God."

The Hasidim recount that Rabbi Nahum used to flagellate his own body before studying the Torah. Once an angel appeared who wanted to reveal to him certain secrets of the Torah, but Rabbi Nahum refused, saying: "Whatever I achieve, must be through effort and self-sacrifice."

His book *Maor Einayim* was one of the first Hasidic books and all the genuine Just Men used it for their sermons. A year later another of his books was edited: *Ismach Lev* (Lift up Your Heart), which treats of Talmud legends.

Rabbi Nahum was the founder of a great Hasidic dynasty that extends to the present day. He is revered throughout the Hasidic world as a genuine Just Man.

When he died in Tchernobyl an *ohel* (funeral arch) was erected over his grave, and many Jews still go there to pray that he intercede on their behalf before the Highest, as he did throughout his lifetime.

Rabbi Jacob Isaac Horowitz, The Hozeh of Lublin: Grand Kabbalist and Visionary

Rabbi Jacob Isaac Horowitz, known as the "Visionary of Lublin," was among the outstanding rabbinical figures produced by Polish Jewry in recent centuries. His profound erudition and genius went hand-in-hand with his fearless struggle on behalf of Judaism, which was having to contend with influences that penetrated into Poland and Western Europe after Napoleon's victories. He firmly believed that the Hasidic movement was capable of saving Judaism; he therefore assumed leadership and, jointly with other personalities and his adherents, became the pioneer and disseminator of the movement in Poland.

His father, Rabbi Eliezer, was rabbi in Yazepov; he belonged to an ancient family whose ancestors included Yeshayahu Halevi Horowitz, author of the famous book *Shneh Luchot Habrit* (Two Tables of the Law).

Rabbi Jacob Isaac had shown scholarly talents and powers of concentration since childhood. When still very young, he was accepted as a pupil of the famous Rabbi Shmelke of Nikolsburg, with whom the leading scholars of all Europe studied. His yeshiva was noted for its reliance on the ablest and best-informed minds from all countries. From the very outset, Rabbi Shmelke noticed the youthful Jacob Isaac's versatile talents; his wife predicted that he "would become a great Rabbi with thousands of adherents and that his virtues would shed light on the world."

Through his Rabbi, he became a Hasid of the holy Maggid of Mezricz, and after the latter's death he was the Hasid of Rabbi Elimelech of Lizensk. Through his association with those two great Rabbis, he learned to tread the sacred path of rectitude and fear of God, rising ever higher in both disciplines, but he was modest and self-effacing in the presence of other people.

He could not hide his knowledge for long, since Rabbi Elimelech of Lizensk held him in the high esteem and consulted him increasingly often, which was proof of his virtues and talents. Before his death, the Rabbi appointed him as his successor, and many thousands of Hasidim traveled to meet him. The greatest Rabbis of those times gathered around him; they included his disciples the Id Hakadosh, Rabbi Jacob Isaac of Przysucha, Rabbi Simhah Bunem and others, who made him famous.

His adepts called him Rabenu Hakadosh, and the Rabbi of Apt said of him that "now he raises his eyes to unite with the Maker." Others said that his soul was at one with that of the Patriarch Moses, with that of the Kabbalist Rabbi Isaac Luria (Ari the Saint) and with that of Rabbi Israel Baal Shem Tov.

The Hasidic world called him Hozeh (visionary) because Rabbi Jacob Isaac saw what ordinary men could not see. When people came to see him and the Rabbi looked at them just once, he not only knew what was going on in the heart and mind of each visitor but also in his city and his house. He could foretell what would happen; he always knew beforehand who would come to visit him and what were his thoughts. Someone said of him "that he possessed the Holy Spirit, and that he could see what was going on from one end of the world to the other." One of his disciples declared that "no Just Man has the merit of possessing eyes like those of the Hozeh."

Thousands of Hasidim, from all social strata, came to see him for a variety of reasons. He uplifted the initiated to the sublimest levels of the Torah, while to simple folk he brought help through wise counsel and prayers to the Almighty.

Everyone talked about him, but he maintained that he did not deserve such attention, and never thought himself superior to others. He respected everyone, especially scholars, even if they were not Hasidim; he was great in both heart and mind—a true genius and a genuine saint.

He wrote three books: *Zikaron Zot*, *Divreh Emet*, and *Zot Zikaron*. He endured much hardship because of his fellow men, despite enjoying the great respect of all.

The Hozeh was Rabbi of many Hasidic Rabbis of Poland, Galicia, and Hungary. He died on the day of Tisha Be-Av and his adepts later spread his teachings throughout the world.

After the death of the Hozeh, many of his disciples became Rabbis and most of them followed his Hasidic system.

The famous Id Hakadosh, Rabbi Jacob Isaac of Przysucha, moved away from the Hozeh during the latter's lifetime and created a new system based on reasoned thought, which was carried on by his student Rabbi Bunem of Przysucha and, in turn, by his student Rabbi Mendele of Kotzk, who created a system of his own.

One of the Hozeh's most notable students was Rabbi Meyer Halevi of Apt, who was well versed in all Torah and Talmud disciplines as well as in the Kabbalah. A few months before his disappearance, the Hozeh ordered that on the shabbat when the chapter on Phineas (Numbers 25:10 ff.) would be read, Rabbi Meyer of Apt be called to the Torah as the *Baal Koreh*[1] to read a longer extract than usual and include the following verses:

> Let the Lord, the God of the spirits of all flesh, set a man over the congregation, who may go out before them, and who may come in before them, and who may lead them out, and who may bring them in; that the congregation of the Lord be not as sheep which have no shepherd...and lay thy hand upon him.... And thou shalt put some of thine honour upon him....

---

[1] Person appointed to read the Torah.

The Hozeh's adepts saw in the foregoing a hint and a signal that their Rabbis were amazed at the choice, inasmuch as more suitable persons were available, but years later, when more was known about Rabbi Meyer, the wisdom of the Hozeh's choice was recognized.

To Rabbi Meyer, "love thy neighbor" was one of the principal aims of life. He used to say that there were no wicked Jews, for "the Dispersion was to blame for everything." To love one's neighbor is one of the fundamental principles of the Torah, and this should always be borne in mind.

His genius went hand in hand with his profound piety. Despite being free of worldly passions, he was keenly mindful of the needs and sufferings of his fellow men; he devoted full attention to all who came seeking his counsel.

Rabbi Meyer lived an ascetic life and fasted from one Sabbath to the next.

In his youth he lived in Stafnitze in great poverty. Hasidic legend tells that Rabbi David Lelever came to town and visited Rabbi Meyer, who wanted to offer him fruit, but there was none in the house, so he asked his wife to buy some in the market. Rabbi Meyer and his wife had only one pair of boots; it was raining and the streets were muddy, so the Rabbi gave his wife the boots and she did as he asked. When the visitor returned to his inn, he described the incident to his wife, who asked: "What did you want of poor Rabbi Meyer?" "A day will come," answered Rabbi Lelever, "when wine will flow at his table like water and he will eat from a gold plate."

Years later, when Rabbi Meyer became Rabbi of Stafnitze, he was visited by a rich trader from Warsaw who presented him with a gold plate.

Despite his great piety, he disliked and opposed his old companion Rabbi Bunem of Przysucha, who had departed from the Hozeh's method and created his own very profound one, of which great wisdom was required. It demanded that each precept be fulfilled secretly, in the depth of the heart, and this applied also to repentance, which called for a genuinely contrite heart.

The Przysucha system emphasized the intention behind the

precept rather than its actual fulfillment, and Rabbi Meyer, like other leaders of that period, mistrusted Rabbi Bunem's system on principle, fearing it might prove disastrous for its adepts.

On one occasion Rabbi Meyer sent two of his ablest Hasidim to Przysucha to ask Rabbi Bunem how he could be a Rabbi since he had previously been a trader in Danzig? When the Hasidim reached Rabbi Bunem's home, he greeted them and asked whence they came. They answered that they were Hasidim from Apt and had come to ask him a question on their Rabbi's instructions.

On hearing the question, Rabbi Bunem concentrated his thoughts for a few minutes, then answered: "Return home and tell the Rabbi of Apt on my behalf that it is no great achievement to remain confined to a house day and night, fulfill the precepts, study, and be a leader at the same time. A leader must be aware of the misfortunes of the people and of the sins of his generation, in order to uplift them from their state of impurity."

When the Hasidim returned and reported the interview to Rabbi Meyer, he replied: "Who said that a Rabbi should be a clown? A Rabbi should be the whole congregation's envoy before the Almighty, bring distressed hearts in to His presence, and pray that all their needs be provided for."

Both of them were great figures, who wrote glorious pages into the story of Hasidism and enlighten us to this day.

Elimelech of Lizensk:
Author of Noam Elimelech

One of the most extraordinary figures of the Hasidic world, the principal founder of Hasidism in Galicia, and spokesman for the new line in Hasidism was certainly Rabbi Elimelech of Lizensk.

He was one of the mainstays of Polish Hasidism, but whereas his companions lived and worked in the Ukraine, Russia, and Poland, Rabbi Elimelech ushered in a new epoch for Hasidism in Galicia.

He first traveled to the home of the Maggid of Mezricz, considered the continuator of the Baal Shem Tov. When the Maggid died, he left a son, known as Rabbi Abraham, whom the Hasidim nicknamed "the Angel," because he was completely devoid of any worldly passion, like an angel. He hardly ate and did not wish to know anything of this world, or of people. He was "pure spirit," living apart from the Hasidim, a recluse wrapped in *tallit* and *tefilin*.

When the Maggid's adepts saw that "the angel" was concerned primarily with celestial matters, they realized that he could not be their leader and as nobody wanted the responsibility of taking the Maggid's place, they began to disperse toward various countries.

One group returned to Galicia and set up a number of centers there that attracted the mass of the Hasidim; among them were two brothers of acknowledged fame as scholars: Rabbi Elimelech of Lizensk and Rabbi Zishe of Anapolya, who had been the Maggid's students for many years. When he died, they began to travel, visiting inhabited places in Galicia, teaching the Jews Hasidism and spreading the Baal Shem Tov's doctrine.

It was then that Rabbi Zishe convinced his brother to become a Rabbi, knowing his grandeur as a divine. Thus a new era began for Hasidism in Galicia.

Rabbi Elimelech settled in the little village of Lizensk, near Yaroslav, and this humble place won worldwide fame through the God-fearing Rabbi who was an innovator of Hasidism in that region.

Many people remember that until very shortly before the outbreak of the World War II, thousands of Jews used to travel to Lizensk on Adar 21, the anniversary of the death of Rabbi Elimelech, because he had declared that those who visited his grave would not "die of repentance."

One of his adepts, Rabbi Mendele Pristitzer, recounted that "all the Rabbi's efforts were directed toward keeping people away from sin, purifying the souls of the Jews, and instilling love and respect for the Maker. "I used to see my Teacher," he went on, "as he meditated on fear of God; his teeth used to chatter and his body trembled for fear of God and His glory."

With time, Lizensk became a center of the Torah and Hasidism in Galicia, and hundreds of thousands of Hasidim from all parts of the world used to visit there to know the paths to the Highest. Rabbi Elimelech was famous for his wisdom and for the miracles he performed; his influence grew, not so much for his teachings as for his prayers.

In his principal work, *Noam Elimelech*, published two years after his death, he wrote that the relationship between a Just Man and the masses should be closer. The individual who needed the help of his Rabbi should first of all have faith in him; thus he would make him his advocate before God. The Hasidim were a congregation with a variety of needs, and the Rabbi was its representative.

All worldly needs—health, sustenance, children—could, according to the *Noam Elimelech*, be met through the mediation of the genuine Just Man, whose duty it was to pray to God and win divine mercy for the Jews. It was he who could fill all man's needs. Therefore the Hasidim were obligated to provide for his sustenance, so that he could dedicate himself to divine service and pray on behalf of all.

The book is divided in four parts: (1) sermons based on weekly readings from the Torah; (2) short interpretations of some verses from the prophets and quotations from the Talmud; (3) five letters written to his son and disciple; and (4) a kind of spiritual testament.

Within a very short time the Rabbi's little market town was besieged by thousands of Hasidim; Jewish visitors arrived daily from everywhere. Moreover, many legends about Rabbi Elimelech's miracles were going around, so everyone knew that to travel to Lizensk meant returning with the necessary help.

But the Rabbi said to his son: "Do you perhaps know, my son, why the people besiege me and ask me to ensure their health and sustenance? It is because they know that I am to blame...for the situation they are in, because my sins have put the world into a negative situation...."

In his youth, Rabbi Elimelech used to martyrize and flagellate his body. For a time he "took to the road" with his brother Rabbi Zishe, disguised as country dwellers.

Rabbi Elimelech's great teacher, the Maggid of Mezricz, also martyrized himself in his youth, until the Baal Shem Tov shouted at him: "When the body is weak, the soul too is weak! One cannot pray as one should, and the principle of prayer is intention."

In a letter to his disciple Rabbi Jacob Joseph of Polna, the Baal Shem Tov wrote: "Is the body your property, that you take it upon yourself to torture it? Man has no right over his body."

Although in his younger years Rabbi Elimelech was an ascetic, when he came to know the Baal Shem Tov's system, which taught that God should be served cheerfully, he changed his style. And he noticed in his book that the way to serve God was not by fasting, since nothing was achieved by it.

One day he said to his disciple the Rabbi of Apt: "If I could find another two men to join me in a Tribunal of Three, I would prohibit fasting."

And when one day a penitent who had been jailed for excessive fasting came to him, he ordered him to take nourishment to comfort his body and thereafter to do penitence through prayer and a contrite heart.

It is interesting to point out that in Galicia the Hasidic movement did not meet with difficulty or opposition as in Lithuania, where it was persecuted. On the contrary, most Jews were Hasidim. There were only two cities, Brod and Lemberg, that deferred to the anathemas from Vilna, but although emissaries were sent to the provinces to combat Hasidism, they never found support among the population.

In general the Rabbi did not take part in arguments between the Hasidim and their detractors, saying that the fuss would die down by itself.

He died on 21 Adar 1786 and the anniversary of his death is observed to this day.

Simha Bunem of Przysucha:
Philosopher and Founder of Polish Hasidism

Rabbi Simha Bunem of Przysucha (1765-1836) was one of the most remarkable figures of the Hasidic world and the principal founder of Polish Hasidism. His teacher the Id Hakadosh said of him: "He is the center of my heart and in him there is a wealth of godliness."

Jointly with the three creators and founders of Polish Hasidism—the Maggid of Kozienice, the Hozeh of Lublin and the Id Hakadosh—Rabbi Bunem was the mainstay of the movement. Yet, whereas the three found disciples and adepts in Galicia and enjoyed great popularity, Rabbi Bunem was the founder of a new system that trod lofty ways and which called for great intelligence.

The Przysucha system taught that every precept must be fulfilled in the most secret places of the heart. According to Rabbi Bunem, penitence too should be done differently, since true contrition presupposes a contrite heart with the sole desire that transgressions be pardoned, not like many people who cry "Forgive us, dispense us," demanding an immediate gift from the Almighty.

The Przysucha system consists in the intention behind the precept rather than the precept itself, and Rabbi Bunem used to interpret the verse of morning prayer "Man should always be devout in secret" as follows: "One should be a man of the world, for the world, but one should be devout in secret."

The new Przysucha style spread rapidly in Poland and also in Lithuania, which was opposed to Hasidism, and its influence is strong today, through generations of disciples who created branches of Kotzk, Ger, Vorke, Alexander and other cities. All were due to Rabbi Bunem and to Rabbis who were his students.

The Just Men of those times feared that Rabbi Bunem's style, which was widespread among the Hasidim of Poland, might be harmful and lead to disastrous consequences, but as time passed, it became evident that his system had ensured the continuation of a devout and scholarly form of Judaism in Poland, as nowhere else.

In Przysucha the Hasidim were an affectionate brotherhood: there were no differences between rich and poor; sages and simple people, scholars or not, all were equal and addressed each other on familiar terms. Nor was it customary to tell stories of the Rabbi's miracles; only this or that mark of his genius was mentioned. Many young people used to go on Shabbat to listen to him and were so fascinated that they stayed on for months and would not return to their homes. Then their fathers-in-law, who supported them, would arrive, insisting that they return to their wives and children. The Rabbi would persuade them to do so, but after a short while with their families they eagerly rejoined the Rabbi in Przysucha. The cycle repeated itself frequently.

Those young people wore light-colored jackets, leather slippers, and white caps and socks; they smoked heavy pipes and went around as in a dream, immersed in philosophical considerations.

The Rabbi was a wonderful man, and hard though people tried to fathom his personality, he always remained an enigma to ordinary people; truly not all minds were able to follow his subtlety of thought and the path he pointed.

Rabbi Bunem, who was a pharmacist, held his Hasidim spellbound; they saw in him a being sent from Heaven to cure body and soul, to which his profession contributed.

He also possessed musical gifts, played various instruments, and expressed his intimate feelings through the violin. His maestro the Id Hakadosh was in the habit of praying with great fervor and was subject to fainting fits; he would remain unconscious for some time, until his disciple Rabbi Bunem played the verse "The dead do not praise You"—then he would recover his senses.

Rabbi Ezekiel Kozenitzer, who lived in Przysucha for many years, tells in his memoirs that he once entered the Rabbi's pharmacy, in which there was a piano, and that a woman with a recipe entered at the same time. The Rabbi prepared the medicine with one hand and played the piano with the other. After the woman had gone, Rabbi Ezekiel said to him: "What you have done is wrong." "Come, now, you are a foolish Hasid," answered Rabbi Bunem. Rabbi Kozenitzer went home in anger, but that night he dreamed that his famous grandfather the Pneh Joshua struck him, saying: "Do not find fault with Bunem of Przysucha, for he embellishes all the palaces of Heaven."

Rabbi Bunem was born in Ladislav. Before he was ordained, he was a big timber merchant and traveled extensively in Germany, Austria, Hungary and other European countries. His adepts told many stories in connection with that; they said that he used to dress in the German style in order to bring the assimilated Jews back to the sources of Judaism.

Later he was employed by the wealthy Mrs. Temerl Bergson (grandmother of the French philosopher Henri Bergson) in Warsaw. She was the daughter-in-law of Reb Samuel Zbitkaver, who by means of gold coins saved the Jews from the Cossack pogrom in neighboring Prague, during the unsuccessful Polish rising that was crushed by the Russians. He set up in front of his house two barrels of gold coins, which he used to pay for every Jew that the Cossacks delivered to him alive.

Working in that business, he often had to travel to Germany, so he dressed according to prevailing fashion. He was one of the most intimate adepts of the Id Hakadosh, and they traveled together to the Hozeh of Lublin, where they were among the most prominent students. The Rabbi of Lublin said: "There is a young man who knows me and understands me, but he hides in the wood among the trees...." (He was alluding to Rabbi Bunem's activity in the timber trade in Germany.) Since then the Hozeh called him "the young German."

When the Hozeh died, Rabbi Bunem became an outstanding disciple and the right hand of the Id Hakadosh. Rabbi Bunem used to say: "In an assessment office I saw an ear-of-grain whose seeds were of pure gold; my Rabbi the Id Hakadosh is a golden ear-of-grain like that one."

Rabbi Simhah Bunem was the son of Rabbi Zevi Hersh of Vladislav, author of two books and a descendant of a genuine Just Man. He sent his son to study in the yeshiva of Matesdorf, Hungary. The youth did not want to make his living from the Torah, so he passed examinations in Lemberg and took his degree in pharmacy. He also studied other subjects, including mathematics and music.

How Rabbi Bunem became a Rabbi is worth mentioning. As a grain merchant, he worked in the market and was sent to the city of Danzig. On one occasion at the Vladislav fair, he was negotiating the price of a cartload of grain with a farmer without managing to strike a bargain. The farmer was insisting on a lower price, saying in Polish: "Make it better!" That sank deep into Bunem's mind; he reflected: "An unknown villager is advising me to be better." He realized that he must do penitence and prepare for a mastership, and immediately after the death of the Id Hakadosh, the Hasidim anointed him as Rabbi. Among his students were geniuses in all the religious disciplines, such as Rabbi Mendele of Kotzk, Rabbi Hanoch of Alexander, the Rabbi of Radzimin and many more. Przysucha became a center for the leading scholars of the period, and Rabbi Bunem won more Hasidim than any other Rabbi before him.

Thanks to his experience in business he knew the ways of the world and had a broad outlook on life. He carried on along his predecessor's path, keeping away from miracles and educating and teaching his Hasidim.

Rabbi Bunem's teachings came across in discussions with his students that led to a state of sublime ecstasy oriented toward fear of God. Wisdom flowed from the pronouncements of this brilliant scholar; his personal relationships and immaculate deportment were equally outstanding. He combined the mystical with the transcendent.

His student the Rabbi of Kotzk once said: "Rabbi Bunem is a commentator who explains and clarifies the Baal Shem Tov."

In his old age he went blind; it was said that he had prayed to God to take away his eyesight in order to penetrate more deeply into the unknown and unite with the Eternal; another version was "so as not to see the lie that governed the world."

Two years before his death the Polish government decided to improve the situation of the Jews. To that purpose, a Jewish committee was set up to "bring the light" to the Jews of Poland. The committee consisted of prominent Jewish activists from Warsaw, including Rabbi Simha Bunem of Przysucha, who also dedicated himself to welfare problems.

The Jewish committee's task included drawing up a plan to improve the economic conditions of the Polish Jews and to introduce secular subjects into the schools.

The Hasidim considered it a prejudicial ordinance, since the decree to close the religious schools and force the Jewish children to attend state schools came as a heavy blow to them. Rabbi Bunem, who spoke Polish perfectly, was in the forefront of the resistance, and, after great difficulties had been overcome, the Hasidim succeeded in having the ordinance withdrawn.

Rabbi Bunem delivered to the government a detailed report on the Jews' grave economic plight, advising what steps should be taken to remedy it. He was Rabbi for thirty years. On his sixty-fifth birthday he fell seriously ill; a few days later he was saying the *Shema Israel*, which his students repeated in chorus; when he reached the word *echad*, he died.

Thus ended the career of one of the most sublime figures of Polish Hasidism.

Rabbi Nahman of Bratzlav: Hasid, Scholar, and Kabbalist

Rabbi Nahman of Bratzlav, since whose passing more than 170 years have elapsed, was one of the Hasidism's most illustrious personalities. He was a great scholar and mystic, and a dauntless fighter for Judaism. A true renovator, he was not satisfied with what Hasidism had created, but opened up a new path.

A worthy grandson of the Baal Shem Tov, he inherited many of his renowned grandfather's qualities, above all his spirit of divinity and his love of God, men, and nature. Like the Baal Shem Tov, he enjoyed solitary walks through the fields and woods. To him, every step was like a prayer that brought him nearer to God. He frequently remarked to his adepts that "it is very pleasant to meditate on one's faith amid green pastures and nature."

He never said plainly that no other Rabbi had been appointed to replace him, but hinted at it: "Prepare a lamp (*ner*) for the coming of the Messiah." The letters of the word *ner* were Rabbi Nahman's initials (in reverse). His Hasidim took the hint and continued to practice his teachings even after his death.

Rabbi Nahman enjoyed the privilege of seeing the world

through the original light of the Creation, which had been reserved for messianic times. The Kabbalah and Hasidism taught communion with God, with the world, and with space. And the classic of Jewish symbolism possessed this emotional communion with divinity in the highest degree. He could well proclaim with certainty that "God is with me, beside me, and in me."

Hence the Hasidim of Bratzlav always longed for the pilgrimage to Uman, to pray at his grave, and, to tell him of their sorrows, even at heavy sacrifice. They secretly crossed the most dangerous frontiers to pray at their Rabbi's sepulcher and fulfill his wish, expressed before his death, that they should visit his grave at any time, since "a path must be opened which has not yet been trodden to this day."

He had promised them that for every step they made toward him, they would be duly rewarded. And he wanted to be together with his Hasidim not only in life. He therefore asked them to keep in touch with him even after his material death, "because even then I shall be with you." He used to say: "What is, actually, for a Rabbi, the difference between life and death? Before, he lived here and afterward, there, in the grave. It is as if he had left one lodging to move to another. I want to stay among you. Therefore, visit my grave."

In his will he asked that when they came to his grave they should speak to him as if he were alive—not only about things spiritual but also about problems of daily life. The Hasidim of Bratzlav were richly blessed with the virtue of faith and believed that God would assist them at any moment. "It is not worthwhile to fear for one's living. It is better to have fear of God, than to fear for money." Rabbi Nahman used to say: "Even if I were alone in the field, I would not lose faith that God would provide for my sustenance."

Thus the Hasidim of Bratzlav lived lives of poverty and oppression and were content with the most elementary and necessary things. As their Rabbi recommended: "It is better to be a debtor to oneself and one's own family, than to the tradesman, for life in this world is a transitory thing, with which one should not get too deeply involved."

Our Rabbi praised the poor: "All evil comes from money." A really righteous person could not possess much money, he used to say. It is better to live in want and poverty than in opulence, concerned with making money and keeping it.

Like his famous grandfather, the Baal Shem Tov, he opened the way for simple Jewish people toward the Lord of the World. He uplifted simple, hardworking laborers and brought them nearer to the celestial spheres, detaching them for wordly materialism, giving them a touch of spirituality and a strong belief that they, too, had access to God, even without schooling. He taught that God was all-powerful, near to all and accessible to all, whether at work in the field or the workshop, on the roads or anywhere else, provided only that the Jew had honest thoughts, a pure heart, and a yearning for God.

To that purpose, Rabbi Nahman of Bratzlav created a special prayer: "Help me, Lord of the World, to serve Thee truly, in innocence and simplicity, without trickery or subterfuge."

Like his grandfather, Rabbi Nahman was opposed to melancholy. "A man should not be sad; on the contrary, he should be cheerful, for it is only through joyfulness that a human being can rise to the greatest heights." His Hasidim therefore used to pray cheerfully and happily, and they sang many songs composed by the Rabbi and his adherents.

His Hasidim sat around a table, and the senior among them taught them and interpreted Rabbi Nahman's works. The students listened joyfully and felt their Rabbi close to them and heard his voice. To them, he was like a good father who taught and guided them: "Though my body is away, my soul is among you and each of you shares in my teaching. You need only bring stones and lime, and I will build with them a wonderful building."

Rabbi Nahman Ben Simha was born on a Shabbat the first day of Nissan 5532 (1772) in the town of Medziboz, Podolia government, Russia—in the cradle of Hasidism. Rabbi Simha was the son of Rabbi Nahman of Horodenko, a disciple of the Baal Shem Tov; his mother, Feige, was the daughter of Hodel, the Baal Shem Tov's famous daughter. Born in a Hasidic ambience of sanctity, Rabbi Nahman sought his own original path within the framework of

Hasidism. He "began everything from the beginning." Like his grandfather, he used to leave town to wander through villages, woods or fields, unite with nature and, through this communion, rise to celestial heights. Like his grandfather, he did not write his own works directly. His disciple Rabbi Nathan of Nemirow wrote down the maestro's teachings, immortalizing his thoughts on the Torah, on Talmudic law, and his philosophy. Thus he compiled and edited his *Likute Maharan*, *Likute Etzot*, *Likute Tefilot*, *Hayeh Maharan*, *Shemoth Tzadikim*, *Sefer Hamidoth*, and many other works.

Rabbi Nathan of Nemirow popularized Rabbi Nahman's philosophy, which is based on the books of the Zohar and the Ari. Rabbi Nahman's works have been sanctified in the Hasidic world.

Another endearing quality was his love of Israel. Despite his material poverty he traveled to the Promised Land, where he wanted to settle. But because of Hasidim, who yearned to have him with them, he returned with the aim of staying for a short while and organizing a group of adherents who should "ascend" with him to Israel. A serious illness, however, frustrated his plans, but his affection for the Land of Israel became ever stronger until the end of his days.

At the age of scarcely forty he was stricken with pulmonary disease and died shortly after. His life was like a flame that burns eternally and whose light is never extinguished. He was a true guide, gifted with tremendous interior force. It was not for nothing that he was said to be a spark from the image of the Messiah—a Rabbi who never ceased exerting his beneficial influence. The fire that he kindled burns to this day: he is still the leading figure that points the way for thousands of his adherents, worldwide.

Rabbi Shneer Zalmen
and His Famous Book Tania

Its author was the Chief Rabbi of Lyubavich, Rabbi Shneer Zalmen of sacred memory, or simply "the Rabbi" as he was known, founder of the Lyubavich and Hasidic Habad dynasty. The name is an acronym of *Khohma* (wisdom), *Binah* (understanding) and *Da'at* (knowledge).

The *Tania* is considered sacred by *Hasidim* generally and especially by those of Lyubavich. A paragraph from it is studied daily like a prayer or a chapter from the Psalms. The book was disseminated extensively among Hasidim in manuscript form. It has often been re-edited, with or without commentaries, and translated into Yiddish. As it is not merely a compendium of ideas from the author's sermons, it is also called the *Collection of Spoken Expositions*.

The subject of the *Tania* is religious philosophy, without religious sophistication. It is a book that links man with God, a guide to human conduct, and caused quite an upheaval in the Hasidic world. Rabbi Levi Isaac, the Rabbi of Berdichev, was "dazzled" by its contents: "It is a genuine miracle to include such a great God within such a small book." Rabbi Baruch Mezibover, grandson of the Baal Shem Tov, opined that Rabbi Shneer Zalmen had condensed all the wisdom of Heaven in that book.

Its author, a leading authority on the Torah, was an extraordinary figure who imparted luster to his own 18th century generation and to Hasidism to the present day. He was well known for his expert knowledge of the Talmud and its commentators, his original views, and as a Kabbalist.

In his youth he was a student of Rabbi Ber, known as the Maggid of Mezricz, after whose death he studied under Rabbi Mendel of Vitebsk. When Rabbi Mendel went to the Land of Israel, Rabbi Zalmen took personal charge of the Hasidic movement in the town of Liazne, near Mohilev, and immediately won fame through his book *Tania* and the *Shulhan Arukh*.

Habad Hasidism implies the Lyubavich style, the foundations of which are apparent in *Tania* and the *Shulhan Arukh*, written by the Hasidic leader Rabbi Shneer Zalmen of Liadi, founder of Habad Hasidism and of the Lyubavich dynasty. The force of his genius and his moral personality won the admiration of Jews to this day.

The first Rabbi of Lyubavich was a remarkable personality both as a Jew and as a person; in him were combined wisdom and Hasidism, philosophy and faith, Maimonides and Baal Shem Tov.

Habad Hasidism was not a new movement. It was based on the fundamental ideas of the Baal Shem Tov, but the Rabbi added extra erudition, amplifying and deepening the philosophical side; thus it exerted a telling influence on educated Jews. The Habad movement attracted many young students from the Lithuanian area, which was why it engendered opposition among educated Lithuanians.

The opposition was led by the Gaon of Vilna, Rabbi Elihau, who later declared that the foundations of the Habad trend were very different from the Hasidism of the Rabbi of Berdichev, of Rabbi Nahum Chernobyler, of the Lubliner, the Karliner and other Hasidic leaders.

According to the Habad movement, intelligence holds a dominant place: "Intelligence is the content of the soul and even faith gains strength through intelligence. Moral virtue based on intelligence is superior to the morality of human nature." The Halacha

(Talmudic law) and the Torah are the light, and in them is the wisdom of God. The Rabbi of Lyubavich ordered his adepts to study Gemara and to distribute Mishna tractates in every town, so that the people could study them in full, within a few years.

The Torah is above prayer. The Habad is a mixture of intelligence and feeling, but the Torah has precedence.

Rabbi Shneer Zalman was a great master; the grandeur and purity of his personality shine forth as a guide and example.

His life story is extraordinary. He was born in 1747 in Liazne, in Mohilev province. His father, Rabbi Baruch, came of a family of Rabbis. When he was about twelve, his teacher, a noted scholar, marveled at this intelligence. "He can only be my friend," he said, "but not my pupil. He does not need a teacher for anything; with his extraordinary intelligence and knowledge he can transmit knowledge to others." He was married at fifteen and was attracted by the Hasidic movement, which had begun to spread under the leadership of Rabbi Ber, the Maggid (a student of the Baal Shem Tov). Rabbi Shneer Zalmen became his adherent, and ultimately his favorite student. Old Hasidim used to say that people who visited the Baal Shem Tov heard him exclaim when the "Baal Tania" had reached the age of three: "A great soul—Shneer—has come into the world." Shneer was the name of the Rabbi of Lyubavich. The two parts of his name, *shneh* and *or*, denote two lights. The first is the revealed, or Hasidism, which is accessible to all: second is the Cabal, hard to fathom, secret.

After the Maggid's death, the Baal Tania was a student of Rabbi Mendel of Vitebsk, and when Rabbi Mendel went to the Land of Israel, the Baal Tania became the Hasidic leader in the town of Liazne.

Violent quarrels erupted between his adepts, the Hasidism, and their opponents, to such an extent that the Gaon of Vilna excommunicated the Hasidim. Rabbi Mendele of Vitebsk tried to bring about a reconciliation before he went to Israel. He traveled to Vilna with his student the Baal Tania, hoping to make clear to the Gaon the essence of Hasidism, but the Gaon refused to see them, and under his influence the struggle between the Hasidim and the *Mitnagdim* (their opponents) became even more bitter. Despite that, immediately after the Gaon's death the Baal Tania wrote to his Hasidim, asking them not to curse him, although to his last breath he had stuck rigidly to his belief that the Hasidim were a danger to traditional Judaism.

The Baal Tania and his adepts firmly believe that the Gaon of Vilna's struggle against them was caused by fear that the Hasidim, with their different style of prayer and other customs, would split Judaism and weaken study of the Torah. It was also feared that Hasidism might be a continuation of the sect of the false messiah. Denunciation went so far that Rabbi Zalmen was arrested during the month of Tishre in 1799 and jailed in St. Petersburg. That episode aroused a great tumult in the Hasidic world and he was finally released on 19 Kislev that same year; the government admitted that the charges were bogus. He was released just as he was reading the verse of the Psalms "Restore my soul in peace." The Hasidim of Lyubavich celebrate that date as a symbol of the triumph of Hasidism.

As a result of the sufferings and persecution endured by Rabbi Shneer Zalmen, Hasidism as a whole and in particular the Habad style was greatly strengthened. People came from everywhere to listen to his teachings, his counsel and his divine services.

His personality and knowledge eventually began to impress his opponents, and his humility and wish for peace helped to calm things down. When he returned from St. Petersburg he visited the chief Rabbis of the opposing faction, who received him with much respect, and antagonism died down. In a letter found in the Jerusalem National Library, the Gaon wrote that the campaign unleashed against the Hasidim was a matter for regret.

The news that the Gaon of Vilna had repented from opposing the Hasidim was based on a rumor that a son of his had visited the Jewish communities in Germany, to whom he had reported his father's repentant attitude. The Hasidic world firmly believed that if both personalites, the Gaon of Vilna and Rabbi Shneer Zalmen of Liadi, had met face-to-face, the quarrels would have ended.

During the Napoleonic invasion the Rabbi and his entire family evacuated Liadi, and on 24 Tevet 1813, during the journey, he died at the age of sixty-six.

The personality, who in life was a model of moral grandeur and who lit a flame in hundreds of thousands of Jewish hearts, won due recognition: his meritorious, honored heritage has been preserved and maintained.

The present Rabbi of Lyubavich not only carries on the tradition bequeathed by those generations of great and honorable men, but is also the initiator and renovator of a Hasidic period. He has renewed Hasidism, guided it along new paths, and created new forms. He envisions the future of Judaism and Hasidism. He has expert knowledge of the Torah and is highly intelligent. His personality attracts thousands of Hasidim and admirers in the United States and throughout the world. The flame that the Tania lit two hundred years ago still burns; it is kept burning today by Rabbi Menachem Mendel Shneer.

In Buenos Aires, too, there is a branch of Lyubavich Hasidism, that is intensely active and strives to attract to religious education children from atheist homes. Its influence and activity in that field are continuously expanding and strengthening.

Recently a spiritual leader has arrived from the United States: Rabbi Tevi Grunblat, born in Buenos Aires, a scholar and a dynamic activist, a graduate of the Lyubavich Yeshiva of the United States. As an emissary of such an extraordinary and world-renowned personality as the Rabbi of Lyubavich, there is no doubt of the success of his mission.

Rabbi Moshe Leib Sosover:
"Lover of Israel"

The Jewish world reveres the luminous memory of that outstanding Just Man, Rabbi Moshe Leib Sosover, known as the "Lover of Israel." Born in Brod, he was a student of Rabbi Shmelke of Nikolsburg. He lives in the memory of the Jewish people as a genuine saint, always ready to sacrifice himself for his Jewish brethren. He was gifted with a uniquely kind heart and an unequaled spirit of sacrifice. In Galicia his name was pronounced like a blessing, and beautiful stories of his sanctity were told. For several generations it was the custom to give his name to the newborn—a name that brought a ray of light, faith, and cheer to many a humble Jewish home. He was said to have acquired his love of his neighbor from overhearing a conversation between two Gentiles as he sat in a tavern. One of them asked the other: "Tell me truly, do you care for me?" "Of course," answered the other. "If so, tell me what I most need." "Well, I really don't know." To this, the Rabbi added: "If one really cares for someone, one should know what she most needs...."

Rabbi Moshe Leib heard the message from Above: if you love your neighbor, you should know his needs.

The Hasidic movement produced a number of truly Just Men and leading scholars. All had a strong love of their neighbor; that was one of the hallmarks of Hasidism. But Rabbi Moshe Leib Sosover reached the most sublime heights of love of one's neighbor and love of God.

His was attuned to every need. He would go from house to house, washing the children, curing skin diseases and wounds, applying a variety of treatments.

One who really loved his neighbor, he used to say, should be able to suck with his own lips the infection from the wounds of children, without showing disgust.

His love of the Jewish people was greater than words can tell. The Baal Shem Tov's disciples uplifted the Jewish masses, taking a genuine interest in them and bringing them nearer to Hasidism. They showed ordinary people the way toward the Highest. The Baal Shem Tov saw and felt the Creator in every blade of grass and in every flower and brought the simplest people near to God, detaching them from worldly materialism and instilling into them the feeling and belief that everyone, even without the Torah, could have a part in God. He taught that God is everywhere, near to all and that He could be reached from the most hidden places. "The Lord is thy shadow," says the psalmist. Whether countryman or worker, from anywhere, in any place, "if a Jew's thoughts are clear and his heart pure, even if he is a stranger, an uneducated person too can be a hasid, and God will love him."

They, the weak and downtrodden Jews, sensed their own worth when they heard the Baal Shem Tov's words: "Love the lowest of the low." The virtue of mercy developed among the Hasidim in such manner that it implicitly led them to love their neighbor.

Hasidic legend tells of a humble woman in childbirth, who lived in a cold, poverty-stricken dwelling. Suddenly at midnight Rabbi Sosover appeared, bringing her good clothes and firewood. He chopped the wood, lit the fire and also cooked a meal for her. As he did those things, he said midnight prayer (I.L. Peretz wrote of this legend in his famous story *If No Higher*).

One eve of Yom Kippur the parishioners were waiting in the synagogue for Rabbi Moshe Leib to begin reciting the *Kol Nidrei*.

Time passed and the Rabbi did not appear. It was getting late and they decided to send the beadle to see what was afoot, but he returned saying there was nobody in the Rabbi's house. The people feared that something had happened to him and began to search for him everywhere, street by street: suddenly, as they passed a humble home, they saw the Rabbi bent over a cradle, rocking a baby. All came running to investigate; the Rabbi enjoined silence. "Do not wake the baby," he said, "it has only just gone to sleep." On the way to the synagogue he heard the crying of another baby, went in, but nobody was there; they had all gone to the synagogue. "How can I begin to say Kol Nidrei when a baby is crying?" asked the Rabbi.

This great lover of Israel was always ready to sacrifice himself for any Jew. To appreciate the extent of his total dedication, the incident recounted by Hasidic legend is given.

When Rabbi Sosover finished his seven-year study course under Rabbi Shmelke of Nikolsburg, his grand master provided him with a loaf of bread, a gold coin and a white dust cover for his journey home. On the way, he heard a voice crying and entreating from a cellar. It was a Jewish laborer who had been unable to pay his lease to the landlord on time and had been jailed, there to die of hunger.

The laborer wept bitterly and begged passersby to help him. Rabbi Sosover took his plight to heart. First he gave him his loaf, then he went to the landlord to pay the debt with the gold coin his teacher had given him. The landlord, however, flatly refused to accept the coin in payment for the larger amount that the poor Jew owed him. Sadly the Rabbi withdrew and, reflecting on the unhappy man's critical situation, resolved to petition the nobleman again to release him. The feudal lord (in those times landlords were all-powerful) took the plea as an insult and sentenced the Rabbi to death. To carry out the sentence, he set his dogs on him, but they would not approach him. The nobleman became even angrier and ordered the Rabbi to be taken to a place where he kept a number of wild beasts. When the Rabbi saw the beasts coming, he covered himself with the white dust cover from Rabbi Shmelke, and the beasts stayed at a distance. The landlord took this to be a miracle from Heaven; he immediately released Rabbi Moshe Leib and the laborer from the dungeon.

When this story was told to the devout Rabbi of Chartkov, he sighed and said: "Where can one find a dust cover like that?"

The commandment "Love thy neighbour as thyself" was the foundation stone of the Hasidic movement, and this implied a duty of affection toward each individual person. In that respect Rabbi Sosover used to say: "There must be something good in every person."

The Hasidic leaders opposed those who accused and slandered their fellow Jews. The Id Hakadosh of Przysucha said that when there was talk of penitence, one should not use harsh or offensive words, but approach sinners with kindness. A true Just Man should understand and interpret a sinner's actions and situation, seeking to influence him through love. Only he who could admonish with kind words was worthy to be a spiritual guide.

A Jewish guide should not imagine that the King of the World had chosen him because he was better than other men, for if a flesh-and-bones king wanted to take off his crown, he should hang it on a peg attached to the wall. Would the peg think itself important because the King had hung his crown on it? Similarly, the spiritual guide should realize that he was like a peg, on which the King had by chance hung the crown.

Rabbi Sosover used to say that every person could tell in this world whether he was righteous or not, and know whether he was treading the paths of the Almighty. That was achieved through love of one's neighbor. When a Jew felt that his love for his neighbor was increasing daily, it meant that he was progressing along the path of Judaism and service of God.

Rabbi Sosover learned seven things from a thief: (1) his principal work is by night; (2) do not let a single night pass; (3) do what is possible, but produce something; (4) do not betray a secret; (5) do not confess before those who demand it, even under compulsion; (6) do not denounce a companion; and (7) one can lose in an hour what has been achieved over a long period, at heavy sacrifice.

He liked to learn from every object, every person, every worldly thing. "The world is one big open book, from which everyone can learn. There is nothing in the world from which one cannot learn anything."

The Rabbi's most valuable precept was to help humble young women in getting married. Tirelessly he sought to promote wedlock among humble folk; he always had some impecunious young woman on his waiting list, and most stories about him refer to that aspect. He collected money for the couple, evading thanks dancing among them.

Hasidic legend tells of the marriage that he arranged for a humble couple after lengthy negotiation, and as he listened to the harmonies of the orchestra, he said: "I ask of the Highest that when I die, the melody they are playing now should be played at my funeral."

Many years passed, and the day of the Rabbi's death arrived. It so happened that on that day the orchestra was traveling to a marriage in Brod. Suddenly the horses reared up and started forward at a gallop and came to a stop at the cemetery. When the musicians learned that Rabbi Moshe Leib Sosover was being buried there, they remembered his words and reported them to the Rabbinical court, which ruled that the same piece be played at the funeral.

Rabbi Sosover was a great lover of Israel, forever revered by the Jewish people. His kindness brought light into the hard lives of his contemporaries, and his luminous spirit lives on.

Rabbi Israel, the Maggid of Kozienice: Kabbalist and Mainstay of Hasidism

Among the outstanding figures of Polish Judaism (of recent generations) was Rabbi Israel, the Maggid of Kozienice. He was famed for his knowledge of all the sacred disciplines and for his fearless struggle on behalf of Judaism against the foreign trends that had begun to penetrate into Poland from Western Europe.

Over 160 years have passed since his death.

He realized that Hasidism was capable of saving Judaism and assumed leadership of the movement. Jointly with the Hozeh of Lublin he was the initiator of the movement in Poland.

In the beginnings, the leaders of Judaism were not given the title of "Rabbi" but were called "Maggid." Reb Israel Bar Sabbatai, Maggid of Kozienice, was a native of Ostrivice in Kielce district.

Beautiful legends were told about his birth; here is one of them: Reb Sabbatai, the Maggid's father, was a simple, honest and very poor man. He was a bookbinder by trade, but was getting too old to work. Although he endured great hardship, he was a steadfast believer and did not want to live on charity.

One winter there was no money in Rabbi Sabbatai's house to purchase the needs of the Sabbath; all valuables had long been sold and the situation was truly desperate. Reb Sabbatai was not disheartened; at noon he went to the synagogue in the usual way, trusting in the Almighty as ever.

His wife began to prepare the house for the Sabbath, sweeping and cleaning. Sweeping under the bed, she found a large silver button from her wedding dress, which she had lost many years before.

Cheerfully she set off toward the jeweler and with the money she received, she prepared a sumptuous Sabbath meal. When Reb Sabbatai returned from the synagogue, he noticed that the house shone as never before. He walked happily in; his wife received him with rejoicing. Although the meal consisted of the choicest dishes, he did not ask his wife how she had put it all together. He sang the *Shalom Alechem* and the *Eshet Hail*, then said the *kiddush* reverently; during the meal his wife reported to him how the Almighty had come to their assistance without human help.

Reb Sabbatai and his wife rejoiced, dancing together; in the heavens too there was great rejoicing. And that same night the Baal Shem Tov himself visited with Reb Sabbatai, whose marriage was childless, and secretly made known to his deeply believing host that even in their old age, they would have a son who would bring light to the world. The Baal Shem Tov would be the godfather, and when the child was born, he named it Israel, after himself.

From an early age the lad was a brilliant student and, although physically weak, studied and dedicated himself to the Torah and to Judaism. He traveled much and taught in a small town; he studied the Torah by night and fasted whole days.

The Maggid studied with the greatest geniuses of his time. His name soon became famous; his influence increased, for he was considered a successful intercessor, on behalf of the Jews, like Rabbi Levi Isaac of Berdichev.

Physically unimpressive, he was small and slight and spent much time in bed, but when he spoke before God his tongue became a living flame that "penetrated the heavens."

His style of Hasidism was derived from the Maggid of Mezricz. It was said that before he went to Mezricz he had already read eight hundred books on the subject of the Kabbalah, and that when he met the Maggid he realized that previously he had learned nothing.

He cured the sick by prescribing herbs and ointments, and reciting prayers in Yiddish.

The Hasidim built him a spacious residence that was always full of visitors. He also received Gentiles who sought his counsel. One of his most faithful adepts was the statesman Count Adam Czartoriski, who did not move a step without the Maggid's advice. On one occasion the Polish military leader Count Joseph Poniatowksi came to him for advice.

A Hasidic legend relates that the Maggid had predicted to Count Czartoriski the re-emergence of Poland as a world power, but that the period of splendor would last only 21 years, and would be followed by another unhappy period, involving the destruction of Poland. And the prediction came true with the third partition of Poland among the three great powers: Russia, Prussia, and Austria.

At Yom Kippur he said the three prayers standing from beginning to end, despite continued ill-health.

One Yom Kippur, during the *Kol Nidrei*, on reaching the verse: "And God said, I forgive you according to your wish," the devout Maggid addressed the Almighty in these words:

> Lord of the world, You have power unknown to any creature in the world, only You know its extent; nobody knows my weakness better than You. Nevertheless, throughout the month of Elul I have prayed and You, great God, know that nothing has mattered more to me than Your people of Israel, for whom I have prayed. I therefore ask You, Lord of the world, why nothing is too hard for me to do on behalf of the Jews, although I am so weak, while You, who have such power, find it so difficult to pronounce the few words 'I forgive you'?

The Maggid instituted certain customs that were accepted and have endured in the Hasidic world. Melodies from Kozienice are noted for their profound and touching accords.

The Maggid died on the eve of the Sukkot on 14 Tishri 1825. A little pavilion was erected over his grave, where thousands of Jews came to pray for salvation. The Kozienice dynasty continued until the Holocaust; last in line was Rabbi Arele, who initially trod in the footsteps of his great predecessors but after a few years as Rabbi changed his style, ousting the scholarly and well-to-do adherents. He surrounded himself with simple people: craftsmen, workers, the needy, maintaining that they would provide support. The old Hasidim and adherents generally felt estranged by this revolution, but with time they came to appreciate that it was brought about by his piety and spiritual grandeur.

He was Rabbi for twenty years. When the Germans invaded Poland he moved to Warsaw and there endangered his life on behalf of the Jews, assisting them in every possible way. In particular he was like a father to the homeless children, trying to get food to them as shells and bullets flew overhead.

He played the violin and sang for the orphans, helping them to fight sorrow and tears.

Concerning Rabbi Arele's death, there are different versions. In his book *Ele Ezkera* (They Will Remember), Rabbi Isaac Levin narrates that Rabbi Arele died on the eve of Yom Kippur before an open Gemara in the synagogue, exclaiming "I don't want to live any longer!" He died as he spoke.

According to another version, the Nazis tried to make him play the violin (he was known throughout Poland for his musical talents), but Rabbi Arele destroyed the instrument, rather than comply with the order, and the Nazis murdered him.

According to Zelechow's *Holocaust*—and to the testimony of others who had miraculous escapes—the Hasidim sent the Rabbi of Kozienice to Zelechow, which was in a less dangerous area, but here, on the eve of Rosh Hashana, the Rabbi, stricken with typhoid and after much suffering, died.

Noted Figures
of the Jewish Golden Age in Spain

Rabbi Saadya Gaon: Philosopher and Talmudist

Rabbi Saadya may be designated one of the luminaries of Judaism. A leading Talmudist and *Posek*,[1] he was also among the first and most outstanding Jewish philosophers and the author of *Emunot ve-Deot* (Of Beliefs and Ideas), an influential work to the present day.

Rabbi Saadya was an excellent linguist, especially in Hebrew and Arabic, a noted Bible researcher and lexicographer, a religious poet, and the author of a *siddur* (prayer book) that bears his name. His personality has traits in common with that of another Jewish scholar who appeared several centuries later—Maimonides, who paid tribute to the spiritual and intellectual grandeur of his illustrious predecessor.

For better understanding of his life and work, a look at Jewish circumstances during his lifetime in the city where he lived is in order.

---

[1] Authority with the power to decide in matters of *Halacha* (Jewish law). His judgment is accepted by the Rabbis.

About 589 of the Common Era, a start was made in Babylon with preparing the final version of the Babylon Talmud (as distinct from the Jerusalem Talmud), a task that devolved on the Saboraites, Jewish scholars who decided on the inclusion of certain fragments and added explanations to passages that they held to be unclear.

This work is generally estimated to have lasted some three hundred years, until the period of the *Gaonim*.

Jewish community life in Babylon enjoyed a fair degree of autonomy. The exilarch (*Rosh Hagolah* in Hebrew; *Resh Galuta* in Aramaic) exerted the civil power, and the *Gaon* (principal of the Talmudic academy) of the city of Sura the religious power. The *Gaonim* were appointed by the exilarchs.

The next most important position, that of community leader, was held by the Gaon of the city of Pumbedita. Jewish life in Babylon was organized on those lines until 1038, when the yeshiva in Pumbedita was closed following the disappearance of Rabbi Hai Gaon, who was the forty-eighth principal of that Talmudic academy.

Until 943, Sura had thirty-six Geonim. A third yeshiva, that of Nahardea, was united after a brief existence with that of Pumbedita.

Rabbi Saadya was the last Gaon of Sura. His appointment to hold that position and his dispute with the exilarch provide interesting and valuable insights into his personality. He bowed only to reason, and never before those who wielded power and influence, emerging victorious over his detractors and persecutors, who ultimately asked his forgiveness.

Rabbi Saadya was the only Gaon who was not a native of Babylon; he was born in the village of Dilas, in Fayoum, Egypt, in 882. His father was a well-known scholar and merchant.

Rabbi Saadya studied under the most learned Jewish and Egyptian teachers, including the famous Egyptian historian Masud, and thereafter continued his education in yeshivot in Israel. He was still young when he began to create works of significance. The first was *Igaron*, a poets' dictionary and guide that contained a sample of rhymes. He also wrote a series of pamphlets against the Karaites, who had begun to play an important role is Israel, Egypt and Babylon. The pamphlets quickly went the round of Jewish scholarly circles and won him well-deserved prestige. On his arrival in Babylon he was already well-known and was received with high honors. The exilarch David Ben Zakai, a noted Talmudist, invited him to a talk on Jewish questions and on sciences generally and was astonished at Rabbi Saadya's knowledge, which was without equal in Babylon; he therefore appointed him to the position of Gaon of the Sura yeshiva, which had been vacant since the death of his predecessor.

In 921 the scholarly Rabbi Aaron Ben Meyer of Jerusalem intended to reform the Hebrew calendar created in Babylon, asking that all the Jewish festivals be celebrated two days earlier in the Dispersion.

In Israel, at that time, Passover, Rosh Hashana, Yom Kippur and Succot were celebrated two days earlier than in Babylon and elsewhere. The time lag remained for two successive years and threatened to lead to a schism among the Jews.

Then Rabbi Saadya, who was an expert mathematician and astronomer, wrote his *Sefer Ha-Moadim* (Book of Festivals) in which he proved scientifically, in clear and accessible language, that Rabbi Ben Meyer was mistaken. That work served to bring agreement and settle the difference.

At the age of twenty-three he won fame for his pamphlets against the Karaites. His readily understandable writings in both Hebrew and Arabic, fully documented and based on irrefutable logic, successfully exposed the fallacy of Karaite ideology and teachings, which were aimed at attracting the Jewish masses.

The Karaites were a Hebrew sect that rejected Oral Law and accepted only Written Law. They therefore did not recognize the authority of the Talmud, nor of the commentators and interpreters of the Torah. They were the perpetuators of the ancient Sadducees, who lived at the time of the Second Temple, and of the Hasmonean King Alexander Janus, who had supported them to the point of eliminating the sages who did not agree. The Karaites had their own book of precepts and observed a different calendar.

They differed from traditional Jews through not lighting candles on the Sabbath—they remained in darkness; through non-recognition of the *tefillin* (phylacteries) precept; through modified practice of the precepts of *tzitzit* (fringes), circumcision, ritual sacrifice and unclean food. Moreover, they did not recognize any festival or commemoration introduced since the end of the Bible, and their prayers were based strictly on Bible verses.

The Karaites gave the Jewish people a good many problems through repeated efforts to attract adherents. First Rabbi Saadya, and after him the Rambam, took effective countermeasures with writings proving that the oral traditions compiled in the Talmud and subsequent works were entirely valid. Rabbi Saadya's declarations led to stormy arguments among the Karaites, and his ideological triumph over them, saving thousands of his brethren from assimilation, made him a leading figure of the Jewish world.

Under Rabbi Saadya's leadership the yeshiva of Sura regained its former splendor, for it attracted many students and was able to improve its economic situation. His activity as its principal, however, was seriously affected by differences that arose between himself and the exilarch David Ben Zakai concerning budget appropriations for the yeshiva.

The *Resh Galuta* received the monies collected from the trustees and appropriated ten percent for the yeshiva, whereas Rabbi Saadya wanted twenty-five percent. Ben Zakai, determined to enforce his decision, sent an advisory through his son confirming the appropriation in an amount according to the percentage he had set. Rabbi Saadya did not accept it and challenged the exilarch's authority. The exilarch's son Yehuda reacted so violently that he had to be removed from the yeshiva. Opinions were divided; Rabbi Saadya steadfastly declared that he would not yield to the rich and powerful. Both were then dismissed from their positions.

Counting on the support of the cultured sector of the Jewish world, Rabbi Saadya Gaon designated Yehoshua Hazan, a younger brother of Ben Zakai, as exilarch. In turn, Rabbi Saadya was replaced as head of the yeshiva by a mediocre scholar, Joseph Ben Jacob; this was due to pressure exerted by the wealthy sector. The dispute went on for two full years; finally, judgment went against Rabbi Saadya because he was a foreigner. Up to the last moment, he was urged to change his mind but he refused to renounce his principles because, as he expressed it, "it is better to die of hunger than to betray one's own conscience." With those words he left Babylon to settle in Baghdad, where he lived for four or five years with his wife and two sons.

During that short period he wrote (in Arabic) a scientific commentary on the Torah and a philosophical work. The latter was translated into Hebrew by Ibn Tibon under the title *Emunot ve-Deot*; it thus became accessible to the Jews as a whole and aroused such interest that during the initial period it was copied in manuscript continuously; later, with the advent of printing, it was one of the first books printed (in Constantinople in 1562). Tens of reprints at later periods bear witness of its popularity, which has not waned to this day.

A significant event in Rabbi Saadya's life occurred when Ben Zakai came to Baghdad to ask his pardon and went on to appoint him Gaon of the yeshiva of Sura, after admitting that there was nobody so well fitted for the position. The two adversaries were reconciled. And in Sura, on the eve of Purim, Ben Zakai invited Rabbi Saadya to his festive meal, and Rabbi Saadya reciprocated. Times had changed and one who profited was Rabbi David Ben Zakai, who on that occasion played host to Rabbi Saadya.

Soon after the reconciliation of the two personalities, Ben Zakai died, followed a few months later by his son Yehuda, who had made a furious outburst against the Gaon at the yeshiva. Yehuda left a son of eleven, whom Rabbi Saadya adopted, brought up, and educated as his own son.

The series of vicissitudes had affected the Gaon's health and he died in Sura a few years later (on 26 Iyar 942).

Rabbi Saadya Gaon's distinguished biographer B. Malter maintains that Rabbi Saadya wrote no fewer than one hundred works in Hebrew and two hundred in Arabic.

His fundamental work, today as pertinent as ever, was the *Emunot ve-Deot*, which has been sanctified by the Jewish people and translated into many languages. A philosophical creation, it aimed at setting forth clearly the principles of Judaism, in order to avoid confusion and deviation.

First and foremost, Rabbi Saadya Gaon laid down three sources of cognizance: the senses, understanding, and tradition bequeathed by our forefathers. Following this summary introduction, the author set forth the ten foundation stones of his religious and philosophical system:

(1) God created the world out of nothing, contrary to what Plato maintained.
(2) The uniqueness of the Creator.
(3) Man is the crown of Creation and was endowed with a soul in order to know truth and distinguish between good and evil.
(4) God delivered the Torah to the Jews on Mount Sinai. There are precepts that we can understand and others that are beyond human understanding, but which men likewise fulfill.
(5) The Torah was given for all generations and never loses its validity.
(6) The prophets were sent by God so that sinners could repent and not perish. In this respect, the case of the prophet Jonah is highly illustrative.
(7) Man has free choice; thence come reward or punishment according to his deeds. In life on earth, however, there is no total reward, which is received only in the other world. Therefore death does not mean the end of existence but moving to a new life.
(8) Resurrection will occur with the coming of Messiah.
(9) Bodies will revive after the atonement of sins.
(10) Spiritual life, like material life, must be governed by ethical principles that provide the human being with a balanced and harmonious life.

The points listed are a bare outline of the great spiritual legacy contained in the *Emunot ve-Deot*; through it, Rabbi Saadya Gaon made perhaps the first attempt in Judaism to set the religious principles of the Jewish people on a rational basis, in an effort to prove that those principles did not contradict the philosophy and science of his time. The work ends with these words:

> They know that I have compiled, set forth and investigated the principal subjects and problems in order to reach a true solution. I therefore ask Jews belonging to all generations to read this book thoroughly and study it until they find the truth.

Menachem Ben Saruk:
Author of the First Dictionary of the Bible

The lexicologist and scholar Menachem Ben Saruk was one of the outstanding spiritual figures among the Jews of Spain, whose imprint on Jewish life has lasted to the present day.

He was born in 910. He led a life of hardship, as we learn from his fellow citizen Rabbi Abraham Ben Ezra, with whom he studied and whose company he enjoyed from an early age.

Throughout his life, success alternated with failure. He spent his early life in solitude and poverty and thereafter depended on the support of well-wishers. He was never lucky enough to attain a level of well-being commensurate with his merits. It was only through a miraculous stroke of luck that he was able for a time to win freedom from poverty and his difficult situation, and to turn his brilliant intellect to account, but his good fortune did not last. In his old age he lapsed into poverty, enduring humiliation and moral injury caused by one with whom he had formerly been linked in close friendship: the poet and lexicologist Dunash Ben Lavrath.

As a youth he had been befriended by the patron, sage and Torah scholar Rabbi Isaac Ibn Shaprut, who took him into his home and provided him with all the necessary help so that he could dedicate himself unhindered to study and research in the Hebrew language, in which he took such a deep interest.

In the meantime Hasdai Ibn Shaprut, son of Rabbi Isaac, had become a notable political personality at the court of the Caliph Abderrahman III. Gifted and able, like his distinguished father, he was a lover of the Torah and seeker after knowledge; he, too, was a well-known patron. He knew both Hebrew and Arabic well and asked Rabbi Menachem to be his personal secretary.

Rabbi Menachem went to Córdoba, where he became the house poet of the Shaprut family, with whom he felt an emotional bond. He praised his benefactor in several poems and became used to the aristocratic Shaprut dynasty—first with the father, then with the son. Freed of the worries of providing for his own upkeep, he created a work that won him immortality: the *Machberet Menachem*, a genuine masterpiece that is considered the first dictionary of the Hebrew language.

His fame as a scholar and poet spread quickly around the Jewish world through this many-sided work, the product and reflection of the author's detailed researches in the Torah and the original language of the Bible. Contrary to customary practice at the time in Spain, he wrote his *Machberet* in Hebrew, not because he did not know Arabic but because he considered it sacrilegious to use any other than original Biblical language for a work involving research in the Torah.

All the other scholars of the Golden Age in Spain wrote their works in Arabic, a language practically unknown in the rest of Europe. Rabbi Menachem's dictionary, however, was quickly disseminated because it was written in Hebrew, which was widely known not only among the Jews but also among Gentile scholars.

The *Machberet Menachem* became a standing reference work for such authorities as Rashi, Rashbam, Rabbenu Tam and Rabbi Joseph Kimche. Rashi frequently utilized the results of Rabbi Menachem's patient lexicological studies for his noted Torah commentary.

None of Rabbi Menachem's contemporaries could compare with him in expert knowledge of Hebrew. In his dictionary he entered and arranged all the words, including those of Aramaic origin, that appear in the Bible, and classified them according to a grammatical and philological system of his own. To that purpose, he created an extensive set of grammatical terms that later was used to lay the basis of Hebrew grammar; he created the term *dikduk* (grammar), which is still in use.

His philological researches, far from dampening his enthusiasm for the beauty of the Hebrew language, increased it; he became an unconditional admirer of the language of the prophets.

His Torah commentaries have much that is fine and warm; they radiate originality and beauty like his philological studies. In his time there was hardly a Bible commentator who did not resort to his classical *Machberet*.

In those days, the longing for a home country of their own had reawakened among the People of Israel. When Jewish envoys from other parts of the world reached Spain, Hasdai used to question them on the situation of their brethren in the relevant communities. One day some Jews from Persia told him that an independent Jewish kingdom was in existence in a very distant place, inhabited by the Kuzars and governed by a king named Joseph. Gripped by enthusiasm, Hasdai instructed his secretary Rabbi Menachem to write a letter to the Jewish Kuzar king, asking for full written information on the mysterious kingdom converted to Judasim.

Rabbi Menachem then wrote on behalf of Hasdai Ibn Shaprut:

> If I knew that our people had a kingdom of their own in the world, I would abandon my high position and my family and cross valleys and mountains, seas and continents to reach you and live with my brethren. I would see the remnants of the Jewish people living in peace and lift up my soul in praise of God for not withholding His mercy from His disinherited people, who have long hoped in redemption while wandering from country to country. Our dignity has been outraged, we are subject to humiliation in the Dispersion, and there is nothing we can say in reply to those who reproach us that every people should have its own country.

Hasdai was eventually informed in reply to his message that the Kuzar kingdom had ceased to exist. The Russian Prince Svyatoslav had seized its territory and its possessions.

With the disappearance of that Jewish kingdom, one of the fondest dreams of the people of Israel vanished. On the other hand, but for the letter written by Menachem Ben Saruk, Jewish history would probably never have recorded that remarkable event.

Throughout Rabbi Menachem's period with Hasdai he enjoyed the confidence of his noble patron and was shown proper consideration. Hasdai was happy that his expectations from his secretary had been fully justified. That situation lasted until the arrival of Dunash Ben Lavrath, another noted scholar and researcher in the Hebrew language, who traveled to Córdoba at Hasdai's invitation to settle in his house and work there as a scholar and poet.

Ben Lavrath was the antithesis of Rabbi Menachem. He came of a well-to-do family; in his youth, he had never known the bitter taste of poverty. He was well versed in Hebrew and a brilliant stylist, but against that, he was overly ambitious and aggressive. From the outset, though lately arrived, he envied Rabbi Menachem for his privileged position and for the honors accorded him.

Ben Lavrath wanted to oust his predecessor; he wanted to be the only scholar and poet in the Shaprut household. He therefore criticized Rabbi Menachem's *Machberet*, claiming that it was conceived on erroneous lines and full of errors, aiming to belittle it in Hasdai's eyes.

Rashi's brilliant grandson Rabbenu Tam was one of the most steadfast defenders of Rabbi Menachem's monumental work. With his expert knowledge of Hebrew he had fully understood the philological system created by Rabbi Menachem and was in complete agreement with the results of his patient and exhaustive researches: he rejected all the charges, defending Menachem's work with extraordinary energy and sharply attacking the aggressor, of whom he said that he had never succeeded in understanding Rabbi Menachem.

But Ben Lavrath's intrigues had produced the desired result. He got together a small group that aimed not only to rob Rabbi

Menachem of his prestige by criticizing his work but also by resorting to outright slander. And these evil men carried out their shameful plan.

One late Sabbath the group visited Hasdai and advised him that they had ascertained that Rabbi Menachem belonged to the Karaite sect of Córdoba, which did not believe in the Talmud. The charge was unquestionably slanderous, for Rabbi Menachem was a genuine Jewish saint who had frequently quoted Rabbi Saadya Gaon in his works. If he had belonged to that sect he would never have mentioned Rabbi Saadya, whom the Karaites hated deeply for having opposed them with great vigour.

Nevertheless, Hasdai fell into the trap and dismissed his personal secretary. The slanderous gang next went to Rabbi Menachem, beat him cruelly, tore his hair out, devastated his lodging, and stole his valuable manuscripts.

Rabbi Menachem endured his distress with fortitude and took the oath before Hasdai, in God's name, that he might thoroughly investigate the matter, moreover reporting to him on his state of mental and physical distress. Finally Rabbi Menachem was proved innocent and Hasdai sorrowfully begged his forgiveness. Although he lived to the age of sixty, he experienced very few happy times.

His name will be remembered by the Jewish people as an outstanding scholar and divine, who stoically endured the many sorrows that afflicted his existence, perhaps that he might reach in total purity the shores of the other world.

Rabbi Moses Ben Hanoch: Initiator of Jewish Religious and Cultural Life in Spain

The kingdom that the Moslems had set up in Spain in 711 developed on a considerable scale in the 10th century. It occupied the central-southern part of the Iberian Peninsula, where important cities such as Córdoba, Seville, Toledo and Granada flourished. There the Jews lived among the friendly Moslems, not only without alarms but under the protection of the Caliphs, whose capital city was Córdoba.

After the Jewish decline in Babylon, a new Jewish life began to develop and flourish in Spain. Spanish-Jewish culture succeeded in harmonizing the Torah with science and the Talmud with philosophy without weakening the Jewish religion; on the contrary, this culture was notable for its wealth of color and variety. There famous personalities contributed on a generous scale to its creation: Moses Ben Hanoch, Menachem Ben Saruk and Dunash Ben Lavrath.

Rabbi Moses Ben Hanoch came from Babylon, where he had been a prominent Talmudist and religious personality. The economic situation had become very critical in those days and the Jewish academies were about to close down for lack of material resources. The local community then decided to send four scholars to different countries with well-to-do Jewish populations with the aim of collecting funds to rescue the high Talmudic study institutes of Babylon.

Among the envoys was Rabbi Moses Ben Hanoch. But the ship was captured by a Moorish admiral known as Ibn Rumakis, whose trade consisted in capturing Christian ships and looting coastal towns. The scholars were taken prisoner together with the other passengers, to be sold as slaves wherever convenient.

Now a terrible tragedy befell the Gaon Rabbi Moses Ben Hanoch. He was the only married man among the envoys and was accompanied by his wife and young son Hanoch.

The Moslem admiral had set eyes on Rabbi Ben Hanoch's beautiful wife and began to make overtures toward her. She realized the danger that threatened them all and asked her husband in Hebrew whether persons who died of drowning would be redeemed at the resurrection and have assured places in Paradise. The sage, unaware of the significance of the question, answered with the verse: "Thou shalt return from the depths of the sea."

Hardly had the woman heard the sage's reply than she threw herself overboard and was drowned.

Brokenhearted, Rabbi Ben Hanoch was taken with his son to the city of Córdoba, where the Jewish community paid the ransom demanded for his freedom.

When he first arrived in Córdoba, about the year 950, he did not reveal his identity to anyone. When the Jews finally became aware of his erudition, it was by accident. This is how it happened:

Dressed in slave's clothing he went to that city's Talmudic academy, presided over by the *dayan* (judge) Rabbi Nathan. When Rabbi Ben Hanoch came in, Rabbi Nathan was trying to explain a very complex aspect of the Talmud. The lecturer was not particularly noted for his learning, though he was highly regarded in Spain. The subject, in connection with the Talmudic tractate *Yomah*, was proving difficult for him; he was unable to unravel the problem. Rabbi Ben Hanoch then stood up and asked for permission to explain it. Rabbi Nathan's students were curious to hear what the "slave" had to say and he was allowed to speak. Rabbi Ben Hanoch delivered a masterly lecture, analyzing and elucidating the subject so simply, yet thoroughly, as to astonish his hearers. Then they began to question him on a wide range of subjects and he answered with characteristic clarity and precision.

In the meantime a number of people had assembled; they were waiting to submit their disputes to Rabbi Nathan. The judge appeared before them and said: "Henceforth I shall no longer be your judge, nor head of the Talmudic academy. Him whom you see here dressed in slave's clothing will take my place. I shall be his student and he will be my master."

That was how Rabbi Moses Ben Hanoch became Rabbi and leader of the Jewish community of Córdoba and eventually administrator of Jewish communities in all of Spain.

When the admiral heard that this important personality had been his prisoner, he demanded an enormous sum of money. The community then appealed to the statesman Ibn Shaprut, who was highly influential at court and secured his understanding of how important it was that Rabbi Ben Hanoch should remain as spiritual leader in Spain, since with him in charge, Jewish religious life would develop considerably. Ibn Shaprut mediated in the matter and Rabbi Ben Hanoch stayed on in Córdoba.

Spain had begun to develop into a Jewish cultural and religious center, with hundreds of young people arriving from various points of the compass to drink from the founts of Hebrew wisdom in the light of the teachings of Rabbi Moses Ben Hanoch. The Rabbi was outstanding not only as a Talmudic scholar but also as a researcher and expert in the Hebrew language, which was essential for correct literal interpretation of Holy Scripture.

In the Talmudic academy of which he was principal, spiritual leaders of high merit were trained who began to exert their beneficial influence on the Jewish masses. They succeeded in converting the Torah into a decisive factor of Jewish community life as it existed in those times.

Rabbi Moses Ben Hanoch died in 970 in Córdoba. He is recognized to this day as the initiator and driving force of study of the Torah in Spain.

Rabbenu Gershon

As a luminary and inspiration in the line of Jewish morals and ethical principles, one figure stands out: Rabbenu Gershon, known as *Maor Hagolah* (Luminary of the Dispersion), who lived in the Middle Ages and was outstanding for his wisdom and for the introduction of reforms that have endured to this day. Rabbenu Gershon was born in 960 in the city of Metz. Even after a thousand years the name of Rabbenu Gershon is still fresh in Jewish minds.

He was deservedly known as the "Luminary of the Dispersion," for he brought light to Jewish life that had endured to this day. He owes his fame primarily to his reforms, among which is that a Jew cannot have more than one wife. The Torah permits polygamy and Rabbenu Gershon was the first to introduce reform whereby a man may not marry a second woman so long as his first wife lives or before he has divorced her. That reform was backed up by the threat of anathema.

The fact that his reforms were accepted by all the Jewish communities of Europe to the present day (except the Eastern and

Sephardi) shows the prestige that Rabbenu Gershon enjoyed as Supreme authority. Moreover, his reform was introduced by the Knesset (parliament) of the State of Israel, and the Sephardi Jews, who formerly did not accept it, have now done so. The reform strengthened the position of Jewish women.

Rabbenu Gershon also ruled that a man could not divorce a woman against her will; both had to agree on such an action. Only if the woman was of unsound mind or had not had children after a lapse of ten years, and refused to accept divorce, could a man marry another woman; but he would have to get the consent of one hundred rabbis of the region, which would not be easy.

The reforms concerning polygamy and divorce not only served to strengthen Jewish life, but also did much to safeguard the Jews' good reputation.

Rabbenu Gershon further ruled that anyone who found any object should announce the fact publicly, until its owner claimed it.

Another of his great reforms was a prohibition against the violation of mail. That was of great importance in those times, for there were no postal services and letters were sent through personal emissaries. Thus the bearer could open them if he wanted to know the contents. The threat of anathema, however, made messengers less inquisitive.

Anathema was the severest form of punishment among the Jews and served as a moral weapon in support of ethical Judaism. It was announced in synagogues by lighting candles, sounding the ram's horn and reading out the *Tohaha*.[1] It was a warning to everyone to abstain from relationships with the object of anathema: not to approach him closer than four paces, nor speak to him. If he did penitence, the religious court released him from anathema.

Rabbenu Gershon introduced other reforms that helped to improve and embellish Jewish life; for instance, a man should not stay away from his home more than eighteen months. If a man died, the widow had to observe the *halitza* precept[2] but the deceased's brother was not compelled to marry her.

---

[1] The warning as given in Leviticus 25:14.
[2] The Levirate law according to Deuteronomy 25:5.

Rabbenu Gershon, though born in Lorraine, spent most of his life in Mainz, where he was rector of the yeshiva. Besides instructing his students, he busied himself with checking and improving the Talmud manuscripts, for printing had not yet been invented.

He was more concerned with practical interpretation of the laws rather than with theoretical research into them. The communities of Germany, France and Italy would ask his opinion on religious problems connected with the civil laws; his replies were treated as jurisprudence, so that the European communities did not have to inquire of the spiritual leaders in Babylon. The plight of Jews in that period raised social and ethical problems for which practical solutions had to be found; that was why his moral influence on Jewish life was so decisive.

The Middle Ages were marked by cruel persecution and hatred of the Jews; Rabbenu Gershon described them as a time of heroism and sanctification of the Ineffable Name. In 912 the fanatical Emperor Heinrich I ordered the immediate expulsion from Mainz of those Jews who refused to be converted. A few were converted, but the majority were expelled, and several hundred offered up their lives on the altar of their faith, victims of persecution.

Rabbenu Gershon's feelings in regard to this brutal action were expressed in several *slichot*.[3] One of them reads: "They invent infamous calumnies against us; we are robbed. Disaster follows disaster; the next day is worse than the last."

The most fitting appraisal of the historic significance of this giant of the Torah came from one of his most notable students, Rashi, who wrote: "Rabbenu Gershon brought light to the eyes of the Jews of the Dispersion and through his valuable teachings became the guide of whole generations."

---

[3] Prayers of penitence.

Rabbi Samuel Ha-Nagid and his Protégé, the Philosopher and Poet Solomon Ibn Gabirol

At the end of the 10th century the Jewish center of Torah and learning had been set up in Spain and flourished in full splendor under Arab rule. In favorable economic circumstances, the Jews were able to develop their full creative power. Scholars and merchants, not only from Babylon but also from North Africa and Israel, settled at that time in Spain, which had become a veritable "promised land" for seekers after things spiritual and for traders.

The leader of the Jewish communities of Spain was one who "possessed both wisdom and material wealth" for he was well versed in the Talmud and also a man of wealth who pursued a prosperous trade. This was Samuel Ha-Nagid, the leading Rabbi of his generation and distinguished scientist, known in the Arab world as Ismail Ibn Yussef Ibn Nagdilah.

Rabbi Ha-Nagid's life story sounds like a fairytale. Nevertheless, all that is known about him has been confirmed by historians and by chroniclers of the times. He was born in 993 in the city of Córdoba; his father, Rabbi Joseph, had got there from a little town in southern Spain. Rabbi Samuel studied Judaica with the leading Rabbis and scholars of his time. He also learned Arabic and other languages and took a special interest in sciences. When he was twenty a particularly savage civil war broke out in Córdoba between the Berbers and the Arabs, forcing all the Jews to flee the city. Rabbi Samuel moved to northern Spain and settled in Málaga. In order to make a living he opened a small shop that provided him with very meager means of sustenance. This, however, did not prevent him from dedicating most of his time to intensive study of Judaic and world sciences, including languages; he became a noted linguist with a thorough knowledge of Arabic, Latin, Spanish, and the Berber language, besides Hebrew and Aramaic.

His shop was a short distance away from the palace of the Grand Vizir Abu Alcazar Ibn Alerif, counselor to the Moorish King Habbus of the Granada faction, and this led to events that were both unusual and profitable to Rabbi Samuel.

One of the grand vizir's servants, who was illiterate, came to his shop and asked him to write some letters for her to send to her relations. The shopkeeper did as he was asked and the servant, happy, showed them to her lover and master who, marveling at the perfection of language and elegant style, persuaded Rabbi Samuel to sell his shop and become his private secretary and adviser, which indirectly made him the king's assessor.

Before his death the grand vizir confessed to King Habbus whence his wise counsel had come; as a result, Rabbi Samuel was appointed grand vizir.

One day the king and his Jewish grand vizir passed in front of the shop. The owner, embittered by poverty, violently insulted Rabbi Samuel. Instead of having the offender's tongue cut off, as the king had suggested, Rabbi Samuel ascertained what the poor shopkeeper's needs were and gave him an abundance of riches. In reply to the king's question, the grand vizir told him that he had not ordered the Arab's evil tongue to be cut off, but instead had changed it into a good one, and as a result he would henceforth receive blessings instead of abuse.

The Moorish king was highly satisfied with his grand vizir, whose effective and intelligent administration enabled Granada to achieve economic superiority over the other provinces, surpassing them also in other aspects. His predecessor Abu Alcazar, who had sensed Rabbi Samuel's capacity for politics and the art of government, had proved to be highly perceptive.

Rabbi Samuel Ha-Nagid was the author of several dozen writings on the Talmud and the Hebrew language, in addition to a philosophical work, the *Ben Kocheleth*. But his most important activity was the assistance he provided for the leading Jewish scholars of his time—especially for the philosopher Rabbi Solomon Ibn Gabirol, enabling him to write his masterly works.

Rabbi Solomon Ibn Gabirol (in Arabic, Abu Iyov Suleiman Ibn Ihiya Ibn Gabirol) was one of the greatest philosophers of the glorious period of Spanish Judaism. Nevertheless, although his Hebrew-language philosophical works, especially the *Keter Malchut*, were famous among the Jews, his most important creation, *Mekor Chayim*, remained unknown for a long time. Translated into Latin under the title of *Fons Vitae* (Source of Life) it lay for some 800 years in the Bibliothèque de Paris; Avicebron appeared as the author. That translation, from the Arabic, had been done by two scholars: a monk and the converted Jew Jean Hispalensis (formerly Abraham Ben David). The Jewish scholar Rabbi Solomon Munk discovered by chance that the real author of the work was Rabbi Solomon Ibn Gabirol. At the same time the Hebrew version was found, which had been translated from the original Arabic by the learned Rabbi Shem Tov Palkira in 1260.

During the Middle Ages the *Mekor Chayim* exerted a pertinent influence especially in the non-Jewish world; its affirmations were disseminated by Christian theologians who seemed unaware that the author was Jewish.

Rabbi Ibn Gabirol's life had legendary connotations. The date of his birth is unknown, but he is known to have lived in Córdoba in Rabbi Samuel's time and, like him, fled from that city to settle in Málaga. Despite poverty, he studied sciences, Talmud, and Hebrew, Arabic, and other languages. He was still in his youth when he began to write poems in Hebrew, many of which the people included in holiday prayers. In one of those poems, *Asharoth*, which is recited on *Shavuot* and refers to the *mitzvot* (precepts), the author says: "I am scarcely sixteen years old and I have the wisdom of a person of eighty."

Ibn Gabirol wrote many poems, divided into the sacred (*shirey kodesh*) and the profane (*shirey hol*). His creation *Keter Malchut* is considered a masterwork, in which he expresses his philosophy on Divinity. He was also the author of *Mivchar Hapninim*, an Arabic selection of extracts from Greek philosophers on ethical problems.

It would seem that Ibn Gabirol was never married, probably because of his consumptive condition or his extreme poverty, but he always received generous aid from Rabbi Samuel Ha-Nagid and other patrons.

His precise age at the time of his death is unknown. According to some scholars of the period, such as Alharizi and Ibn Ezra, Ibn Gabirol died before he was thirty, but Arab sources give his life-span as 1021 to 1058.

As to the manner of his death, the *Shalsheleth Ha-Cabala* relates that Ibn Gabirol once wrote a superb poem and took it to an Arab friend who was eager to write poetry but lacked Ibn Gabirol's creative power. This "friend" could no longer repress his envy and murdered him, burying the body under a fig-tree that grew in his garden. The fig tree began to bloom and to yield fruit earlier than usual, arousing widespread astonishment. The King ordered an investigation of mystery. The Arab, under interrogation, confessed his guilt and was sentenced to the gallows.

Rabbi Ibn Gabirol's poems were and still are sung by the people. Many of his sacred writings became part of the *zemirot* (Sabbath songs) and his *piyyutim* (religious poems) are recited with other prayers.

His philosophical works are a different matter, for his ideas set forth in the *Keter Malchut* (in Hebrew) and in *Mekor Chayim* (in Arabic, although a Latin translation and a partial Hebrew translation have been preserved) do not agree with those upheld by Judaism. Thus under neo-Platonic influence he believed, like Plato, that matter existed before the Creation, albeit without image or form. This definitely contradicts the Jewish belief in *Yesh Meayin*, or Creation out of nothing.

Rabbi Shlomo Yitzhaki (Rashi)[1]*:*
Commentator of Holy Writ

There can be no doubt that his name and his memory have been graven in Jewish history in indelible letters, for he wrote a commentary on the Bible and the Talmud that opened a new horizon for the interpretation of Holy Writ, and which truly is without equal.

One may definitely say that, but for the Rashi, the Torah would have remained a sphinx to future generations; that was the opinion of his famous grandson, the Rashbam.

Nobody was so famous and popular. Intelligence, wisdom and the sanctity of his person made him great; he was venerated not only by Jews but also by many Roman Catholics.

The work he did opened up a new stage in Jewish life; he became the most famous personality of the Middle Ages.

Many stories were told about his life, even covering events before his birth. In that respect he is comparable to Biblical heroes like the patriarch Isaac, Samson, and the prophet Samuel, of whom

---

[1] Initials of his name.

there are reports full of miracles in connection with their birth.

Those stories should not, however, be considered mere legend, for they are based on true historical facts.

One hundred miles from Paris lies the ancient city of Troyes. It was there that in 1040 a child named Solomon was born. His father, Rabbi Isaac, was a scholar, but he was very poor, because he did not want to earn a living from a rabbinical position. Thus he became a grain merchant, dedicating part of the day to his occupation and the remainder to studying the Torah.

One notable fact is that Rashi's birth coincided, to the day and the hour, with the death of Chief Rabbi Gershon, which is interpreted as meaning that when one divine light is extinguished, another is lit immediately and the Jewish sky does not remain in darkness.

Young Solomon showed outstanding scholarly ability from childhood, and his teachers perceived the purity and sanctity of that sublime soul.

Rashi founded a yeshiva, which attracted students from France and Germany and also from distant Slavic countries, and quickly became the most important center of Torah studies. With numerous caravans transporting goods along a variety of European routes, many took the opportunity to make the tiring journey to Troyes in order to study there.

The Rashi's students questioned him in close detail; he treated them as if they were his sons, and they felt happy. He never left them and provided support that made for spiritual union between teacher and students.

Rashi's originality lay in simplicity and clarity. He did not seek complex sophisms, but set himself to clarify the details. He maintained that one should first understand the straightforward meaning of each verse and that the Torah had been written in a language "of men and for men." That was how to interpret its contents, and with that in mind he composed his commentary.

In addition to his expert knowledge of the Talmud, he was skilled in Hebrew and introduced grammatical laws. His interpretations quickly spread to all countries with Jewish populations and the other commentaries were left aside.

Thanks to his simple way of putting things, both the Bible and the Talmud began to become more accessible to the Jewish masses. All the scholars admitted that but for Rashi's commentary, the Babylonian Talmud would have suffered the same fate as the Jerusalem Talmud, which is accessible only to privileged minds.

Studying the Torah with Rashi makes everything seems clear; not a verse is beyond understanding.

The commentary was a corollary to the manuscripts of the sages, which the Rashi most skillfully corrected, systematized and completed. He also composed other works and much of the *Mahzor Vitri*.

At the age of twenty-five he was world famous and the spiritual leaders of his generation spoke of him as "a light that illuminates the darkness of the Dispersion." He travelled to a number of countries to disseminate his commentaries.

To elucidate better the meaning of a verse or word, he showed what amounted to genius in using words from other languages, especially from German and French. In 1 Kings we also find a Slavic word, which, according to Rashi, is of Russian origin.

Before he died, he had the satisfaction of knowing that the Torah was being disseminated ever more widely. The persecution suffered during the Crusades brought the Jews closer to their Torah, their only comfort during those terrible times.

His descendants and students also gave him much cause for satisfaction.

Rashi had three daughters: Rachel, Miriam and Yocheved. Yocheved was studious, and when Rashi fell ill she read his correspondence to him and wrote the letters that he dictated.

Yocheved married Rabbi Meyer Ben Samuel, and they had three sons who became famous: Rabbi Samuel Ben Meyer, known as the Rashbam; the renowned Rabbenu Tam; and Rabbi Isaac Ben Meyer, known as the Ribam.

Rashi was unable to finish his commentary on the Talmud, for at the age of sixty-five death wrested the pen from his hand. In that respect, in the tractate *Makot* (19b), Rashi's commentary ends with the following words: "Our Rabbi was physically pure and gave up his soul in purity."

Rabbi Yehuda Halevy:
Physician, Philosopher, and Poet

In 1975 we celebrated the 900th birth anniversary of one of the greatest Jewish poets and scholars, who lived during the Jewish Golden Age in medieval Spain and illuminated the Jewish firmament with his wisdom and knowlege: Rabbi Yehuda Ben Samuel Halevy.

The marks he left are profound, his heritage is eternal, his life quasi-legendary. His work *Kuzari* reached to every corner of the Jewish Dispersion, and through it tens of generations were afforded light, comfort and hope in the darkness of exile.

His religious verses and other poetry, his ideas generally, are as fresh today and have as much force as when they were created. Rabbi Yehuda Halevy was one of the first who in times of distress and dejection encouraged and revived the national conscience. He bitterly deplored Jewish destiny, but also spoke in happier terms of coming redemption (*Kuzari*, II). He felt convinced that the Jews had been chosen by Divine Providence to attain eternal redemption, for God was on the side of the oppressed. On that basis, he called on the people not to lose heart and, like the Rabbi of Berdichev, known as the "intercessor for Israel," set forth his complaint before the Almighty for having abandoned His people. As regards the genius that is apparent in his poetry and compositions and his philosophical work *El Cuzari*, enough has been written to fill an enormous library. Nevertheless it is difficult to know and characterize the many-sided influence of his spiritual heritage over the Jews during the course of history.

Kuzari, which in the original Arabic is titled *Book of Explanations to Protect a Disparaged Creed*, contains a conversation between the king of the Kuzaris and a Jewish scholar, who discuss the loftier aspects of faith and particularly of Judaism. The book sets out to disprove false philosophical speculation on the subject of God and the world. The true facts of the Jewish faith are highlighted as concrete factors, founded on the historical experiences of the Jewish people. Its system is based on the fundamental principle of faith. Creation is a product of God, who conceived it out of nothing. The Highest is omniscient and His Providence is everywhere. God is the center of all our yearnings. The Jewish people is the heart of mankind and the Jews suffer more than others, just as the heart suffers more than the other organs (*Kuzari*, 11).

Not for nothing did God say to the People of Israel: "I have chosen you among all the peoples and I therefore make greater demands on you, because of your sins." God is stricter with the Jewish people than with other peoples.

To understand clearly Rabbi Yehuda Halevy's point of view, it is important to point out that, to him, the Jewish faith is the revelation of the national conscience.

Although the fundamental ethical principles of the Torah of Moses have a universal human significance, the Torah constitutes an exclusive property of the Jewish people, to which it is firmly attached by an infinity of psychological and cultural bonds. *Kuzari* is one of the fundamental books of Jewish religious philosophy. It was written in Arabic and subsequently translated into Hebrew by Rabbi Yehuda Ibn Tibon.

As the narrative goes, the king of the Kuzaris want to adopt a new religion and sends for representatives of the Christian, Moslem and Jewish beliefs for talks about each religion.

The Jewish representative, Rabbi Isaac Singari, explains to him during their talk that although the Jewish faith is so disparaged, it is the true one. The explanations and thoughts of the Jewish sage prove convincing and the king as well as his people adopt the Jewish faith.

Rabbi Yehuda Halevy defines two fundamental principles of Judaism: the Torah, as the property of the Jewish people, to which it is linked by historical and spiritual bonds: and the sanctity of the Land of Israel. He concludes that sanctity can be attained only in Israel, and illustrates this point with an example: a vineyard can bear fruit only in the right ambience and climate.

He was the first to set Jewish existence in the Dispersion on a theoretical basis. Any people, when uprooted, perishes. Israel, however, lives because it bases its existence on a spiritual principle. The Jews, wherever they are and in whatever generation they live, remain linked with Israel. In his religious poetry, especially his *Songs of Zion*, Rabbi Yehuda Halevy reveals his longing for the Land of Israel, his thoughts on the destiny of the Jewish people, and his yearning for Divinity.

His delicate emotional poems, born of creative inspiration, are of incalculable literary value. Some of them are said on the night of *Tisha Be-Av*.

Rabbi Yehuda Alharizi wrote that one could sense a Holy Presence in his writings. He composed more than 700 secular poems and many others of a liturgical character.

Yehuda Halevy was born in Spain, the only son of Don Samuel of Castile, who sent him to study in Rabbi Isaac Alfasi's famous yeshiva. He also studied other sciences, especially medicine. His analysis of Greek philosophy led him to conclude that it was meaningless for the Jewish spirit, because it was internally void. "Do not yield to the attraction of Greek wisdom, for it bears no fruit, only flowers," he wrote in a song. He rejected Plato's philosophy because it denies God. In its place, Rabbi Yehuda Halevy teaches a Jewish philosophy and way that do not come from outside, from the Greeks, but from inside, from Judaism itself, and that culminate in *Kuzari*. He wrote his books in Arabic so that they might reach all the Jewish sectors of the Islamic world and convince them that God was the Lord of the world and of its inhabitants, and that He had chosen the People of Israel and crowned it with a divine prophecy.

To him, Zion not only was the historic country of his forefathers but also the sublime symbol of the beauty to which his soul aspired.

In his poem *My Heart Is in the East and I Am in the West*, he grieves at his situation and longs for the moment when he will be able to kiss Zion's stones.

At the age of fifty-four he left Spain to settle in the Land of Israel. He reached Alexandria, where he stayed for about a year, then continued his journey to Israel.

Concerning the manner of his death, there was a story that when he reached the gates of Jerusalem he tore his clothes and became ecstatic, beginning to recite his famous poem *Zion, Pray for the Well-Being of Your Captives*, and an Arab horseman passing by became furious at the Jewish invocation and killed him.

The moral heritage that Rabbi Yehuda Halevy bequeathed contains ideas that live on and still serve as a guiding light.

Rabbi Samuel Ben Meyer (Rashbam) and His Brother Rabbenu Tam

Rabbi Samuel Ben Meyer, or Rashbam (from the initials of his name) is considered one of the outstanding Talmudic personalities of all time. His mother, Yocheved, was Rashi's daughter; his father was a distinguished Talmudic scholar. He had two famous brothers: Rabbi Isaac Ben Meyer, known as Ribam in the Talmudic world; and Rabbenu Jacob Tam, a great Torah and Talmud commentator who surpassed his brother in that field, won distinction for his knowledge of Hebrew, and amazed the Jewish world with his erudition.

The Rashbam was born in Ramerupt, France, in 1083, at a time when his grandfather Rashi had entered his fourth decade of life. He began to study the Torah with his father, Rabbi Meyer, but the main influence in his education was that of his grandfather Rashi, whose commentaries have been studied for generations as part and parcel of the Torah and the Talmud and remain to this day the delight of readers whether children, young people, or adults. The Rashbam may thus be said to be the first Jew who studied Humash (Pentateuch) and Gemara with Rashi.

His famous grandfather helped him to explore the depths of the Talmudic "sea" and to discover genuine secret treasures there.

Having had teachers of the standing of Rashi and other notable Rabbinical authorities of the period, Rabbi Samuel won increasing renown in the Jewish world, which began to consider him a new rising star.

He was still a young man when he began to argue with his grandfather on points of Halacha and interpretation of the Torah. And in not a few instances, the grandfather came to accept his grandson's opinions. The Rashbam tells us that his illustrious predecessor admitted after certain discussions that it was time to revise his commentaries in the light of his grandson's remarks.

After the death of his grandfather and father the Rashbam virtually took their places. He had already won recognition in the Jewish world as a religious and spiritual authority, and the most prominent Rabbis of France and Germany began to send him inquiries on Halachic questions.

Rabbi Samuel interpreted Biblical verse on a strictly logical basis, literally and without sophistry; this won him a privileged position among Jewish commentators. Jointly with his brother Rabbenu Jacob Tam he was among the first *tosafot* commentators (authors of additional Bible commentaries).

Although Judaic sciences were his main interest, he did not neglect secular matter. He understood the world—and his neighbor—through experience accumulated in Rashi's house. He was in frequent touch with people belonging to a variety of professions, cities and countries. He traveled widely and was in permanent contact with many Jewish scholars of the period.

He had many friends in Paris: Rabbi Matityahu, Rabbi Yehuda Ben Abraham, Rabbi Yehuda Ben Yom Tov and Rabbi Yechiel had settled there and with them he took part in many get-togethers dedicated to the Torah. In that city there were many public study classes on Halachic subjects. In that way he began to see more of the outside world and learned to know it better.

He often got involved in arguments with Christian students who claimed to show that in the Bible there were definite allusions to the coming of their messiah; they intended, moreover, to make fun of the Jewish religion. Rabbi Samuel, far from giving way to their arguments, defeated them with his irrefutable logic. Later, in his Torah commentaries, he used the same arguments as in those debates.

The Rashbam successfully completed his grandfather's monumental work, filling in those parts of the commentary on the Babylon Talmud that had been left unfinished. He had working methods of his own; he went his own way, using entirely original interpretation systems, whose main feature was rigorous logic.

His love of simple, straightforward interpretation was such that he took the liberty to write commentaries that contradicted his grandfather's concepts.

He dedicated his life not only to the Talmud and Halacha, but also to study of the Hebrew language and its grammar. For his commentaries he used the *targum* (Aramaic translation of the Bible) by Onkelos, who was also an outstanding linguist. He also studied the Vulgate, by Jerome.

His brother Rabbenu Tam said of him: "He is the sun that lights our generations."

Rabbenu Tam, whose actual name was Rabbi Jacob Ben Meyer and who lived in the cities of Ramerupt and Troyes in 1100-1171, was the leading Talmudic authority of his time. He was rich and influential, for he was in close touch with the highest government spheres. He was one of the most noted Jewish leaders of his time, in both the civil and the religious fields. Since the conclusion of the Talmud nobody has equalled him in *pilpul* (an ingenious dialectical method for study of the Talmud) according to the authoritative opinion of Rabbi Isaac Ben Sheshet, one of the most prominent Rabbis of his time. He solved the most difficult and complex problems that arose from study of the Gemara in matters of double meaning. His renown spread rapidly throughout the Jewish world; he received inquiries on religious questions from all points of the compass.

In Ramerupt he was the principal of the large local Talmudic academy, whose fame he helped to spread.

On the second day of Shavuot (Jewish Pentecost) of the year 1147, the Crusaders unleashed a massacre among the Jews, during which he would have been killed but for the providential intervention of a well-known nobleman, who saved his life. Thereafter he went to Troyes, the city of his grandfather Rashi, where he took charge of Talmudic academies and assumed leadership of his people, setting up a series of regulations (*takanot*) that bear his name, aimed at elevating the status of women and making more accessible certain all-too-rigid religious practices.

Like his brother Rabbi Samuel, he was a noted Tosafist. He won renown in the Jewish world through his idea that the four sections of the Pentateuch that deal with phylacteries should be arranged in a different order from that established by his grandfather Rashi. Therefore many religious Jews utilize both types of phylacteries, those of Rashi and those of his grandson Rabbenu Tam.

His innovations in interpretation of the Torah and his replies to various Talmudic questions were compiled in his principal work, the *Sefer Hayashar*. His teachings appear also in the *tosafot* (addenda or supplements) printed in the Babylon editions of the Talmud.

Rabbenu Tam was noted for his tolerant and benevolent interpretation of the Jewish law in view of the difficult moments that the people were going through at the time. Since the Jews were prohibited from engaging in trade and it was increasingly difficult for them to make a living, he allowed them to lend money to Gentiles against moderate interest. "We are increasingly burdened with the taxes," he wrote, "payment of which the State exacts from us, and there is no other way of finding the required amount. It would therefore be absurd to maintain the prohibition of charging interest."

To strengthen Jewish community life was a constant preoccupation with him, and in Rabbinical conventions he exerted his influence to ensure that strict disciplinary rules were introduced to safeguard this fundamental aspect of Jewish existence and survival.

Through his close ties with high government circles he strove to obtain cancellation of the many anti-Jewish decrees dictated at the time. He trained many students who continued his system of study, the analysis and interpretation of Holy Writ known in the Jewish world as the *"tosafist* commentators' method." This method consisted in logical and exhaustive analysis of the significance of the Gemara, in order to reach conclusions that should be accessible to all.

His name, like that of his illustrious brother the Rashbam, will live in the memory of the Jewish people.

Rabbi Abraham Ibn Ezra: Jewish Poet of Spain

Rabbi Abraham Ibn Ezra (ca. 1091-1169) is considered one of the greatest poets and scholars of the Jewish Golden Age in medieval Spain.

His spiritual legacy is inestimable. Beloved of the people, he became a legendary figure. In times of despair and dejection, he succeeded in arousing national feelings and conscience in the Jews. In his poems he expresses sorrow at the cruel fate of his people, whom he believes were chosen by God to enjoy eternal life, for the Almighty is always on the side of the oppressed.

Little is known about his youth, but most historians agree that he was born in Toledo, Spain, in about 1091, twelve years before the death of the Rashi, the great commentator. His private life, like that of many other Jewish personalities of olden times, is shrouded in mystery.

In his time Spain was the most important center of Jewish culture in the world. Famous sages, scholars, linguists, mathematicians and astronomers, physicians and poets, philosophers and statesmen came together there. Jewish genius was revealed in its full splendor, harmonizing world science and philosophy with the principles of the Jewish religion in a well-balanced whole.

Abraham Ibn Ezra stood out among the giants of his generation. He was deeply versed in the Torah besides being a poet, philosopher, physician, astronomer, mathematician and lexicologist of note. Hardly a branch of science eluded his observant eye and nimble mind. One of the leading Talmudic scholars, Rabbenu Jacob Tam, held him in high esteem. "Ibn Ezra is close to nine of the ten sources of wisdom that descend on earth," he wrote. Maimonides held that he was as great as the patriarch Abraham in his generation and advised his son to study his works.

Rabbi Abraham Ibn Ezra's humility was proverbial. He wrote tens of books, but his major creation comprised commentary on the Pentateuch, the minor prophets, Isaiah, the Five Rolls, the Psalms, Job, and others, which won him the gratitude of his people to this day, since his monumental work on the Bible helped to bring Holy Scripture nearer to people at all social and intellectual levels.

Ibn Ezra was also a distinguished researcher in the Hebrew language and wrote several works about its grammar; he was virtually the first to attract the attention of the Roman Jews to Hebrew, of which they knew nothing. He translated from Arabic a book on the grammar of the Hebrew language by Yehuda Ibn Hayug and campaigned to safeguard the beauty and purity of "the language of sacred things."

His knowledge of astronomy and astrology won him deserved renown. He maintained that the heavenly bodies influenced the destiny of human beings. As a noted astrologer, he predicted future events. As soon as he entered a town, people crowded around him to hear his predictions. He soon won such fame as a fortune-teller that he was invited to serve in that capacity in the royal palace.

Nevertheless, despite his fame, Ibn Ezra went through many hard times. He wandered from place to place without a definite purpose. His poverty was as great as his genius, and he never succeeded in getting a stable occupation. All his plans to settle down and make a regular living ended in failure; he wrote in one of his poems: "If candlemaking was my trade, the sun would never set / And if I traded in shrouds, no one during my life would die."

Nevertheless, his misfortunes could not quell his cheerful spirit; he took his setbacks with a smile. When he wept, it was at the disasters that befell his people.

Ibn Ezra was neglectful of his person and restless by nature. Restlessness was apparent not only in his thoughts and creations, but also in his private life. A tireless traveler, he went to Morocco, Egypt, Israel, Persia and India, where he was arrested. His intelligence secured his release. He also visited Italy, France and England. An insatiable internal urge prevented him from staying in the same place for any length of time. The more he traveled, the more he wanted to see of the world, despite the dangers that dogged travelers in those times. Between journeys, he found time for study and for the creation of different works. In one of his poems, he characterized himself in these words: "Everywhere I live,/books I write,/and secrets I reveal."

His most transcendent work, which aroused the greatest interest, was certainly his commentary on the Torah, which strongly influenced the Jews of his own and later generations. His writings did much to help people understand the Hebrew language better and to know the Bible in the original. He also wrote hundreds of beautiful secular and religious poems in clear, rich, colorful language; his *piutim* (liturgical poems) were considered sacred by the people. Through them, down the centuries, the Jews, beset by worries, could seek succor from the Almighty.

Owing to his love of travel, his works were written in Hebrew and not in Arabic, a language unknown to Jews outside Spain. His philosophic-religious book *Yesod Morah*, which he wrote in a few weeks, attracted the attention of the leading scholars of the period. It has been estimated that he created some two hundred works on various subjects and disciplines, including, in addition to those mentioned, mathematics, astronomy and chess.

Ibn Ezra was gifted with a delicate sense of humor. He liked to joke, to compose riddles, to talk to freethinkers and tease them with his sharp-witted banter, and he enjoyed chess, at which he was an expert.

According to some researchers, Abraham Ibn Ezra was closely related to Rabbi Yehuda Halevy; some claim that he was his son-in-law.

A legend tells how the two poets met. Rabbi Yehuda Halevy knew Ibn Ezra's works, but did not know him personally. One day a poor tramp entered Yehuda Halevy's house. The Rabbi did not notice him, for he was absorbed in writing a poem whose last lines were proving particularly difficult; he could not find appropriate rhymes. Each stanza began with another letter, in alphabetical order. On reaching the letter *resh* he gave up, unable to finish the poem, and went to bed. Next morning, as he sat down at his desk to continue his work, he saw in amazement that the line had been completed in masterly fashion and, scarcely able to believe his eyes, he exclaimed: "This marvel could only be the work of an angel from Heaven, or of Abraham Ibn Ezra." At that moment, the tramp introduced himself.

He was in lively demand from all sides, and in many places there were people who wanted to have him with them permanently. One rich Jew was ready to give up his wealth and go out on the road with Rabbi Abraham Ibn Ezra, despite the dangers he would have to face; he wanted to be beside him and listen to his sermons.

After lengthy travels and having completed his Bible commentary, he decided to return to Spain. Before he reached its frontiers, he repeatedly fell ill. He was then seventy-five and, feeling that he had not long to live, he paraphrased a verse of the Pentateuch that referred to the patriarch Abraham: "And Abraham was of seventy-and-five years when he left the shores of the world." That brief sentence was a summing-up of his life story, fraught with suffering; he left to posterity a gigantic spiritual legacy, which new generations would do well to know.

The Great Maimonides (The Rambam)

Down through the centuries so much has been written about the vast range of knowledge, the personality and genius of Maimonides, whether in the realms of medicine, philosophy, or Talmudic writ, that a giant library could be amassed in tribute to his universal spirit, piety and intellectual creative power. And still it would be difficult to encompass the enormous influences he has exerted over the Jews for so many centuries, like the column of fire guiding the Jewish people as ordained by Divine Providence.

The Rambam's life was a triumph of human genius, a revelation of the Divinity that lies in the nature and powers of man. One may safely assert that throughout Jewish history no one else has penetrated so deeply and widely as Maimonides into the Talmud and the treasures of the Torah.

His life history is well known, but it is worthwhile to consider more fully certain aspects that have not been adequately analyzed and explained. Two of those aspects appear to have been neglected: his longing for the Land of Israel and why he did not live there; and his vision of a Jewish nation.

It is known that in his youth he had to leave his native city of

Córdoba in Spain, because it had been overrun by Arab tribes whose king introduced anti-Jewish laws. The Jews were given an ultimatum: convert to Islam or perish. Most of the Spanish Jews left the region, including the Rambam, who with his family moved to Morocco, and from there after wandering through deserts and unknown lands to avoid discovery as a Jew, finally reached Jerusalem safe and sound with his family. For three days he prayed before the Wailing Wall and thereafter visited the tomb of the Patriarchs in Hebron. He fasted and wept over the destiny of the Holy Land, in particular because Divine Providence did not allow him to stay in Israel (as is known from the will that he left with his son). He therefore accepted the invitation of the Egyptian Jews and settled in Cairo, the capital of Egypt. The Rambam was then twenty-five years old, but his name was already famous.

The Jews of Alexandria honored him with an appointment as spiritual leader of the community, but, like the sages of the Talmud, he maintained that "the Torah should not be used to gain material profit" and was content to make a living in other positions or in trade. He also feared that such a position would take up much of his time and he would be unable to study or create. In his letters he complained of not having enough time to study the Torah because of his multiple occupations attendant to his appointment as physician to the Sultan and his court.

Despite his knowledge of many of the scientific disciplines of those times, he dedicated most of his time and his great intellectual powers to the Torah. In one of his writings he declared emphatically that "the Torah had chosen him in his mother's womb before he was born" and that he was chosen by destiny to disseminate the Torah worldwide.

The Rambam was a voracious scholar—he usually studied fifteen hours a day—and he possessed an extraordinary memory. He remarked that "the angel of oblivion had no power over him" so that everything that he studied or read remained forever graven in his memory.

He studied and read much, in various languages. At the age of sixteen he wrote a book about logic; at eighteen a book about mathematics and another on astronomy, dealing in particular with the principles on which the Jewish calendar is based. Later he began to compose his wonderful interpretation of the Mishna, and thereafter interpretations of the Torah. His *Letters about the Yemen and the Conversation* strongly influenced the estranged Jews of Yemen who had abandoned their faith and later reverted to Jewry.

Later he wrote *Guide of the Wayward*, a work of profound philosophical content. But his greatest work was *Yad Hazakah* in fourteen volumes, also entitled *Mishne Torah*. In that work he recapitulated all the precepts of the Written and Oral Law, arranged so that anyone could find and understand the law clearly.

All the scholars of his time recognized him as the greatest of them all, and agreed that everything he said should be taken into account. To this day, Rabbis as well as ordinary people study the Rambam, to know and understand what the Torah demands of the Jews.

Many of his manuscripts remained unknown and were lost. Hundreds of them are preserved in the famous *Geniza* of Cairo. The *Yad Hazakah*, on which he worked for ten years, confirms his yearning for the rebuilding of a Jewish homeland and his vision of redemption. The twelfth of his Thirty Principles of Faith proclaims: "I fully believe in the coming of the Messiah, and though it be delayed, I shall expect it every day until his actual coming." Those principles became the foundation of the Jewish belief and of hope of freedom and resurrection.

In the *Mishne Torah* he unfolds a marvelous vision: Jewish life within a country, a kingdom, a Holy Temple, Jewish tillers of the soil, a Sanhedrin and priests, Jewish kings and judges. That work outlines the ideal constitution for the day when the Jewish people are newly redeemed. Nor did he forget the practical demands of daily life and held that Israel is sacred even after its destruction and "that the sabbatical year reigns even after the hecatomb."

The Rambam also conceded great importance to the Hebrew language, holding it to be sacred and created as the Jew's language to enable him to express his choicest thoughts and feelings. Moreover, it should serve as the spiritual instrument of mankind. That is why Jewish scholars call it "the language of things sacred," for its words are intended to express a pure and sacred way of life.

The Rambam was the first to say that to study Hebrew was the duty of every Jew, since it was precept of the Torah, and those who considered it a minor matter were mistaken. The Mishna, he wrote, teaches that a simple precept should be observed as if it were the strictest and to study Hebrew is equally as important as the precept of circumcision or *tallit* since nobody knows what is the reward for fulfillment of each precept.

All the foregoing became apparent through his feelings of repentance in the last days of his life for having written his books (except the *Yad Hazakah*) in Arabic, and his longing for the day when he could begin translating them into the sacred language.

He was also unhappy at having lived in Egypt, which brings the principal enigma: why did he not move to Israel. This was clarified through the will that he left with his only son, Abraham. On 20 Teveth 1204, when he was about seventy, after attending the sick, he called his son, ordered the doors to be closed and said to him:

> Know, my son, that I have only a few hours to live. My soul will return to God, to the holy source whence it came and only by body will remain on earth. I therefore ask of you, my son, to promise me that you will do the same as the sons of our patriarchs Jacob did with the body of their father: bury my body in the Land of Israel. And, just as Joseph had to apply for a dispensation from the Pharaoh to transport his father's body, do you similarly apply to the Sultan. All my life, I wished to live in our Holy Land, to study and become attached to the sanctity of Israel in order to die there. But in Heaven it was decided otherwise: that I should live among my brethren of the dispersion and help them in their need.... Now it is my wish that my bones should rest in the country for which I have longed all my life...in the land of the Patriarchs.

Then he went to his writing desk and wrote to the Sultan, bidding him farewell in courteous terms, thanking him for the favors granted to himself and his brethren who lived within the Sultan's dominion, and finally requesting permission for his body to be taken out of Egypt in order to "rest in the land for which I have yearned all my life: in the land of the patriarchs, in the Land of Israel."

Then he said the night prayer and laid himself to rest, murmuring the words: "Into Thy hands I deliver my spirit." The Column of Fire was extinguished, but only on the material plane. So long as the Jewish people exist, the Rambam's teachings will shine forth like a beacon of light.

The news of his disappearance aroused worldwide emotion; a day of fasting was proclaimed in Jerusalem. He was buried in the city of Tiberias, near the tomb of Rabbi Yohanan Ben Zakai. The inscription on his tombstone read: "Here rests our Rabbi Moses, son of Maimon, the elect of Mankind."

And since then there has been a saying: "Since Moses (our Teacher) and until Moses (son of Maimon) there has not been a personality so great as Moses."

The Rambam's Monumental Work Yad Hazakah

More than 800 years ago the Rambam completed his work *Yad Hazakah*, also known as *Mishne Torah* and recognized as the greatest spiritual creation and heritage of the generations. It is not a single book but actually fourteen books. The Rambam called it *Yad Hazakah* because the numerical value of the Hebrew word *Yad* is fourteen. It is a compilation of the laws, moral and scientific teachings dispensed by the Babylonian and Jerusalem Talmud, as also by the books of the Tannaim and Amoraim; of certain religious principles and studies of Divinity; of good behavior, table manners, customs in attire, hygiene and other things.

The Rambam wrote in his introduction that he compiled this work because the Jews were faced with great problems and nobody had time to study all the different commentaries and opinions; hence the need to concentrate it all in one place. He thus became the teacher and guide of all the Jews of all the generations and in all the fields of endeavor: *Halacha* (Jewish law), philosophy, ethics, and sciences. He worked tirelessly for ten years on the master book *Yad Hazakah*; many stories and legends were woven around it.

The *Mishne Torah* is a book in which the Rambam compiled all the commandments that God gave to the Jews through the written and oral Torah, arranged so that anyone could find what he sought directly and understand it clearly. Through that book, the Rambam not only became the Rabbi of Egypt but also the teacher of all subsequent Jewish generations.

All the scholars of his time agreed that the Rambam was the greatest among them and that due attention should be given to everything he said. His book *Yad Hazakah* became the foundation on which all built for generations. All the scholars and sages study the Rambam to the present day, to know and understand what the Torah demands of the Jews. "The Rambam says," "It is a difficult Rambam"—such expressions are heard at times.

Enough has been written about Maimonides to form a vast library: his breath of knowledge; his great intellect, which created immortal works in Halacha, medicine and philosophy; his charity, universal spirit and creative power. Nevertheless, it is difficult to characterize and encompass the many-sided influence exerted over the Jewish people by this spiritual giant, to whom Providence granted the privilege of turning into a column of fire.

The Rambam's life was a triumph of human genius, a divine revelation of human nature and human powers. It may be said without hesitation that in all Jewish history one cannot find so great a human spirit that immersed itself so fully and profoundly as the Rambam in the sea of the Talmud and the treasures of the Torah.

Thus it is only natural that the Jewish world should so devoutly sanctify his name and his creation, and that on the 800th anniversary of his *Yad Hazakah* festive occasions and commemorations, symposia, book shows and publications specially dedicated to his great historic work were organized in Israel, in the United States and in London.

The British Museum, which arranged an 800th anniversary commemoration of Maimonides, exhibited the actual manuscript and over thirty editions of the *Yad Hazakah*. The first printed edition is from Rome, dated 1475. It is worth noting that the museum's brochure describes the Rambam as the greatest human spirit that ever existed.

His *Mishne Torah* provides insight into his great longing for the rebirth of the Hebrew state. The Rambam was a man of astonishing vision. He wanted full-scale Jewish life in a country, a state and a *Bet Ha-Mikdash* (Holy Temple), Jewish farmers and leaders, a Sanhedrin with priests, Jewish kings and judges. The Rambam's *Mishne Torah* is an ideal constitution for the time when the Jewish people return to prosperity. Nor did he forget the practical demands of everyday life.

To the Rambam, Israel would remain sacred even after its destruction. Thus he wrote: "*Shmitah* (resting the soil every seventh year) means that in the seventh year of cultivation, the soil is accessible to all." The agricultural laws are as valid after the destruction as before it.

The Rambam paid homage to and idolized the Hebrew language as the most valuable ever created, for it was the individual's language, made to express the most delicate thoughts and feelings of mankind and to serve as a spiritual inspiration for all mankind. According to the Rambam, that was why our scholars called it the "language of things sacred," for its treasury of words was destined to express a pure and sacred life.

The Rambam's death caused deep distress. Everywhere, the Jews wept and mourned the loss they had sustained through the death of the great leader. There was particular sorrow in the city of Jerusalem. A fast was decreed there as soon as the bad news was known. All the Jews, men, women and children, assembled in the synagogues, took out the Torah Roll and read the Pentateuch section of *Tohacha* (chapter of maledictions) ending with the Haftarah in I Samuel 4, which tells how the Holy Arc was captured and the honor of Israel was lost when God's Arc was taken from them.

The Rambam's Letter to His Son Abraham

Serve God with *love*, since *fear* only prevents one from falling into sin. Love of God, on the contrary, is conducive to good deeds.

Know that a man is judged by everything that he does. He who does good deeds is well treated in *this* world; all those that see him praise him and until the end of his days he rejoices in his successful work, is satisfied and does not fear death, for he does not fear punishment but instead is confident in the well-being that is granted to all those who are God-fearing. But if a man seeks evil, it will pursue him, people disapprove of him, and before he dies he feels pain at oncoming darkness and knowing that his name is despised.

I therefore ask you to understand that the light is better than darkness, that life is better than death, and that you should therefore choose life and light. Get accustomed to doing good, for man's nature depends on habit, and the latter turns into nature.

You should know that soundness of body precedes that of the soul, and the first-named is like a key that opens the palace. Therefore the principal aim of morals is to keep your body health and improve your way of life. Be honest and straightforward, keep away from frivolity, from consorting with loafers, from the game of the unmarried, since from them come all evil. Consort with scholars, be humble and listen carefully to what they say, do not show conceit nor contradict except only when and where it is appropriate. Weigh every word before you speak, for thereafter you cannot withdraw your words. Seek for knowledge, frequent scholars to hear their moral teachings and the innovative suggestions and ingenious arguments of their students; emulate those with learning and shun the ignorant. In asking questions or giving answers, do not become confused, or shout, or stutter. Speak in clear language, in a calm voice, analyze things like a master who seeks the truth and not like one who is stubborn and seeks only to win the argument.

Study when young, for then you may profit from the experience of others, when your mind is still clear and unencumbered by thoughts, and your memory is unaffected. A time will come when you have the will but not the power, and even that which you know is recalled with much effort and little result.

Love truth and justice and thus you will be like one who builds on rock; abhor lies and injustice, for they mean building on sand or attaching with saliva. There may be situations when the truth brings you losses and lies bring you profit, but safety comes only from truth. And when you have to pass on my legacy, you will pass on my rectitude, that I have inherited from God; rectitude takes me where my family members cannot go, bequeathing to me a heritage superior to that of my progenitors; it helps me to win success and brings profit to me and to others.

My sons, take due care even in cases for which the Torah does not provide; keep your word, whether pledged publicly or in secret, do not trust in falsehood nor in deception, live in innocence and purity, do not touch anything that belongs to another, do not benefit from anything that does not belong to you with certainty, keep away from anything dubious and better leave it to your opponent. He who has a mere taste of the dubious will end by taking a bigger bite; he who takes a little will take much, and one who steals in secret will steal openly until he is exposed as a liar, thief and scoundrel. Keep away from such persons, and may they live and die in the mire of their shame and disgrace. He who has a load of hay will produce straw, and he who seeks rectitude will reap justice.

Value your morals and be happy with your rectitude, for there is no ancestry better than morals or more venerable than rectitude. Draw nearer to the outcast, bow before the humble, smile at those who are shamed, derive piety from the oppressed and share their joys, remember them at your festivals and take care not to offend them with your gifts. Abhor idleness, for it leads to corruption, poverty, sorrow and slander; it is a ladder toward Satan and his servants; all that comes of sloth. Will you not become abhorrent through quarrels that corrode a man's body, soul and property? And afterward, what remains?

I have seen happy men turn sullen, noblemen lapse into brutality, families crumble, men of power and influence humiliated, cities razed, communities dispersed, religious men corrupted, honest people perish; all as a result of quarrels. Keep away even from a family member who is involved in disputes, so that you do not suffer through his sin. Pride yourself in the virtue of patience, for that is real proof of heroism and true victory. If you seek vengeance you may fail to achieve it; a prolonged wait for it will make you ill. If you achieve it, you have fallen into error before God. Moreover, if you are possessed by feelings of hatred, your intelligence will be blunted, you will become confused when at work and all your faults will be exposed.

Through patience, even your enemies will come to consider you a saint. Those that sought to harm you will repent and consider you noble; if they are honorable they will change for the better, if they are evil and corrupt, they will be hurt and will worry at the realization that you did not become abhorrent, that you are not like them, that you dominate them with the crown of your integrity. Be humble, for humility is the ladder of access to greatness. There is no jewel more precious than humility. That is proved by the fact that Moses, greatest of all the prophets, did not boast of any of his virtues; he was a humble man.

Put a lock on your mouth and a bridle on your tongue. God, in his infinite love, gave to man the gift of speech so that he, through his profound comprehension, should thank Him, praise Him and narrate His miracles. Therefore it is not fitting that the tongue should cause damage through lies and slander.

Eat as much as you need to live, and no more. Do not imagine that much food and drink strengthens the body and increases the intelligence. On the contrary, if one does not eat much, the stomach has power to receive and enough natural warmth to digest; man is strengthened, becomes healthier, and his intelligence develops. And if someone eats to excess, his stomach will neither tolerate nor digest it. As a result, that man is weakened and his intelligence is debilitated. Take care not to eat before you have digested the last meal, for the body and the stomach will be damaged and this causes most illnesses. Work before your meal and rest after it. Do not eat in a hurry like gluttons, do not stuff your mouth with food, avoid spoiled food like an enemy that you wish to eliminate. Do not eat in the street or nibble like mice, but eat at regular hours in your home. Avoid frequent meals with youthful companions. Know that meals taken in company reveal a man's character, good or bad; and many times have I gone home hungry and thirsty for fear of seeing my neighbor's shame.

Beware of wine, which corrupts the strongest and shames even the best men. I do not advise you to abstain totally from wine, but destroy its strength with water, drink it during meals and without exaggeration. Not in vain does the Torah relate the ignominy of Noah, for us to point the moral.

Dignity is like a gift in which to clothe the body. Therefore dress according to your possibilities and eat less than you are able—only enough to keep alight the flame of the spirit. Avoid gambling altogether and give to the poor more than the state of your fortune allows.

Rabbi Joseph Kimche: Defender of the Jewish Faith

Rabbi Joseph Kimche was one of the most significant Jewish personalities of his time in France. Among Jewish centers of the Middle Ages, Provence had features of special interest. Great scholars lived and created there, including the well-known commentators Rabbi Moses Hadarshan (mid-11th century); Rabbi Nathan Ben Yekhiel of Rome, author of the *Arukh*; Rabbi Kalonymus Bar Todros; Rabbi Joseph Ibn Kaspi; the Rabad, author of the *Sefer Ha-Kabala*; and others.

Rabbi Kimche was born in Spain in 1105. The situation prevailing there compelled him to emigrate to Provence in France, where he settled in the city of Narbonne, known as an important center of the Torah and as a place of residence of noted Jewish scholars.

The Kimche came of an ancient family of scholars who, with the passing of time, settled in Italy, Turkey, Syria and Britain. The first to impart luster to that illustrious surname was Rabbi Joseph, whom the Jews of Provence honored with the title of Rabbi Joseph Gaon.

Although he was one of the most famous scholars of his time, he was by no means well-to-do. Rabbi Abraham Ibn Ezra, who during is world travels spent some time in Narbonne, where he and Rabbi Kimche became friends, frequently quoted the latter's valuable commentaries on the Pentateuch in his own Torah commentaries.

Rabbi Joseph Kimche had expert knowledge of the Arabic language and of Hebrew grammar. His *Sefer Ha-Zicaron* enjoyed enormous popularity because it so greatly facilitated comprehension of the Torah. He also wrote the *Sefer Ha-Galui*, a commentary on the books of the first prophets.

In his works he sought to interpret Holy Writ on strictly logical lines, without sophisms. He wrote many books, among which may be noted the *Sefer Ha-Torah*, a commentary on the Pentateuch; the *Sefer Ha-Mikneh*, on the prophets; and commentaries on the Book of Proverbs, the Song of Songs and Job. He also translated from Arabic into Hebrew Rabbi Bahye Ibn Paquda's *Hovot Halevavot* (Duties of the Heart) which was the Jews' first ethical system and is considered a classic of its kind to this day.

He was particularly noted for his brilliantly effective arguments in debates on the subject of Christianity. In his time public debates about religion were fairly frequent, with the participation of representatives of the Church, some of whom were converted Jews, and of the Jewish faith. Christian priests deliberately sought to stir up feeling against the Jews, aiming to convince the masses that Catholicism was not only the true faith but the only one.

The Rabbis had no wish to take part in debates of this kind and tried to avoid them, but mostly without success, for they were virtually compelled to appear and take part in them together with Catholic religious authorities. Refusal to do so would have angered the Catholics, exposing the communities to violence and other moral and physical dangers.

As a result of those experiences Rabbi Kimche wrote a pamphlet-like work, the *Sefer Ha-Brit*. There are various suppositions as to what reasons impelled him to do so; the most probable is that he wanted to leave to future generations a guide to defense of the Jewish faith, containing replies to the Christians who sought to turn the Torah and the prophets to their own advantage, aiming to show that they foretold the coming of Jesus and concluding that all religious Jews who believed in Holy Scripture should recognize Christ as the true and definitive Messiah. Rabbi Yehuda Halevy must have had the same purpose in mind in writing his *Kuzari* in dialogue form against the detractors of the Jewish religion.

Through his *Sefer Ha-Brit*, Rabbi Kimche did much to disprove the flimsy, albeit subtle arguments of the Gentiles. In that work he pointed out that the true religion is known from its results and, since the Jews were a people that behaved in accordance with the highest ethical ideals, their faith was beyond discussion. Nobody could doubt that the descendants of Abraham strove to live by the laws of the Torah and that they believed in one single God, without recognizing any other kind of divine power. Their behavior was moral: they did not kill or steal, practiced charity and were hospitable, all in contrast to the behavior of the Gentiles.

He particularly emphasized Jewish morality, pointed out how the Jews observed the Sabbath, obeyed their parents, did not give way to their passions, protected the sanctity and purity of family life, educated their children in the spirit of the Torah and paid high ransoms for the release of their brethren captured by the Crusaders, the self-styled fighters for Catholicism.

The Christians could not fail to admit that in those respects Rabbi Kimche was absolutely right, or that in those times the Jews were outstanding for their lofty moral standing, but they also argued that the Jews were not believers in the true faith because they did not recognize the divinity of Christ. What use were their good deeds, contended the Christian representatives, if they did not believe that Christ was born of Mary to redeem mankind? It was true that Christian men did evil deeds, but they were redeemed and purified by faith. The Jews could not be redeemed because they rejected the essential thing: belief in Christ. Thus Rabbi Kimche described the passionate religious arguments of that controversial period in his *Sefer Ha-Brit*.

The Rabbi went on to argue that the people of Abraham believed in God, creator of the world, whom no man could see, nor imagine, because "no man nor live being shall see Me." "How, then, can we believe that your great God entered a woman's womb and came out of it as a child, without the power of reason, mindless, ignorant, hungry and thirsty, a sucking babe at the mother's breast, that cries, sleeps and dies like any other human being? No, we cannot accept such a belief. My mind," he went on, "does not allow me to diminish by one iota the grandeur and sublimity of God."

The Christian scholars raised the question of the meaning of the verse: "The scepter shall not depart from Judah, nor a lawgiver from between his feet, until Shiloh come" (Genesis 49:10). They said that according to their faith it meant that the Jewish people would prosper from the time when they begin to believe in Jesus. On the other hand, they lost their kingdom, were expelled from their country and dispersed throughout the world because they had treated the son of God badly.

To that, Rabbi Kimche answered that "Shiloh" did not allude to Jesus, but to the patriarch Jacob's blessing of his sons, which meant, in his words, that the prosperity of the Jews would last until King David's time. And only then would the kingdom come into being. Therefore, what was the relationship between Jesus and that fact, since the kingdom of the House of David had been destroyed four hundred years earlier?

The arguments of the Christian scholars were refuted one after the other by Rabbi Kimche in his *Sefer Ha-Brit*. It is, moreover, interesting to note that he was allowed to attack so openly and directly the fundamental principles of the Catholic faith; this points to the existence of great religious freedom, which seems implausible for those times. Neither side was able to convince the other, but Rabbi Kimche's courageous pronouncement on Christianity in a fervently Catholic country is worthy of tribute.

This outstanding scholar and polemicist died in 1170 at the age of 65. His two sons, Rabbi Moses and Rabbi David Kimche, were also noted scholars. The elder, Rabbi Moses, was a prominent commentator and Hebrew grammarian. He wrote commentaries

---

*Many Jewish scholars prefer the translation "The scepter shall not depart from Judah, nor the ruler's staff from between his feet; so that tribute shall come to him and the homage of peoples be his."

on the Proverbs, Ezra, Nehemiah and Job. Of special interest is his book *Mahalach Shevileh Hada'at*, a methodical and accessible textbook, considered to be the first synthesized Hebrew grammar, which was translated into Latin with commentaries by the grammarian Rabbi Eliahu Bachur.

His second son, Rabbi David, was also a fine scholar, known in the Hasidic world as Redak.

Rabbi Moses Ben Nahman (Ramban): Kabbalist, Philosopher, and Renovator of the Jewish Community of the Land of Israel

Rabbi Moses Ben Nahman, known also as the Ramban and to Gentiles as Nahmanides, was one of the most prominent figures of his time. He was born in Spain in 1195 and died in Israel in 1271. He exerted a notable influence on religious Judaism through his authority as a scholar, interpreter of the Torah, prominent Kabbalist, philosopher and renovator of the Jewish community of the Land of Israel.

In the 12th century Spain was the leading Jewish cultural center in the world. The Talmudic nucleus of Babylon had disappeared and, although other centers existed in Italy, Germany and France, they did not attain the stature of the Sephardi.

The Jews of Spain had already won an important place in the Hebrew cultural world through such distinguished personalities as Rabbi Saadya Gaon, Rambam (Maimonides), Rabbi Abraham Ibn Ezra and Rabbi Yehuda Halevy.

In the 13th century there appeared in the Jewish firmament of Spain a new star that shone with a powerful light: Rabbi Moses Ben Nahman. He created a number of important works, including a commentary on the Torah, another on several chapters of the Talmud and the *Sefer Milhamot Hashem* (Book of God's Wars). He was among the first to teach the Kabbalah, and some researchers even attribute to him the authorship of *Ha-Emunah Ve-habitachon*, an important Kabbalistic work.

Moses Ben Nahman came of a family of intellectuals who lived in Gerona, in Catalonia. At the age of fifteen he was considered an authority on the Talmud, since he had already written several treatises on the subject that earned outspoken praise from the well-informed, who thought them truly masterly.

His brilliant mind, his sense of logic, and his capacity for investigative inquiry in approaching the most varied subjects became apparent from his early youth, when he dedicated himself to science and philosophy, studied medicine, and mastered several languages.

He also made a thorough study of the Kabbalah, for he was fascinated by a mystic world in which every word and even every letter of the Torah held a secret of Creation that he hoped would be revealed.

Among the most serious problems that the Jews had to face in the Gentile world were public arguments between representatives of Christianity and Judaism. The Jewish authorities had to appear at all the debates, where attendance was obligatory, in order to defend themselves against the insidious and imaginary charges brought by their adversaries. The Christian authorities were trying to convince the people that the Jews were evil and that their books contained denigrations of Christian faith and ethics.

Rabbi Ezekiel of Paris had participated in a religious dispute of that kind in 1240. That debate had resulted in an official order to burn the Talmud publicly. Nahmanides had to take part in a similar confrontation in Barcelona, in the presence of the King and his courtiers. His Christian opponent was the converted Jew Pablo Cristiani. Rabbi Moses Ben Nahman put up a fiery defense of the Jewish faith, showing marvelous skill in proving the falsity of the accusations put forward by his opponent. The debate, in which the Catholic spiritual leaders had so confidently expected victory, ended in a crushing victory for the Ramban and reassurance for the Jewish population. Nevertheless, a few religious fanatics refused to accept this defeat and, through intrigues and with the help of Pope Clement IV, succeeded in getting a decree ordering the expulsion of Rabbi Nahman from Spain. He was then about seventy and had to leave his home, his children and his yeshiva.

He decided to go to Israel, of which he had always dreamed. In his works he maintained that it was the sacred duty of every Jew to settle in the Promised Land, and then, in his old age, destiny paved the way for him to fulfill the precepts that he held to be the most important in the Torah.

In the late summer of 1267 he set out toward Israel and on 9 Elul he reached Jerusalem, the city of the luminous past, which he found in a state of utter dereliction. The entire Holy Land had been in ruins since the destruction of the Second Temple in 70 of the Common Era. Thereafter it had undergone the devastations of the Mongol invasion, with the slaughter of the Arab, Jewish, and Christian inhabitants. In that situation Rabbi Nahman fell prey to dejection. He walked the streets of Jerusalem weeping and mourning the death of his innocent brethren, put to the sword by a ruthless enemy.

Finally he overcame his grief and decided to reorganize Jewish community life. He arranged for the building of synagogues, houses of study and a large yeshiva, to which students began to arrive from various countries. The Jewish community gradually began to recover its former importance.

The Ramban was becoming increasingly famous among Jews everywhere. In addition to his initiative in seeking to restore the grandeur of the Land of Israel, he strove steadfastly to awaken love of Israel among the Jews of the Diaspora. He wrote to his children and friends in Spain and through his emotional descriptions of the Holy Land, he further strengthened the bond between his Spanish brethren and Israel. Perhaps he did not possess the poetic talent of a Yehuda Halevy, whose poems had succeeded in kindling a deep love of Zion, but the influence of his captivating personality was equally effective in sowing and strengthening the idea of a return to Israel among the Jews of Spain and the remainder of the Dispersion.

Some researchers assert that the Halukah (the fund collected in the Dispersion for the sustenance of the Jews in Israel) was erroneously called the "Rabbi Meyer Baal Hanes Fund" when it should have been called the "*Kupat* (Fund) Ramban."

The creative genius that had characterized Nahmanides in his youth was ever-present until the end of his days. In addition to the works mentioned he wrote the *Sefer Hazchuth* and *Sheelot Utshuvoth*, in which his wisdom, frankness of approach, and high moral standing were strongly apparent. He also wrote a philosophical treatise on the subject of family life and *piyutim* and *slichot* (religious poems).

Before he went to Israel his students and adepts begged him to give them a sign that should enable them to know the date of his death. Rabbi Nahman told them that on that day the tombstone on his mother's grave would be split. Several years later his students found a fissure on the spot indicated: the maestro had disappeared. This occurred in 1271; his remains were buried in Haifa.

Rabbi Moses Ben Nahman enriched the Jewish world with valuable spiritual treasures. His own sons and his disciples won fame through his wisdom and teachings, and by his works he lives on in the memory of the Jewish people.

Rabbi Bahye Ben Joseph Ibn Paquda: Religious Philosopher and Author of Hovot Halevavot

This famous Spanish-Jewish religious philosopher was the author of *Hovot Halevavot* (Duties of the Hearts) whose popularity has not decreased with the passing of the centuries.

Little is known about the life of Rabbenu Bahye, whose work just mentioned had an enormous influence on many generations of Jews during the passing of some eight hundred years since its publication down to the present day. Nor is it known with certainty in what years he lived; some historians place him in the 12th century and others in the 13th. Nevertheless, there is unanimous consensus regarding his *Hovot Halevavot*, which is generally considered an ethical work of the first magnitude, full of poetry and sanctity without equal; reading it, one feels impelled to observe elevated moral standards.

A profound thinker, the author believes that for man to believe in God and learn to love Him, he must have a lofty concept of Divinity. That was why this book was dedicated to extensive consideration of this theme and others of an ethical and religious nature.

Rabbenu Bahye was considered one of the greatest philosophers by the Jews as well as by the Arabs. His *Hovot Halevavot* appeals to the heart rather than to the mind. That is why it is read as if it were a poem, an exalted spiritual song, a hymn to God that arouses in the human breast a deep love of one's neighbor and of the Supreme Maker.

In his time, Spain had become the greatest Jewish cultural center in the world. The Talmudic center of Babylon had by then disappeared and the Jewish centers of Italy, Germany, and France had only just begun to develop. The Jews of Spain moved along a broad and richly productive path, guided by luminaries who shone with lights of their own.

Rabbi Bahye was a typical exponent of Spanish Jewry, outstanding for mental qualities and knowledge in both secular and Judaic fields, which made him one of the most illustrious personalities of that Golden Age.

Jewish life was becoming endangered, for the people's faith was weakening: free thinking, the investigative spirit and philosophy had taken root among the Jews, especially in Spain and Provence. Rabbi Bahye decided to take steps to counteract that influence and guide his brethren back into the right path.

Although he was well-versed in the Talmud and *Poskim*, he did not write any Halachic works (on Talmudic law), apparently because he took no particular interest in the subject. He liked to bring out the old ethical values of Jewish creation and the underlying wisdom of the Pentateuch—an aim that he achieved in his Torah commentary known as *Midrash Bahye al Ha-Torah*.

He brought new and original ideas to Judaism. He was not only a Talmud scholar but also a strong-minded philosopher who succeeded in dissipating the storm clouds that had gathered over the Jewish people, in putting an end to religious anarchy, and in defeating the enemies of the Jewish faith.

All his life he used his great spiritual resources in defence of the Torah and Judaism.

The system he used in explaining the Torah was far-reaching and eclectic, ranging from the literal to Kabbalistic interpretation with investigation of the secret meaning of the words.

His book *Hovot Halevavot* deservedly won fame through the Hebrew translation by Rabbi Yehuda Ibn Tibon. It comprises ten chapters. In his introduction Rabbi Bahye points out that he had read many books on the precepts and Talmudic law, but that none of the authors had thought necessary and ultimately did not take the trouble to explain things logically. He had therefore decided to be one of the first to tackle that task.

The first chapter, under the title *Sha'ar Haichud* (Gate of Uniqueness) contains philosophical considerations and sets forth reasoned arguments on the existence of a single, unique God, who created the world with a definite purpose. He further enumerates the attributes of the Divinity with following explanations, all of which are illustrated with examples taken from the Bible, the Talmud, and the Midrash.

The second chapter, *Sha'ar Habechina*, approached the subject of Divine Providence and its influence on nature, and also that of the precepts on human behavior.

Next comes the chapter *Sha'ar Avodath Elohim* (Gate of Divine Worship) which teaches how to serve God. Here the author takes the opportunity to combat the opinions of the heretics who reject the immortality of the soul, the concepts of punishment and reward, paradise and hell, knowledge of good and evil, and free choice. This "Gate" contains a beautiful dialogue between man's spirit and his body about virtues and sins, shame and cruelty, love and hate, happiness and sadness, and other things.

The fourth Gate, *Sha'ar Habitachon*, analyzes the virtue of faith, reiterating that by trusting in God the human being wins peace of mind. The author also considers the old ethical theological problem of the virtuous who lead harassed lives and the wicked who have a good time.

In the other chapters Rabbi Bahye teaches the virtues of modesty, of penitence, of spiritual equilibrium, of isolation, of love of God, and other things, illustrating his thoughts with examples taken from the Bible, the Talmud, the Midrash and a number of philosophers.

The influence of *Hovot Halevavot* on the Jewish world down the centuries has been enormous. The leading preachers still quote whole paragraphs from it, and in many Jewish communities special circles have been created under that name, in order to study that monumental creation night after night.

The scholar Chaim Joseph David Azulai (1727-1806) mentions in his famous work *Shem Hagdolim* (The Name of the Great) the custom of studying the *Hovot Halevavot* during the ten days of penitence between Rosh Hashana and Yom Kippur. Also the 16th century Rabbi Joseph Caro, author of the *Shulhan Arukh*, narrates in one of his works that a preacher sent from Heaven gave him advice on how to lead a life of purity, and his advice included studying every day a chapter of *Hovot Halevavot*.

The Hasidic movement considered it the most important Jewish ethical treatise. It is worth noting here that in the book *Tzena Urena* dedicated to Jewish women, Rabbenu Bahye is quoted repeatedly.

The *Tzena Urena* (Go Forth and Behold) was written by Rabbi Isaac Ashkenazi, of Janow, about 1623. The title was derived from a verse of the Song of Songs that reads "Go forth, O ye daughters of Zion."

The Jewish women were practically inseparable from this book, which was written in clear and accessible Yiddish. It contains narratives from the Pentateuch and samples of weekly readings from the Torah, alternating with legends and interpretations put in simple and very attractive form.

On Sabbath afternoons the Jewish women used to display their finest raiment and, in an atmosphere of peace, goodwill and purity, gathered together to read the *Tzena Urena* to the accompaniment of music. Rabbenu Bahye was frequently mentioned at these devout gatherings: "And saith Bahye, in the name of the Midrash, that King Solomon was the wisest of all men...."

When a maiden was married, the custom was to present her with a *Tzena Urena*—a work that was reprinted many times and is still a companion for Jewish women to this day.

The legacy of Rabbenu Bayhe has set its eternal seal on Judaism.

Rabbi Abraham Ben Samuel Abulafia: Philosopher, Kabbalist, and Jewish Community Leader

The Kabbalist Rabbi Abraham Ben Samuel Abulafia (1240-1300) was one of the most original scholars of his time. The Abulafia family lived in Spain for many years and produced outstanding Rabbis as well as noted commentarists, philosophers, Kabbalists and physicians (Abulafia in Arabic means "father of health").

Rabbi Abulafia was born in Saragossa, Spain, in 1240. Although he was educated with great care, he felt the lure of travel, from early childhood. Wherever he went, he sought the benefit of new experiences and as much knowledge as he could garner. His thirst for knowledge was insatiable. What fascinated him most were the secrets of Creation and of life, the search for which gave him no rest and urged him to explore paths of knowledge never before trodden. Finally he plunged his whole being into Jewish mysticism, a path he would follow to the end of his days. Study of Maimonides' *Guide for the Perplexed* did not fully satisfy him, because the matter-of-fact arguments set forth did not satisfy the feverish searchings of his restless mind, nor satisfy his longing to probe the deepest secrets of existence—a subject that the Kabbalah tackles extensively.

His effervescent imagination, the product of a highly emotive nature, impelled him to visit the Land of Israel, to seek out there the ten lost tribes that according to legend lived on the other bank of the river Sambatyon.[1] His efforts proved vain, and he returned from his journey depressed and disillusioned. Not only had he failed to achieve this aim but he had barely escaped the bloodthirsty Crusaders engaged in unrelenting battle against the equally cruel Moslems.

Rabbi Abulafia's restless investigative spirit was greatly stimulated through knowledge of the *Sefer Ha-Yetzira* (Book of Creation), which led him along the infinite path charted by the Kabbalah. After long study and introspection he decided in favor of practical Kabbalah, which he considered superior to the theoretical because through it one could ascend from one level to another on the way to the Holy Spirit. On the other hand, one who knew its secrets and techniques could, through combinations of words and letters, work miracles, orienting secret divine forces to produce supernatural things, even to hastening the coming of the Messiah.

Rabbi Abulafia was a fervent preacher of those ideas and set up yeshivot to propagate them systematically. He maintained that in order to attain spiritual ecstasy it was not enough to study; cleanliness, fasting and a life of extreme purity were needed, and to approach a state of sanctity physical desires had to be repressed. These were not mere words in his mouth; he set the example, becoming a genuine ascetic.

He diffused his teachings both by word of mouth and in writing. It is known that he created many works that strongly impressed the mystics of his and later times, but very few of them have survived. Notable among these are the *Sefer Olam Haba* (Book of the World to Come), in which he recommends isolation and asceticism; the *Sefer Hayashar* (Book of Rectitude) and the *Imreh Shefer* (Expressions of Gratitude), in which he approaches different Kab-

---

[1] A legendary river whose torrent-like waters tore up stones all week and rested only on the Sabbath.

balist problems in relation to the mysteries of Genesis, prophesying, according to his calculations, the date of the coming of the Messiah. This prophecy caused him serious problems, since it did not agree with other religious authorities of his time.

One authority, known as Rashba (initials of Rabbi Shlomo Ben Adereth), who held the position of Chief Rabbi of Barcelona, was his most virulent opponent, going so far as to call him a false messiah. Rabbi Abulafia remained unruffled and responded with two books: *Vezoth Lihuda* and *Sheva Netivot Ha-Torah*, in which his wisdom and lofty intellect shone forth to turn defense of his ideas into objective and crushing attacks against his accuser.

With his writings and sermons Rabbi Abulafia won many adepts and perpetuators and set his seal on the world of Jewish mysticism. His influence was felt for centuries, especially among the Kabbalists of Safed, among whom he held a privileged position.

The following anecdote is characteristic of his interesting personality: in 1280 Rabbi Abulafia visited Pope Nicholas IV in Rome. During the interview, he dared to point out that the Pope's belief was erroneous and invited him to convert to Judaism. As a result, he was sentenced to be burned at the stake; he must have escaped, since there is evidence of his presence in Messina, Sicily, ten years later and thereafter in Greece. He died about 1300.

Rabbi Jacob Ben Asher: The Baal Ha-Turim

In the Baal Ha-Turim's time, Spain was the most important Jewish cultural center in the world. The Talmudic center of Babylon had long ceased to exist, and the other Jewish centers in Italy, Germany and France did not have a high cultural level because the leading Jewish personalities of those times had emigrated to Spain.

There, the Jews encompassed a wide-ranging spectrum of creative activities. They could point to brilliant antecedents—men of genius, great minds, prominent figures, and sages who exerted their beneficial influence of a world of lofty aims, demonstrating the viability of reasoned harmony between the Torah and science, philosophy and religion.

The Baal Ha-Turim was typical of these fine Jewish scholars. His genius and his universal knowlege put him in the forefront of them.

Rabbi Jacob Ben Asher—this was the Baal Ha-Turim's real name—was one of eight sons of the great Talmudic academician Rabbi Asher Ben Yekhiel, known in the Jewish cultural world as *Ashre* or *Rosh*. He was born to a scholarly family in Germany. His father, Rabbi Yekhiel, was a recognized Torah and Kabbalah authority whom the people believed was a genuine worker of miracles. His son the Baal Ha-Turim inherited his fine qualities.

Initially the family lived in Germany, where they became one of the mainstays of German Jewry, but they went through one of the most harrowing times in history. Under the Emperor Rudolf I the Jews were subjected to relentless persecution and massacres. Many communities were decimated, and only part of them managed to escape and emigrate to other countries. Among them was the Rosh and his son the Baal Ha-Turim.

The family decided to settle in Spain, famous at the time as a Jewish spiritual center. Shortly thereafter the Spanish Jews got to know Rabbi Jacob, who won growing distinction in the world of the Torah.

Rabbi Jacob Ben Asher became one of the most influential personalities of all time and a highly original Talmudic scholar. His sole and exclusive world was that of the Torah and Halacha; for him, no other center of attraction was worthy of his attention.

A creative genius of the first magnitude, he possessed an astonishingly systematic turn of mind and produced a monumental work that for volume, range, form and content holds a prominent place in Halachic literature and became the principal guide to Jewish religious life. The work, titled the *Arbaah Turim*, is a compendium of religious laws divided in four sections, each of which is called a *tur*, or "row." The first section, *Tur Orach Chayim* (Way of Life), lists religious laws on prayers, benedictions, the Sabbath day, holidays and the days of atonement and fasting. Next comes the *Tur Yoreh Deah* (Teacher of Knowledge), which comprises religious rules covering the ritual slaughter of animals and birds for food, prohibited foods, the salting of meat, meat and dairy foods and other matters. The third section, *Tur Even Ha-Ezer* (Stone of Help), sets forth the rules that should govern marital life, betrothal, divorce, levirate and other things. The last part, the *Tur Hoshen Ha-Mishpat* (Breastplate of Judgment), deals with civil law, witnesses, judges, lawsuits, and the like.

The four *Turim* became the foundation of the *Shulhan Arukh* compiled at a later period by Rabbi Joseph Caro, who wrote a commentary on the *Turim* compendium under the name of *Beth Yosef*.

In elaborating his vast compendium of religious laws, the Baal Ha-Turim pursued the same purpose as the Rambam (Maimonides) with his *Mishne Torah*, which was considered a masterpiece and a model of its kind for its admirable construction and profound spiritual content, in addition to its clarity of exposition and power of synthesis. Since many Rabbis experienced difficulty in locating the less well-known Halachic elements, the Rambam undertook the task of ordering and arranging them in his *Mishne Torah*, extracting essentials and noting final conclusions. For these reasons his work had become a source of Torah and Halacha and was considered sacred by the Jewish people.

It was in the same spirit that Rabbi Jacob Ben Asher compiled his own monumental work, codifying the religious laws that governed Jewish life. The *Arbaah Turim* became a guide of the first magnitude for Jewish religious life and a permanent reference work for many Jewish scholars, who consistently relied on it.

The author of the *Turim* not only interpreted and codified the religious laws but also elaborated a Torah commentary based in every way on the Rambam and Rashi. He commented on the Torah with the elements of the Midrash and Kabbalah, aiming to interpret it through the *gematriah* (a method that consisted in finding the hidden meaning of the words by means of the numerical values of their component letters) and other Jewish mystical systems.

Initially he found it difficult to adapt to the cultural and religious life of his brethren in Spain, for the scholars of Germany, his home country, had followed very different paths. They avoided getting enmeshed in the maze of science and philosophy, subjects in which the Jewish scholars of Spain were masters, having created an admirable synthesis between religious and scientific knowledge. Rabbi Ben Asher could not understand why the great Rabbinical authorities of Spain devoted so much attention to teachings and philosophical systems foreign to the Hebrew spirit when they had the Torah and the Talmud, those inexhaustible sources of Jewish knowledge.

His Torah commentary known as *Baal Ha-Turim* (a name later applied to the author) has been source of spirit and intellectual delight to many generations. It appears in small print in many editions of the Pentateuch.

His life was rich in creative work but also in sorrow and suffering. He was physically weak and ailing, besides being very poor, though his father had been extremely rich. He gradually lost what money he possessed, so that his only source of income was his salary as a Rabbi in Toledo and he gave that to the poor.

His brother Rabbi Yehuda, who was also a noted religious authority, shared his destiny of poverty an ill-health.

The Baal Ha-Turim had many good friends who were ready to lend a hand, but he refused their offers, preferring to lead an exemplary life of humility and poverty.

Rabbi Ben Asher died in Spain in 1340. The work that he left to posterity brought him eternal fame and has had a marked influence on Jewish life.

Don Isaac Abravanel:
Sage, Statesman, Poet, and Interpreter of the Bible

On the anniversary of the death of Don Isaac Abravanel and 500 years after the Spanish Inquisition, it seemed appropriate to recall aspects of the life of one of the major personalities who became an eternal symbol.

The greatest among the spiritual personalities of his time—statesman, poet, Biblical interpreter and scholar—known among the Jews as Abravanel, was born about 1437 and died in 1510. He lived and created his works during the Golden Age in medieval Spain. He was one of the major figures in Jewish history, a luminary of the Dispersion who brought light to the Jewish firmament through his teachings and knowledge. In addition, through the important official positions he held in both Spain and Portugal, he several times saved Jews from conversion or from physical destruction or spiritual persecution.

But the great Jewish statesmen of Spain and Portugal not only dedicated themselves to politics but also realized that they belonged to a people that could only exist under the protection of the Torah and its laws.

They therefore did everything possible to ensure that the Jewish people did not depart from the Torah and its precepts. Rabbi Hasdai Ibn Shaprut formerly protected the yeshivot of Babylon and later ordered that similar yeshivot be built in Spain. Rabbi Samuel Ha-Nagid, without neglecting his responsibilities toward the Spanish state, found time to dedicate himself to teaching the Talmud in his yeshiva and to write a book on the subject.

A similar line of conduct was followed by Don Isaac Abravanel. Although he held the highest official position as minister of finance and saved the governments of Spain and Portugal from bankruptcy, he had a high regard for the Jewish people, Holy Writ and the Jewish faith and traditions. The important tasks of government did not worry him; as a cabinet minister, he continued his studies.

Don Isaac Abravanel was born in Lisbon, Portugal. According to the prologue to his book *Ma'aseh Hayeshua*, he descended from King David and his family moved to Spain after the destruction of the First Temple (586-587 before the Common Era).

In Don Abravanel's time, Spain was the leading Jewish cultural center in the world. The great Talmudic center of Babylon had long been in decline, but in Spain and Portugal it revived very strongly.

Down the generations Spanish Jewry produced scholars who earned world renown—authors of notable works that set their seal on Jewish life down to the present time, famous grammarians, experts on Holy Writ, mathematics, physicians, astronomers, poets, philosophers and statesmen.

At that time, Jewish genius was revealed in its full brilliance and beauty in all the fields of spiritual creation. That was why this period of Jewish history was known as the Golden Age.

Don Isaac Abravanel was typical of that Golden Age with his genius, his erudition, his significant and varied works as an interpreter of the Bible and as a statesman. His name became famous, even sacred among the Jews; he became a legend. In times of despair, he aroused the Jewish national feeling of conscience. He believed that the Jews were God's chosen people to enjoy eternal life and contentment, because God helps those in distress.

Little is known of his childhood. It is accepted that he was born in Lisbon, in the aristocratic cradle of Rabbi Yehuda's family. As with many other personalities of that period, Isaac Abravanel's youth is shrouded in the mists of history. It is known, however, that he published the philosophical treatise *Tsuroth Hayesodoth* and *Hemdath Hazkenim* on the subject of the faith. His teacher was Rabbi Joseph Ben Abraham Ibn Hiyyun, Chief Rabbi of Lisbon. In addition to his Torah studies, he dedicated himself to philosophy, enhancing his knowledge from the Rambam's *Moreh Nevuchim* (Guide for the Perplexed), Yehuda Halevy's *Kuzari* and other philosophical works of world significance.

Thanks to his popularity and fame, he was invited by King Alfonso of Portugal to become the kingdom's minister of finance, enjoying full confidence. With his lucid intelligence he quickly became a favorite of the court and the palace. It was rare for a Jew to enjoy such admiration and respect, especially at a time when the Spanish Church was beginning its anti-Jewish provocations. He was respected not only for his personal virtues but also for the vitally important services he rendered to the state. He rescued the royal treasury from bankruptcy and rose to the highest position that a Jew could attain. Everyone considered him to be the savior of Portugal.

In his moment of splendor, Don Isaac Abravanel did not forget that he was a descendant of the dynasty of David and that he was in duty-bound to uphold the tradition of his forefathers. At that time the king had occupied the coastal town of Tangier and taken many Arab prisoners who would be sold as slaves; among those prisoners were two hundred and fifty Jews. When Abravanel learned of their plight, he at once set up a committee to collect funds with the aim of securing their release. But after the death of King Alfonso, his son and successor Juan II unleashed a wave of persecution, bloodshed and tyrannical decrees and ordered the arrest of Isaac Abravanel.

Thanks to his friend Abravanel succeeded in escaping to Spain with his wife and two sons, José and Samuel. There he was welcomed by King Ferdinand and Queen Isabella and became their minister of finance, raising the kingdom's finances to a state of prosperity.

It was natural and inevitable that his position should awaken the resentment of enemies of the Jews. Their own kings had violated Catholic Church law that prohibited the Jews from holding public office. This had occurred when hard times lay not far ahead—the Inquisition and expulsion of the Jews from Spain were on the way. Money, however, proved stronger than the Christian government. As Abravanel could fill the empty coffers of the royal treasury to sustain the wars against the Arabs and ensure the country's maintenance, the ecclesiastic decree was not implemented.

For eight years Isaac Abravanel was a leading figure at court. Under his capable management, the whole country flourished. Trade developed; the country became rich. But amid the splendor and power, fear came to the Jews. Everywhere they contributed to the reconstruction and enrichment of countries, created cultural values, developed new ideas, forged ideals, yet when their creative work had been completed they were told that they were unwanted. Spain at that time was a typical example of ingratitude, moral decadence, dehumanization and brutality. Thus arrived the disastrous year 1492, when the Spanish king, to whom Abravanel had given so much financial and moral help, gave the order that all the Jews should leave Spain—those who wanted to stay would have to convert. Don Isaac Abravanel, together with his family, shared the unhappy fate of thousands of Spanish Jews who left their homeland. Abravanel settled in Naples, Italy, where he became the king's political counselor. Later he went on to Sicily and Corfu. The tragedy of his life was that he seemed predestined to save each country from its difficult situation but was unable to settle in any of them.

Abravanel wrote many books, but the most notable was his Bible commentary. For his interpretations, the Jewish people have sanctified him; his work brought the Bible to the people at all levels. In his explanations he sought to clarify from a historical point of view the different Jewish customs and the procedures of a government in the times when the Jews were in the Land of Israel. He also raised philosophical questions of interest to Jewish scholars concerning the resurrection of the dead, the eternity of the soul and divine protection. As a scholar and politician he described scenes of Jewish life in the times of the Judges, Kings and Prophets and based his interpretations on Rashi and the Rambam. In addition to his Biblical commentary he wrote twenty-four works on various religious subjects, seeking to lift up the hearts of the Jewish people, strengthen all those who had lapsed into despair and show that redemption was nigh. His comforting words were much needed in view of the disasters that had struck the Jewish people.

In his book *Sheeloth* he wrote: "Throughout the time that I spent beside kings in palaces I was never able to study the Torah; my time was wasted on vain things...to win success and honours, but it all disappears as if gone with the wind...." His Bible commentaries as well as his other works are full of sorrow and unhappiness, reflecting the situation of his exiled brethren.

In the history of the Jewish people his name is remembered as that of a saint, who dedicated himself completely to the people from which he emerged.

Rabbi Joseph Caro:
Compiler of the Shulhan Arukh

The year 1975 marked the 400th anniversary of the death of one of the outstanding figures of all time, whose genius and wisdom shed light on the Jewish cultural firmament: Rabbi Joseph Caro, the famous Sephardi sage and Kabbalist who compiled the *Shulhan Arukh*.

This grandiose work, sought after and acknowledged by the whole people is based on Rabbenu Jacob Ben Harosh's famous *Four Columns*. It was known in all the corners of the Dispersion, and its influence is as strong as ever after 400 years. Hardly a Jewish traditional family is without its own copy of the *Shulhan Arukh*, which serves as the daily guide of our people. Less well-educated Jews use the *Compendium of the Shulhan Arukh*, which has been edited without commentaries in order to be accessible to everyone. The scholar, however, can undertake detailed study in the four large volumes, which include the explanations and commentaries of the most renowned Ashkenazi sages.

To this day all the Rabbis and sages base their rulings on the principles of the *Shulhan Arukh* bearing on Jewish life throughout the Dispersion.

And although its text includes the commentaries of the famous Polish scholar Rabbi Moses Isserles of Cracow (the Rema) and of other Ashkenazi sages, the original text is largely the work of the compiler and remains thus today.

It is difficult to characterize this genius, whose words carried weight in tumultuous times and even today are law to religious Jewry. The most appropriate thing to say is that everything created during previous generations was uplifted by his pure and noble spirit, to serve as a guide for future generations.

His rulings were sanctified as if they had been handed to Moses in Sinai, and there is no doubt that Rabbi Joseph Caro, compiler of the *Shulhan Arukh*, has justly won fame in Jewish history for having clarified and defined Jewish law for the whole Jewish people.

In his preface to the *Shulhan Arukh*, Rabbi Caro pointed out that his book comprised all the laws and rulings of the Babylon and Jerusalem Talmud, of the *Tosafot, Safra, Mekhiltah* and others. Truly one needed a remarkable memory and the brain of a genius to research the origin of each law and ruling, as also to revise and check the different commentaries. Often Rabbi Caro had to deal with laws and problems on which there were different opinions, all coming from distinguished scholars and usually contradictory. To determine which was right he set up a kind of Clarification Court consisting of three scholars considered the greatest researchers of Jewish law: Alfasi, Rambam and Rashi. If two of these scholars agreed on any ordinance, their opinion was adopted as a ruling and the author established it as practice of law. Rabbi Caro worked for twenty years on this vast compendium, which initially was edited under the title of *Beth Yosef* and in commentary form under the title *Arbaa Turim 1* (Four Columns).

Later the author was able to determine that the form and content of his work were viable for scholars and not for the people, who did not need investigative details of each law but a practical guide setting forth the laws clearly and briefly.

Rabbi Caro thereupon abridged his work and edited another under the title of *Shulhan Arukh*, which contained the practical side accessible to all. This work was first edited in Venice, in four parts: *Orah Hayim*, laws bearing on prayer, the Sabbath and other festivities; *Yoreh Dea*, the laws of animal processing and unclean animals; *Even Ha-Ezer*, laws governing family life; and *Hoshen Mishpat*, laws governing economic problems.

The Ashkenazi scholars immediately recognized the importance of the *Shulhan Arukh* and the grandeur of its author, as well as its value for the broad Jewish masses; but they held that their own rulings should be added.

It should not be forgotten that in those times Poland was the center of Torah learning, and Jews from all parts of the world went there to get authoritative opinions. That was why the contributions of Ashkenazi scholars and Ashkenazi customs were so important.

Two years after the appearance of the *Shulhan Arukh*, the acknowledged leader of the Polish Rabbis, the noted scholar and sage Rabbi Moses Isserles (the Rema) introduced it in Poland and added new laws, statutes and addenda, since many customs of the Jews of those regions, which were respected and venerated by the Rabbis, had not been taken into account by Rabbi Caro.

Since Rabbi Caro's law compendium was titled *Shulhan Arukh* (The Prepared Table), the Rema called his addenda *Mapah* (Tablecloth). With those addenda, the *Shulhan Arukh* became the foundation of the future development of religious Judaism.

And since then, to live according to the *Shulhan Arukh* has been practically axiomatic for every observant Jew. It may be reliably stated that for generations the *Shulhan Arukh* has been one of the most popular books in Jewish homes and remains ever present in synagogues and places of study, where it has been one of the books most frequently consulted.

Being accessible alike to the scholar and the man-in-the-street, it guides and sets its seal on the conduct of every Jew.

The *Shulhan Arukh* became the book most widely accepted by the whole people and was held to be "celestial law."

Some scholars initially opposed the rulings of the *Shulhan Arukh* and of the Rema's *Mapah*, believing they might exert a negative influence on subsequent study of the sources, but in time the scholars of both East and West began to acknowledge it as the practical law governing Jewish life.

With regard to the Rema's addenda, a legend narrates that Rabbi Joseph Caro, a leading Kabbalist, dreamed that was urged to speed up his work, because there was a noted scholar in Poland who planned to write a similar work. The legend adds that when Rabbi Caro wrote down a law in Safed, it was mystically communicated to the Rema, who immediately wrote his commentary to it.

Rabbi Joseph Caro was born in Toledo, Spain, in 1488, that is, four years before the Expulsion. His father, Rabbi Ephraim, who was among the victims of the unjust law, emigrated with his family to Portugal, but they were expelled from there also. After much hardship they managed to reach Turkey and settle in the city of Adrianople. There the young Joseph won fame: at the age of thirty he was considered an outstanding scholar, known as "Maran." It was then that he began to write his famous work, which he finished in Safed together with other writings.

Many Sephardic Rabbis and other Jews had begun to settle in Israel during that period, and both Jerusalem and Safed became Torah centers. Safed especially became known as the "city of the Kabbalists." Rabbi Caro arrived in Safed in 1536 and lived there until 1575, when he died at the age of eighty-seven.

Rabbi Moses Isserles (The Rema):
Commentator of the Shulhan Arukh

The year 1972 was the 400th anniversary of the death of one of the great luminaries of the Dispersion. His memorial stone bears the inscription: "From Moses son of Maimon, the Rambam, till Moses the Rema, there was no other equal to Moses."

Until 1939, when World War II broke out, the Polish Jews used to commemorate his death, which occurred during Lag Ba-Omer. Many would come to the city of Cracow to visit the grave of this genuine saint, which proves the significance of the person and his work. As the most prominent leader of his generation, he earned worldwide recognition; his every word was law to posterity. The most fitting description of his personality is to say that everything created in earlier generations was concentrated in his figure, for revision and projection to posterity. His name, Rabbi Moses Isserles, is not thus remembered, nor are the titles of the thirty-three books that he wrote; all are known by his acronym Rema. And Rema holds the same rank as the Rambam.

His laws were accepted as if they had been given by Moses at Sinai; and there is no doubt that he won an eternal place in Jewish history through his explanations and adaptation of the *Shulhan Arukh* for the Jewish masses.

In those times Poland was the center of study of the Torah, and the whole Jewish world made their inquiries there for rulings on religious questions.

No Jews had lived in Spain or Portugal for several decades, except for the few crypto-Jews. Those in France and Italy were oppressed; nor was it different in Germany.

Study was therefore concentrated in the distant eastern countries of Asia and Africa. Poland was the only European refuge where study of the Torah went on and the results were passed on among the broad Jewish masses.

The chronicles of those times describe Jewish life in the Rema's time, emphasizing its spiritual nature. Every important community had a yeshiva and provided its principal with upkeep of needy children, whose families required help. They also pointed out that the honor of the Torah was sustained at a high level, since all the rules of Talmudic law, like the laws of the Torah, were applied in practice in the lives of the Jews in Poland. On the other hand, they were given a measure of self-rule through a Rabbinical court by royal decree, so that the spiritual leaders, who knew the laws of the Torah and Talmud, practically became official leaders of the communities, as in the times of the Amoraim and Geonim of Babylon.

The Rema was born in Cracow in 1520. His father, Israel, was one of the richest men in Poland and a member of the Community Council. Of German descent, he built a large synagogue with his own money in 1533 in memory of his wife Malka, daughter of Eliezer, who had died prematurely. Initially it was known as the New Synagogue. Soon after the death of the great genius it was renamed Rema's Synagogue.

From an early age Moses showed admirable qualities and an enormous appetite for study. His teachers soon realized that here was a pure and noble heart that would shed light on the world. He was a student of the famous principal of the Lublin yeshiva, Rabbi Shalom Shakhneh, who later married him to his daughter. Young

Moses remained faithful to his teacher's method of study, which consisted in adopting the sentences of those judges that coincided with the opinions of the Talmud sages and creating sophisms to resolve the controversy between the Gemara and the judges.

After his marriage he founded a yeshiva in Cracow and, as he was also very rich, he generously provided the means of upkeep for a large number of students. Immediately students and scholars from all over the world began to arrive at the yeshiva, and Cracow became the counterpart of Sura and Pumbedita, the ancient study centers of Babylon.

The Rema's name became world famous as a judge and for his commentary on Rabbi Joseph Caro's *Shulhan Arukh*; this commentary was convincing proof of the Rema's genius.

His profound knowledge enabled him to detect some shortcomings in the religious laws as published at the time, and he undertook to correct them, composing a new series of laws that were clear, precise, and suitable for the people as a whole.

At the same time the great Sephardic scholar Rabbi Joseph Caro was working on the same problem; he composed an interpretation of the Turim that he published under the name of *Beth Yosef*.

Rabbi Isserles was not in full agreement with that book and worked out his own interpretation, which served to complete many laws. And when the popular *Shulhan Arukh* appeared at a later date, the Rema pointed out the fact that the author, being Sephardi, had not taken into account the rulings of Ashkenazi scholars and had omitted many customs of the Polish and German communities. He completed it all in the form of "Remarks" that were introduced into the *Shulhan Arukh*, and in the same way added new rulings based on popular customs that to him were as important as the laws of the Gemara.

Just as Rabbi Caro's compendium of laws was titled *Shulhan Arukh* (The Prepared Table), so Rabbi Isserles's "Remarks" bore the title of *Mapah* (Tablecloth).

With those additions, the *Shulhan Arukh* became the foundation of religious Judaism in future generations. All his life, the Rema concerned himself with the problem of what is permitted and what is prohibited. In his spare time he studied philosophy, Kabbalah and scientific disciplines, firmly believing that secular studies were not an end but a means to know the Torah better.

Many considered Rabbi Isserles a reincarnation of the Rambam, since the writings and efforts of both these geniuses were aimed at making the laws more accessible to all.

He had a special fondness for the Hebrew language and even in the face of opposition from other scholars, allowed treatises on astronomy or stories to be read on the Sabbath simply because they were written in Hebrew.

Although he was very strict in matters of observance of the precepts, he sometimes showed flexibility—for instance, he did not allow divorce on grounds of childlessness, arguing that "it is a worse transgression to destroy a family than to die childless."

In consideration of the 400th anniversary of his death, one feels bound to mention the miracle that occurred at the Rema's synagogue and grave, which are still in good condition.

The fury of the Nazi killers and their Polish helpers not only fell upon live Jews but also upon the dead. Nearly all the synagogues in Poland were razed and Jewish cemeteries in towns and villages were desecrated. Tombstones could be seen in the roads, where they were used for paving materials, and inscriptions with Jewish lettering were plainly visible.

There was one exception: the Jewish cemetery of Cracow and its synagogue. Before leaving Poland I saw the synagogue and the adjacent cemetery. In both places busy hands were at work preserving and renovating the ancient structure. The inscriptions on the tombstones of the Rema, his father and his adherents or relations were easily legible, as were those on the graves of other famous personalities.

A particular source of interest was the synagogue's fine library, of which a former student of a Lithuanian yeshiva was the custodian and which catalogued famous titles brought in from a number of places, including private libraries.

The Communist government met all the costs of restoration. That occurred before 1960, when thousands of foreign tourists visited and the Poles were seeking to rehabilitate themselves from their guilt in the eyes of the world. At that time the Rema's synagogue and the adjoining cemetery were considered centers of attraction and historical treasures.

But it was not long before anti-Semitic persecution broke out afresh against the tiny remnants of the Jewish population of Poland. The Rema's synagogue was closed, and the cemetery was left in a state of neglect.

The Rema's light shone for fifty-two years: it was extinguished on the day of Lag Ba-Omer in 1572, but his memory lives on in the hearts of the people, both for his monumental work and for the pure and holy life that he led.

Index

Aaron, 121
Abai, 105
Abba, Samuel Bar, *also known as* Samuel Yarhinai, 94-96
Abderrahman III, Caliph, 203
Aboab, Isaac, 44, 84, 85
Abraham, Rabbi, of Kalisk, 43, 70
Abraham, Rabbi Yehuda Ben, 225
Abraham, the Patriarch, 28, 97, 98, 104, 123, 124, 230, 232, 247
Abravanel, Don Isaac, 101, 265-269
Abulafia, Rabbi Abraham Ben Samuel, 18, 25, 126, 258-260
Abulafia, Rabbi Jacob, 59
Adereth, Rabbi Shlomo Ben, 260
Aggadah, 29, 62
Ahab, King, 29, 31, 32
Ahiah of Shiloh, 28
Akiba, Rabbi, 98, 99
Alerif, Grand Vizir Abu Alcazar Ibn, 214-215

Alexander Janus, 197
Alexander the Great, 39
Alfasi, Rabbi Isaac, 73, 222, 271
Alfonso, King of Portugal, 267
Alharizi, Rabbi Yehuda, 222
Alkabetz, Rabbi Solomon Ben Moshe Halevi, 43, 58, 69-72, 120
Alroy, David, 35
Alsheikh, Rabbi Moses Ben Chaim, 43, 61, 71, 120
Amimar, 106
Amran Gaon, Rabbi, 125
Ananias, 39
Antiochus Epiphanus, 39
Apiriyon Shlomo (by Rabbi Solomon Alkabetz), 72
Arbaa Turim 1 (Four Columns), by Joseph Caro, 271
Arbaah Turim (by Rabbi Jacob Ben Ashef), 262, 263

Arele, Rabbi, 191
Ari Noem (of the Mahari Modena), 59
Ari, *see* Luria, Rabbi Isaac Ben Shlomo
Artzot Hachaim (by Rabbi Meyer Libush Malbim), 134
Arukh (by Rabbi Nathan Ben Yekheil), 245
Asharoth (by Rabbi Solomon Ibn Gabirol), 215
Asher, Rabbi Jacob Ben, *also known as* Baal Ha-Turim, 261-264
Ashi, 106
Ashkenazi, Rabbi Bezalel, 57
Ashkenazi, Rabbi Chaim, 61
Askari, Rabbi Elazar, 120
Atar, Rabbi Chaim Ben, *also known as* Or Hachayim, 73, 74, 76
Auerbach, Rabbi Chaim, 135
Avrothi, Abraham, 58
Azariah, 39
Azulai, Chaim Joseph David, 62, 257

Baal Ha-Turim, *see* Asher, Rabbi Jacob Ben
Baal Ha-Turim (by Rabbi Jacob Ben Asher), 264
Baal Shem Tov, Rabbi Israel, *also known as* Besht, 28, 48, 54, 75, 76, 85-88, 123, 140-142, 144, 146, 148-154, 156-158, 161, 165-167, 173, 174, 176, 179, 180, 184, 189
Baal Shem Tov's Testament, 85, 86
Bachur, Rabbi Elihu, 249
Bait Hadash (New House), by Rabbi Joel Sirkus, 129
Baruch, Rabbi, of Mainz, 47
Bavah Bathrah, 97

Be'er Hagolah, 114
Beirow, Rabbi Jacob Moses, 43
Belshazzar, King, 38
Benhamu, Don Shelomo, 9
Benjamin of Tudela, 39
Ben Kocheleth (by Rabbi Samuel Ha-Nagid), 215
Bergson, Mrs. Temerl, 171
Berith Halevi (by Rabbi Solomon Alkabetz), 120
Besth, *see* Baal Shem Tov, Rabbi Israel
Beth Hashem (by Rabbi Solomon Alkabetz), 72
Beth Yosef (by Rabbi Joseph Caro), 120, 263, 271, 276
Bezalel, Rabbi Yehuda Liwa (Loew) Ben, *also known as* Maharal of Prague, 77-81, 114
Bible, 17, 23, 25, 28, 83, 95, 104, 110, 118, 134, 198, 203, 225, 230, 232, 256, 268, 269
Biyani, Samuel, 58
Bunem, Rabbi Simhah, of Przysucha, 161-164, 169-173

Caro, Rabbi Joseph, 43, 56, 69-71, 120, 257, 262, 270-273
Clement IV, Pope, 252
Cohen, Rabbi Shlomo David, 45
Compendium of the Shulhan Arukh, 270
Cristiani, Pablo, 251
Cyrus, King, 33
Czartoriski, Count Adam, 190

Daniel, 17, 23, 34, 35, 38-41, 124, 127
Daniel, Book of, 38
Darius, King, 40
David, King, 123, 248, 366

de León, Rabbi Moses, *also known as* Rabbi Moses Ben Shem Tov de León, 18, 22, 25, 126
Derech Hachaim (by Rabbi Yehuda Liwa Ben Bezalel), 114
Deuteronomy, Book of, 100, 101, 110
Divreh Emet (by Rabbi Jacob Isaac Horowitz), 167
Dybbuk—Between Two Worlds, the (by Samuel An-ski), 59

Eidelis, Rabbi Samuel Eliezer, *also known as* Maharsha, 129
Elijah, *also known as* Eliyahu Ha-Navi, 21, 28-32, 34, 35, 57, 59, 119, 130, 154
Elimelech, Rabbi, of Lizensk, 88, 89, 161, 165-167
Emden, Rabbi Jacob, 90-92, 125
Emek Bracha (Blessed Valley), by Rabbi Abraham, 65, 130
Emunot ve-Deot (Of Beliefs and Ideas), by Rabbi Saadya Gaon, 117, 195, 199-201
Esau, 104, 123
Etz Hachaim (Tree of Life), by Chaim Vital, 62
Exodus, Book of, 104
Eybenschütz, Rabbi Jonathan, 90-92
Ezekiel, 34
Ezekiel, Rabbi of Paris, 251
Ezra, 124
Ezra, Book of, 249
Ezra, Rabbi Abraham Ben, 202
Ezra, Rabbi Abraham Ibn, 98, 229-232, 246, 250

Falger, Rabbi Jacob Joseph, 158
Falkon, Rabbi Elyah, 58

Ferdinand, King, 267
Four Columns (by Rabbenu Jacob Harosh), 270
Francis, Rabbi Mordecai, 57
Frank, Jacob, 19, 91
Franz Josef II, Emperor, 145

Gabirol, Rabbi Solomon Ibn, 72, 80, 215, 216
Gamliel, Rabbi, 124
Gemara, 17, 22, 34, 35, 47, 80, 85, 100, 101, 106, 110, 111, 134, 135, 143, 148, 156, 180, 224, 226, 276
Genesis, Book of, 94, 98, 115, 248
Gershom, Rabbi, of Kitev, 75, 76, 148
Gershon, Rabbenu, *also known as* Maor Hagolah, 210-212, 218
Grunblat, Rabbi Tevi, 182
Guide for the Perplexed (by Rabbi Moses Ben Maimon), 258, 267
Guide of the Wayward (by Rabbi Moses Ben Maimon), 235
Gur Aryeh, 114

Habbus, King, 214
Hacohen, Joseph, 86
Hacohen, Rabbi Moses, 54
Hacohen, Rabbi Sabbatai, 121
Hadarshan, Rabbi Moses, 245
Ha-Emunah Ve-habitachon, 251
Hafni, Rabbi Samuel Ben, 101
Ha-Hasid, Yehuda, 18
Hai Gaon, Rabbi, 101, 196
Halacha (Talmudic legislation), 47, 226, 263
Halevi, Rabbi Meyer, of Apt, 162-164
Halevy, Yehuda Ben Samuel, 220-

223, 232, 250, 252, 267
Halperin, Meyer Libush Ben Yeheiel Michael, 134
Ha-Nagid, Rabbi Samuel, 213-216, 266
Hananiah, Rabbi, 113
Hanasi, Rabbi Abraham Bar Hai, 98
Hanassi, Rabbi Yehuda, 95
Ha-Navi, Elyahu, 27
Hanes, Rabbi Meyer Baal, 253
Hanoch, (Enoch), 30
Hanoch of Alexander, Rabbi, 172
Hanoch, Rabbi Moses Ben, 207-209
Harosh, Rabbenu Jacob Ben, 270
Haruveni, David, 35, 120
Hatash, Rabbi Hirsch, 22
Hatora Vehamitzvah, 134
Hayeh Maharan (by Rabbi Nahman of Bratzlav), 177
Hayug, Yehuda Ibn, 230
Hazan, Yehoshuah (brother of David Ben Zakai), 198
Heinrich I, Emperor, 212
Hemdath Hazkenim (by Don Isaac Abravanel), 267
Herman, Professor, 102
Hersh, Rabbi Zevi, 172
Hezikiah, 124
Hidushe Aggadah (by Rabbi Samuel Eliezer Eidelis), 129
Hidushe Halachoth (by Rabbi Samuel Eliezer Eidelis), 129
Hilchot Akum, 107
Hilhot Teshuvah (by Rabbi Moses Ben Maimon), 157
Hilhot Yetzirah (Laws of Creation), 114
Hispalensis, Jean, (formerly Abraham Ben David), 215

Hiyyum, Rabbi Joseph Abraham Ibn, 267
Horowitz, Rabbi Jacob Isaac, *also known as* Hozeh of Lublin, 160-163, 169, 171, 172
Horowitz, Rabbi Yeshayahu Halevi, *also known as* Shela, 64-68, 130, 160
Hosea, 43
Houdini, Harry, 102
Hovot Halevot (by Rabbi Bahye Ben Joseph Ibn Paquda), 246, 254, 256, 257
Hozeh of Lublin, *see* Horowitz, Rabbi Jacob Isaac

Id Hakadosh, *see* Isaac, Rabbi Jacob, of Przysucha
If No Higher (by I.L. Peretz), 184
Imreh Shefer (Expressions of Gratitude), by Rabbi Abraham Ben Samuel Abulafia, 259
Isaac, the Patriarch, 28, 123, 124, 217
Isaac, Rabbi (author of *Or Zarua*), 47
Isaac, Rabbi Jacob, of Przysucha, *also known as* Id Hakadosh, 161, 162, 169, 171, 172, 186
Isaac, Rabbi Levi, of Berdichev, 123, 159, 178, 189
Isaac, Rabbi, of Vienna, 126
Isabella, Queen, 267
Isaiah, 230
Ish Hasid Hayah (There Was Once a Hasid), 27, 32
Ismach Lev (Lift Up Your Heart), by Rabbi Nahum of Tchernobyl, 159
Isserles, Rabbi Moses, *also known as*

Rema, 114, 116, 128, 129, 271-278

Jacob, 104, 124, 248
Jacob, Joseph Ben, 198
Jehoiada, Benyahu Ben, 111
Jeremiah, 34
Jezebel, 31, 32
Job, 230
Job, Book of, 117, 246, 249
Jonas, 123
Joseph, 105
Joseph, Rabbi Jacob, of Polna, 148, 167
Josephus Flavius, 34, 35
Joshua, 123
Judges, Book of, 269

Karteh Uphalteh (by Jonathan Eybenschütz), 92
Kaspi, Rabbi Joseph Ibn, 245
Katz, Rabbi Elihau, 159
Kav Hayashar, 111
Keter Malchut (by Rabbi Solomon Ibn Gabirol), 215, 216
Keter Shem Tov, 148
Khmelnitsky, Bogdan, 91
Kimche, Rabbi David, 248-249
Kimche, Rabbi Joseph, 203, 245-248
Kings, Book of, 269
Kochba, Bar, 35
Korban Minha (Book of Prayers for Women), 125
Kozenitzer, Rabbi Ezekiel, 171
Kuzari (by Rabbi Yehuda Ben Samuel Halevy), 220-222, 247, 267

Lachmi, Rabbi Abraham, 58
Lakish, Rabbi Simon Ben, 94
Lamentations of Jeremiah, 21

Lavrath, Dunash Ben, 202, 205, 207
Lecha Dodi (by Rabbi Solomon Alkabetz), 45, 69-72, 120
Leib, Rabbi Moshe, 146
Leib, Rabbi Yehuda, 134
Lelever, Rabbi David, 163
Letters about the Yemen and the Conversation (by Rabbi Moses Ben Maimon), 235
Levi, Rabbi Isaiah Ben Levi, 119
Leviticus, Book of, 110-121
Likute Etzot (by Rabbi Nahman of Bratzlav), 177
Likute Maharan (by Rabbi Nahum of Bratzlav), 177
Likute Tefilot (by Rabbi Nahman of Bratzlav), 177
Lisser, Rabbi Jacob, 125
Luria, Rabbi Isaac Ben Shlomo, *also known as* Ari, 19, 25, 28, 43, 44, 54, 55-66, 69, 70, 85, 106, 117, 120, 125, 127, 130, 139-141, 156, 157, 161, 177, 257
Luria, Rabbi Solomon, *also known as* Maharshal, 119, 128, 129
Luzzatto, Moses Chaim, 20

Ma'aseh Hayeshua (by Don Isaac Abravanel), 266
Machberet Menachem (by Menachem Ben Saruk), 203-205
Maggid of Mezricz, *also known as* Rabbi Ber, 86, 144, 156, 161, 165-167, 179, 190
Mahalach Shevileh Hada'ot, 249
Maharal of Prague, *see* Bezalel, Rabbi Yehuda Liwa Ben
Maimon, Rabbi Moses Ben, *also known as* Rambam, Maimonides,

14, 35, 36, 66, 73, 98, 100, 101, 102, 104, 106, 107, 117, 118, 122, 125, 128, 129, 157, 179, 195, 198, 230, 233-240, 250-253, 258, 263, 269, 271, 274
Maimon, Rabbi Solomon, 83
Maimonides, *see* Maimon, Rabbi Moses Ben
Malachi, 29
Malbim, Rabbi Meyer Libush, 132-135
Manot Halevi (by Rabbi Solomon Alkabetz), 72
Maor Einayim (Splendor of the Eyes), by Rabbi Nahum, 159
Mapah (by Rabbi Moses Isserles), 272, 276
Margulis, Reuben, 22
Matityahu, Rabbi, 225
Meir, Morenu Harav, Rabbi, 65
Mekor Chayim (Source of Life), by Rabbi Solomon Ibn Gabirol, 215, 216
Menachem, Rabbi, 204
Mendele, Rabbi, of Kotzk, 162, 172, 173
Mendelsohn, Moses, 145
Mendel, Rabbi Menahem, of Vitebsk, 43, 70, 179, 180
Mendes, Grace, 71
Menorat Hamaor (Chandelier of Light), by Rabbi Isaac Abohav, 84, 85
Meshulan, Rabbi, the Hasid, 54
Meyer, Rabbi Aaron Ben, 197
Meyer, Rabbi Isaac Ben, 219, 224
Meyer, Rabbi Joseph Ben, *also known as* Tam, Rabbenu Jacob, 203, 205, 219, 224, 225-228, 230
Meyer, Rabbi Samuel Ben, *also known as* Rashbam, 203, 217, 219, 224-228
Meyer, Tanna Rabbi, 108, 109
Mezibover, Rabbi Baruch, 178
Midrash, 33, 40, 62, 80, 85, 86, 110, 111, 113, 256, 257, 263
Midrash Bahye al Ha-Torah (by Rabbi Bahye Ben Joseph Ibn Paquda), 255
Mikra Kodesh, 134
Miriam (Moses' sister), 123
Mishna, 17, 22, 36, 62, 78, 80, 100, 101, 120, 151, 180, 236
Mishne Torah, see Yad Hazakah
Mivchar Hapninim (by Rabbi Solomon Ibn Gabirol), 216
Mizmor Shir Leyom Hashabbat, 79, 80
Molho, Rabbi Solomon, 19, 120
Montefiore, Moses, 133
Moses, 17, 24, 27, 28, 29, 123, 161
Moses, Rabbi, of Córdoba, 25, 43, 66, 69, 120, 139
Munk, Rabbi Solomon, 215
"My Heart Is in the East and I Am in the West" (poem, by Rabbi Yehuda Ben Samuel Halevy), 223

Naboth, 31, 32
Nahman, Rabbi, of Bratzlav, *see* Simha, Rabbi Nahman Ben
Nahman, Rabbi Moses Ben, *also known as* Ramban, 18, 122, 124, 126, 250
Nahor, Rabbi Isaac Sageh, 18, 126
Nahum, Rabbi, of Tchernobyl, 155-159
Nassi, Joseph, 71
Nathan, Rabbi, of Córdoba, 208, 209

Nathan, Rabbi, of Nemirow, 177
Natronai Gaon, Rabbi, 125
Nebuchadnezzar, King, 38
Nehemiah, Book of, 124, 249
Nethivoth Olam (by Rabbi Yehuda Liwa Ben Bezalel), 114
Nicholas IV, Pope, 260
Noam Elimelech (by Rabbi Elimelech), 166, 167
Numbers, Book of, 109, 162

"One Hundred Prayers" (by Rabbi Natronai Gaon), 125
Or Hachayim, *see* Atar, Rabbi Chaim Ben
Or Hachayim (Light of Wisdom), by Rabbi Chaim Ben Atar, 22, 74, 75
Or Zaruah (by Rabbi Isaac of Vienna), 126

Palkira, Rabbi Shem Tov, 215
Paquda, Rabbenu Bahye Ben Joseph Ibn, 22, 246, 254-257
Pentateuch, 17, 74, 98, 100, 101, 134, 230, 232, 240, 246, 257, 264
Peretz, I.L., 184
Perle, Rabbi Meyer, 79
Philo of Alexandria, 117
Pirke Avot, 80, 113, 114
Plato, 222
Poniatowski, Count Joseph, 190
Pristitzer, Rabbi Mendele, 166
Prophets, Book of, 269
Proverbs, Book of, 246, 249
Psalms, Book of, 123, 230

Rabad, 245
Rabah, 105
Ralbag, 101

Rambam, *see* Maimon, Rabbi Moses Ben
Ramban, *see* Nahman, Rabbi Moses Ben
Ranay, Rabbi Joseph, 44
Rashbam, *see* Meyer, Rabbi Samuel Ben
Rebecca, 123
Recanti, Rabbi Menachem Ben Benjamin, 129
Reincarnations (by Rabbi Chaim Vital), 63
Rema, *see* Isserles, Rabbi Moses
Rokeach, Rabbi Eliezer Ben Yehuda, 18, 47, 51-55, 126
Rudolph I, Emperor, 262
Rumakis, Ibn, 208
Ruth, 21

Saadya Gaon, Rabbi, 101, 117, 125, 195-201, 250
Sabbatai, Rabbi Israel Bar, *also known as* Maggid of Kozienice, 169, 188-191
Salanter, Rabbi Israel, 124
Saloun, L., 114
Samson, 217
Samuel, 100, 101, 217
Samuel, Book of, 100
Samuel, Rabbi Meyer Ben, 219
Saruk, Rabbi Menachem Ben, 73, 202-207
Saul, King, 100, 101
Scholem, Gershom, 20
Seder Hatefilot, 125
Sefer Ha-Brit (by Rabbi Joseph Kimche), 247, 248
Sefer Ha-Galui, 246
Sefer Hagilgulim (The Book of Transmigrations), by Rabbi Chaim

Vital, 117
Sefer Hairah, 54
Sefer Hakanauth (by Rabbi Jacob Emden), 116
Sefer Hamidoth (by Rabbi Nahman of Bratzlav), 86, 177
Sefer Ha-Mikneh (by Rabbi Joseph Kimche), 246
Sefer Ha-Moadim (Book of Festivals), by Rabbi Saadya Gaon, 197
Sefer Hasidim, 48, 49, 52, 54
Sefer Ha-Torah (by Rabbi Joseph Kimche), 246
Sefer Hatshuva, 54
Sefer Hayashar (Book of Rectitude), by Rabbi Abraham Ben Samuel Abulafia, 259
Sefer Hayashar (by Rabbi Joseph Ben Meyer), 227
Sefer Hayerzirah (Book of Creation), by Rabbi Abraham Ben Samuel Abulafia, 80, 113, 259
Sefer Hazchuth (by Rabbi Moses Ben Maimon), 253
Sefer Ha-Zicaron (by Rabbi Joseph Kimche), 246
Sefer Milhamot Hashem (Book of God's Wars), by Rabbi Moses Ben Maimon, 251
Sefer Olam Haba (Book of the World to Come), by Rabbi Abraham Ben Samuel Abulafia, 259
Sefer Rokeach, 52-54, 83, 126
Sfirat Hagrah (by the Gaon of Vilna), 80
Shaar Ephriam (by Rabbi Jacob Emden), 90
Shaarei Kedusha (Gates of Sanctity), by Rabbi Chaim Vital, 62
Shadur, King, 96

Shakneh, Rabbi Shalom, 275
Shaksheleth Ha-Cabala, 216
Shapira, Rabbi Nathan Ben Solomon, 130
Shaprut, Hasdai Ibn, 203-206, 209, 266
Shaprut, Rabbi Isaac, Ibn, 203
Sheelot Utshuvoth (by Rabbi Moses Ben Nahman), 253
Sheeloth (by Don Issac Abravanel), 269
Shela, see Horowitz, Rabbi Yeshayahu Halevi
Shem Hagdolim (The Name of the Great), by Rabbi Chaim Joseph David Azulai, 257
Shemoth Tzadikim (by Rabbi Nahman of Bratzlav), 177
Shesheth, Rabbi Isaac Bar, 73
Sheshet, Rabbi Isaac Ben, 226
Sheva Netivot Ha-Torah (by Rabbi Abraham Ben Samuel Abulafia), 260
Shivchei Rabbi Chaim Vital (Praise of Rabbi Chaim Vital), 61, 116
Shmelke of Nikolsburg, Rabbi, 160, 161, 183, 185
Shneh Luchot Habrit (by Rabbi Yeshayahu Halevi Horowitz), 65, 66, 69, 130
Shulhan Arukh (compiled by Joseph Caro), 43, 56, 79, 120, 134, 179, 257, 262, 270, 271, 272, 275, 276
Siddur Beth Yaakov (by Rabbi Jacob Emden), 92
Siddur Hatefillah (Order of Prayer), by Rabbi Jacob Emden, 90
Simha, Rabbi Nahman Ben, *also known as* Rabbi Nahman Bratzlav, 174-177

Simon, Rabbi, of Lochwitz, 84
Singari, Rabbi Isaac, 222
Sirkus, Rabbi Josel, 129, 130
Solomon, King, 111, 123, 129, 257
Solomon, Matatiyahu Ben, 129
Song of Songs, 21, 246
Songs of Zion (by Rabbi Yehuda Ben Samuel Halevy), 222
Sores, Rabbi Leib, 143-146
Sosover, Rabbi Moshe Leib, 183-187
Svyatoslav, Prince, 205

Taitatzak, Joseph, 69, 120
Talmud, 21, 23, 24, 33, 39, 54, 62, 94, 97, 102, 105-107, 110, 113, 115, 119, 124, 141, 162, 197, 208, 212, 218, 219, 224, 226, 234, 251, 255, 256, 263, 275
Tam, Rabbenu Jacob, *see* Meyer, Rabbi Joseph Ben
Tania (Collection of Spoken Expositions), by Rabbi Shneer Zalmen, 178, 179
Tibon, Rabbi Yehuda Ibn, 199, 221, 256
Tidros, Rabbi Kalonymus Bar, 245
Tohacha, 240
Toldot Ya'akov Yosef (by Joseph Hacohen), 86
Toldoth Ya'acov Yosef (by Rabbi Jacob Joseph of Polna), 148
Torah, 17, 18, 20, 23-25, 31, 44, 47, 48, 52, 54, 55, 62, 63, 74, 77, 91, 95, 114, 118, 124, 126-131, 134, 135, 153, 157, 159, 162, 163, 180, 197, 203, 210, 212, 218-220, 224, 225, 227, 235, 246, 247, 250-252, 263, 265, 266, 275
Torah Haolah (by Rabbi Moses Isserles), 128

Torah Or, 86, 141
Tsuroth Hayesodoth (by Don Isaac Abravanel), 267
Tzadock, Rabbi, 116
Tzavaoth De Baal Shem, 148
Tzena Urena (Go Forth and Behold), by Rabbi Issac Ashkenazi, 257

Urim Vethummin (by Jonathan Eybenschütz), 92

Velvl, Rabbi, of Zhitomir, 158
Vezoth Lihuda (by Rabbi Abraham Ben Samuel Abulafia), 260
Vilna, Gaon of, *also known as* Elihau, Rabbi, 54, 80, 125, 134, 179-181
Vital, Rabbi Chaim, 18, 25, 43, 54, 60-63, 69, 70, 117, 127
Vitri, Rabbi Solomon, 125
Voloshin, Rabbi Chaim, 80

Yaarot Dvash (by Jonathan Eybenschütz), 92
Yad Hazakah, *also known as Mishne Torah*, 26, 82, 125, 141, 235, 236, 239, 240
Yaffe, Rabbi Mordecai, 129
Yarhinai, Samuel, *see* Abba, Samuel Bar
Yayin Harokeach (by Rabbi Eliezer Ben Yehuda Rokeach), 54
Yechiel, Rabbi, 225
Yehuda, Rabbi, the Hasid of Regensburg, 46, 48, 50, 52, 54, 126, 135
Yekhiel, Rabbi Asher Ben, 261, 262
Yekhiel, Rabbi Nathan Ben, 245
Yesod Morah (by Rabbi Abraham Ibn Ezra), 231
Yitzhaki, Rabbi Shlomo, *also known*

as Rashi, 74, 114, 125, 203, 205, 212, 217-219, 224, 225, 227, 263, 269-271
Yohai, Tanna Rabbi Simon Bar, 18, 21, 22, 24, 25, 28, 44, 62, 71, 91, 116, 126, 127
Yom Tov, Rabbi Yehuda Ben, 225

Zacharias, 105
Zakai, David Ben, 197-199
Zakai, Rabbi Yohanan Ben, 237
Zakuto, Rabbi Abraham, 98
Zalman, Rabbi Shneer, of Lyubavich, 158, 178-181
Zbitkaver, Reb Samuel, 171
Zevi Nahalat, 22
Zevi, Sabbatai, 19, 35, 75, 83, 91, 92, 116, 148
Zikaron Zot (by Rabbi Jacob Isaac Horowitz), 162
Zimrah, Rabbi David Ben, 57
"Zion, Pray for the Well-being of Your Captives" (poem, by Rabbi Yehuda Ben Samuel Halevy), 223
Zishe, Rabbi, of Anapolya, 166, 167
Zohar, 18, 21-25, 28, 36, 62, 71, 91, 106, 117, 119, 126-128, 131, 117
Zot Zikaron (by Rabbi Jacob Isaac Horowitz), 162
Zutra, 106